Models

Russian Women's Aut[illegible]ical Texts

Edited by Marianne Liljeström,
Arja Rosenholm and Irina Savkina

K I K I M O R A   P U B L I C A T I O N S

Series B : 18 Helsinki 2000

Models of Self
Russian Women's Autobiographical Texts

ISBN 951-45-9575-0
ISSN 1455-4828

Aleksanteri Institute
Graphic design: Vesa Tuukkanen

Gummerus Printing
Saarijärvi 2000

Content

Part II: ”Я – Ты – Они – Другие”

Part III: Scenarios

Introduction

By presenting ongoing research on Russian women's autobiographical writing, this anthology aims to contribute to the growing body of scholarship on Russian women's cultural history. The articles of the collection grew out of papers which were presented at a seminar in Helsinki in August 1999, organised by a research project on Russian women's autobiographical writing funded by the Academy of Finland. The purpose of the included articles is to draw images of the female subjects emerging from a large variety of Russian women's autobiographical texts. The texts studied have been written during a considerable time span, stretching from the beginning of the 19th century up to the present day, in different social contexts with prevailing gendered conditions and attitudes.

The articles of this collection explore texts that – from the perspective of the influential Great Canon of Russian literature – are doubly marginalised: firstly, as autobiographical literature, which, since the times of Belinskii, has been given the status of a "boundary" phenomenon, and secondly, as women's texts, the legitimacy of which is still today questioned in the domain of mainstream academic research. Beyond this, Russian women's texts about the "self" (*avtoteksty*) have the role of a "poor relative" as they become objects of research far less frequently than Western women's texts.

The authors of this collection seek to explore the intersection of genre, gender and nationality. Each article analyses material of its own, which as a rule, has not earlier been included in any research field. Notwithstanding the variety of the material and differences in the researchers' methodological approaches, they are involved in a wide range of questions dealing with the theory of autobiography.

First and foremost the term *autobiography* itself is problematic. Although the term figures in the title of this book, only a few of the texts which the articles are concerned with, could without reservation be included in the definition of "autobiography". The texts present diaries (Rosenholm, Savkina, Demidova, Tyryshkina), letters (Tyryshkina, Hoogenboom), memoirs (Rytkönen), a short story, in the multigeneric structure of which the discourse of diary and autobiography play a significant role (Novikova), an epistolary diary (Savkina), poems (Taylor), official Soviet autobiographical sketches and memoirs (Liljeström, Kelly) and sexual biographies based on interviews (Rotkirch, Zdravomyslova, Temkina). Catriona Kelly talks about "biographies in the first person"; Hilde Hoogenboom explores how the writing of a woman writer's literary biography actually becomes a means for the creation of a male author's own autobiography.

Thus, the authors of this book become, directly or indirectly, involved in questions about the borders of generic definitions: how definable and important is the difference between *autobiography* and *biography, autobiography* and *memoirs, letters,* or *diary?* Is it necessary to define differences between various types of autobiographical or self-representational writing in more detail, or should we, on the contrary, talk about a metagenre, a polygeneric continuum, since the borders of different types of autobiographical writing are so diffuse and permeable? If we accept the latter argument, is it possible to define this kind of metagenre as *autobiography* (thus making the definition broader), or would it be more adequate to use and adapt a new term, such as *littérature intime* (Philippe Lejeune), *autogynography* (Domna Stanton) or *autodocumentary literature* (cf. articles by Savkina and Demidova)?

The problems concerning the term *autobiography* come to light especially in the context of Russian texts. It is no longer news that Russian researchers, contrary to their Western colleagues, seldom use the term. This has, as can be assumed, its own, various reasons. The first reason is connected, if we may say so, to the peculiarities of Russian cultural tradition looked upon from a uniform Westernising view, to Russian mentality, which do not have such emphasis on individuality or personality, as the so called "paneuropean" tradition. On the other hand, the course of individualistic confession, which is first and foremost meant in the West by the term autobiography, was embodied in Russia in the autobiographical novel and short story of the 19th and partly 20th century, as for example in S. Aksakov's and L. Tolstoi's famous works. This genre, belonging to fiction, adapted those features which most Western researchers connect with "real autobiography", above all the theme of becoming a personality, emphasis on the personal and the psychological processes of self-identity. In addition, the autobiographical research tradition plays a certain role in presenting the "standards" of the genre and thus also affecting decisions about the texts to be studied.

In Western research the generic canon is most frequently presented by the "holy trinity" of Augustine, Rousseau and Goethe. All these names are important also to Russian authors, but not to the same extent as their own Russian tradition, where the "founding-father" is A.I. Herzen and his book *My past and thoughts*. Herzen's text is a complex, conglomeratic, multigeneric formation, which cannot be defined as autobiography in the same sense as, for instance, Rousseau's text. Social involvement, combination of self-analysis and self-representation, a retrospective Bildungsroman and a journal dealing with the "forth-coming future", a mixture of an organised story – line and fragmentation – these and other special features of Herzen's memoir text have all greatly influenced both the practice of Russian autobiographers and theoretical interpretations of their work. And, finally, Russian researchers' "dislike" of the term "autobiography" is caused by the fact that in Soviet times this term had an official, ideological and formal meaning. Soviet citizens had to write autobiographies when applying for a job or for studying. It was a self-denunciation, or rather, a proof that one is ideologically in accordance with the requirements of a "Soviet citizen". As Elena Zdravomyslova states discussing this question in her article, "such self-presentations during official interviewing or interrogations became part and parcel of Soviet double self-identity" (Kelly and Liljeström touch upon this problem as well).

The question is not only of terminological adaptation of words, but of a national specificity of the genres we are discussing. Catriona Kelly points out in her article that generic conventions cannot be easily translated from one society to another, because autobiography, as she states, is "one of the more nationally idiosyncratic genres". Hence, a question that begs for intensive discussion is the relationship between national specificity and generic laws of genre.

The content of the collection at hand shows that despite the "exotic Russian" material and a distinct feeling that not everything can be opened with the "universal master-keys" of Western methodology, there are quite a number of topics where national specificity does not hinder the inclusion of the Russian material in a more general theoretical discussion. One of the questions of this kind is the relationship between autobiography or autodocumentary and fiction. What is the uniqueness on which autobiographical writing is based? What should we think about some current theories arguing that any text, even a restaurant bill, is a certain autobiographical text? Or, on the other hand, that there is no such thing as autodocumentary, because the referentiality of any text is an artefact, a rhetorical effect brought to life in the intersection of different discourses warped in the text?

If we differentiate non-fiction literature as a special type of writing, what do we mean with it? Are we talking about texts which *sincerely testify to a certain truth?* Or are we talking about texts which lay claims to be *accepted as truth*, as stories about *what really happened?* Or do we mean by non-fiction that the author strives purposefully, with the help of certain narrative strategies, to emphasise referentiality and authenticity of the text, thus creating quite distinct conditions for reading? How do we define authenticity? Olga Demidova suggests that we should decipher silences in writers' autobiographies by turning to their fiction work; Catriona Kelly compares Panova's memoirs with those of Yur'eva. However, the question arises, whether *another text* is capable of being a sufficient referent. After all, it is nothing else but another version. *How many* texts should we read as complements so that it would be sufficient for establishing "how it was"? Can we in the end find an answer to this question? Is the question relevant in the first place?

The authors of this collection participate in the discussion and show the difficulties and ambiguities in confirming the authenticity and identity of the author in the text. They expose how the models of narrating and self-representation (both on the level of the story, and on the symbolic and verbal levels) depend not only on the author's strivings, but also on social and literary conventions. This becomes especially evident in the readings of Soviet material (Liljeström, Kelly). However, as the articles of Savkina, Hoogenboom, and Tyryshkina demonstrate, we can with the same certainty talk about discursive constraints in the contexts of sentimentalism, romanticism and symbolism. Olga Demidova writes that "a woman creates her conception of self in the frame of a foreign discourse". But the question whether there actually is a discourse in which men create their self-conception as their "own" becomes as relevant. How then is gender constructed – as concepts of "own" and "foreign" – in connection to such conditions as class, nationality, culture and religion?

Informed by the papers published in this anthology it is easy to agree with Barbara Heldt's already classical (hypo)thesis that the autobiographical genres belong – among others – to that female tradition of Russian writing where we can find "consistency and evolution in the dramatisation of the female self". The cases illustrated and read in this book show how an autobiographical genre can serve as a forum for aesthetic and philosophical self-construction, and aim at a psychological self-reflectivity for intellectual Russian women who – especially in the 19th century – lacked the institutional conditions of Authorship. The articles are varied both according to historical time, scholarly object and methodological approach. However, because gender is of central importance for the authors, a significant common point of view of the readings is an understanding of the importance of *who* is speaking, *who* is considered appropriate as an autobiographical self. This brings up a further question of why and how the self is represented in the autobiographical genres?

The scholars orient themselves towards the historical situations of Russian women as writers, which in a significant way have differed, and still do, from those of men. In doing this the scholars do not aim at any uniform or final solution to the conflicting and tense relations between the author, the text, and the reader. The authors pay attention to the social and cultural origins of the "models of self" that Russian women explicate in different kinds of life-writing, such as diaries, memoirs and correspondence (Rosenholm, Savkina, Tyryshkina), autobiographical portraits as Soviet artists, as exemplary citizens or representatives of émigrés, (Demidova, Kelly, Liljeström), self-writing through fiction, or even lyrics (Rytkönen, Taylor). In this connection, the scholars presume that the "crisis of the subject" announced by post-structuralist criticism, does not necessarily concern women and their subjectivity as authors, because they have not been in possession of institutional autonomy in the way male authors have been. Rather, it seems that the issue of "self-writing" should motivate us to further examine the "author" and to avoid using stereotypical slogans of post-structuralist *or* hermeneutic positions, as is often done, in opposition and contradictory to each other. In order to avoid studying women authors only as textualized objects, we can focus on the various positions the autobiographers speak from. As some scholars point out, there are several aspects we ought to pay attention to which are bound to the public identity of Russian and Soviet woman authors (for example, such as social class, as Hoogenboom suggests).

Besides a social context formed of upper classes with a self-identification of *intelligentsiia*, there are features which are common to many of the female autobiographers. The positions from where they model their lives are often marked by different kinds of dualistic structuring. The dualisms, which can be read in the self-modelling are, for example, those between private and public/official, authenticity and self-censorship, mimicry and revelry, between feelings of dilettantism, on the one hand, and the "burning fire" of creative forces, on the other hand, and the place of individual desire in the moral hierarchy of the community. The structure reminds us of the psychological and cultural phenomenon that the Russian feminist critic, E. Shchepkina, has called the *dvoist'vennost'* of Russian intellectual women: it is a double bind of an intellectual woman "balancing" between the gendered worlds where women in relation to men stand in a position of inferiority, on the one hand, and cultivate the lacking self-esteem into indifference and feeling of uniqueness against "ordinary" women, on the other hand. A significant role in this "balancing act" is given to the male ideal, either real or fictive, as a teacher and a mentor, who participates in shaping the autobiography and is strongly involved in the process of myth-making.

The texts studied in this anthology show that we do not need to put our only hope in unknown archive material to be able to reconstruct Russian women's autobiographical tradition. There are enough texts, already known and published, utilised as documentary material, though many of them have not yet been objects of readings and interpretation. For example, such great memoirs as that of Elena Vodovozova still wait to be examined properly. To ask *how* the women writers are represented in the texts is, according to the authors of this anthology, to look at the narrative strategies the women writers have picked up in acquiring their authorship. Do we find similarities, common "models" of the female selves, or common textual strategies of telling one's experiences in these texts? One field of similarities which can be traced in the articles concerns certain key words embedded in most of them, such as "masks", "roles", "masquerade", "auto-representation", "myth-making", and "the female Self" in relation to "the Other". The key words deal with the status and position of the female "I" who speaks as a displayed self by means of language interpreting the lived experience in relation to time and space.

The autobiographer is not only engaged in finding out effective narrative strategies but she is simultaneously a reader of her life; writing autobiography is also a "cultural act of a self reading", as Janet Varner Gunn has put it. The self-interpretation in images, masks and roles, which are not to be reduced to sociological "roles", shows the complexity of the linkage between masquerade and femininity. Indeed, one may say that the female "models of selves" understood as the genealogy of femininity *(zhenstvennost')* can be identified as those cultural forms, cultural presentations and imaginations of Femininity, which undermine any ontological authenticity, as among many Joan Riviere, Luce Irigaray, Teresa de Lauretis and Silvia Bovenschen have pointed out.

In almost every paper the self-interpreting I-narrator is involved in a process of interaction with the ideal of femininity, both striving to it and opposing it. Since the beginning of the 19th century, Russian women write themselves in close connection to images and expectations of femininity. Hoogenboom shows how Elizaveta Kul'man denotes her public identity by the means of the objectifying third person (*ono*) and creates her literary biography to fit that of the Greek poetess, Corinna. In Savkina's presentation Anna Kern and Anna Olenina write themselves through the "strange speech-roles" of the sentimental literary protagonists Clarissa-Julie-Delphine. According to Taylor Evdokiia Rostopchina and Karolina Pavlova practised identificational role-play by mirroring their selves against the foil of the other female poetess, as did Emma Gershtein in relation to Nadezhda Mandel'shtam in Rytkönen's interpretation. Rosenholm reads Elena Shtakenshneider's "model of self" as something unique compared to ordinary women, shaped as an anti-play with the "masquerade" identified as the "normal" femininity. Novikova takes the image of "the female warrior masquerade" as the route of reading the autobiographical *povest'* of Elena Rzhevskaya. Even though not all authors do explicitly use the terms of masks and roles, the narrative self-modelling they study implies practices of feminine "myth-making" (*mifotvorchestvo)* of the Woman as the Other, the Stranger: Demidova points to this kind of practice by speaking for example of Nina Berberova's self-creation as the "Other, deviant from all the others, not at all similar to other's personality". Liljeström sees in a similar way the "exceptional" Soviet woman as a construction of the "Remarkable", identifiable only as a contrast against other "ordinary" women. Considering these cases of self-modelling, we can ask whether it is the construction of the female self as exceptional and unique in opposition to other ordinary women, which could form one common position among Russian women who work on their autobiographical selves.

What is, however, often present when the focus is on femininity and love, becomes apparent in the diaries and correspondence of Ludmila Vil'kina. Tyryshkina's selection of Vil'kina's correspondence is a revealing case of how myth-making is involved in the definition of ideal femininity, here stronger present than in others' autobiographies, uncovered in its very ambiguity. It shows how the female self-modelling, understood only in relation to others and defined by them, through others'/men's "I"/eyes, which according to Tyryshkina was Vil'kina's strategy as a "life-artist", will be reduced into "applying alien masks and playing strange roles". Mythological sources can be used to expand one's self, as is the case with Shtakenshneider and her Cassandra, but mythical associations can also work as a counter force, as shows Vil'kina's self-modelling. Trying to fulfil the roles of the ideal stranger, the role ascribed to women by their male contemporaries, as *femme fatale* and *femme enfante,* the female self is also subjected to the workings of self-destructive powers.

As already has been noticed, the anthology contains important diversities. They concern both research material (the analysed texts) and ways of interpretation, "reading routes". By analysing specific texts from different theoretical and methodological points of view, and by bringing together researchers on women's autobiographical texts from Russia and the West, the anthology, to sum up, actualises and continues discussion on certain comprehensive questions within the research field.

The most important of these questions concern gender as an interpretative frame in reading Russian women's autobiographical texts. The authors understand the relationship between male and female speech – an overall historical framework in the articles – as a cultural context in which the enforced silence of women can be read as the norm even when women manage to write and publish, to achieve and have influence. This means, that the female autobiographical subject emerging within historically differing cultural practices of identity production is unevenly authorised – hierarchically and symbolically subordinated to the male subject – by varying modes of dominant discourse. This being a common point of departure for the included articles, there is, however, at least two ways or levels of reading gender in the autobiographical texts written by women. The first perspective concerns figuring the feminine, often as ruptures of phallogocentrism. The other perspective positions women as speaking agents within a world of male institutions, including writing, which are nevertheless possible to resist. On the one hand we have texts dealing with Russian literature as material to explore primarily gendered literary and cultural processes from a gender point of view, on the other hand there are texts focusing on problems of Russian literature with gender as *one* of their background categories. These views are not necessarily compatible, because they depend on different definitions of the category of women, definitions which are themselves unstable. However, both perspectives accentuate and request further discussion on the continuous dilemma within feminist research of grounding the analysis in the identity of women.

Another important question – confirmed by the structure of the anthology – concerns the fruitfulness of a multidisciplinary discussion for advancing the research and formulating new questions within the field. The authors read women's self-representational writings from different conceptual frame-works and with multiple methodological, above all discursive and semiotic-psychoanalytical, approaches. All articles deal, however, with textual analysis, with questions of narrativity, the gendered place of narration in cultural expression, with interactions between inter-, intra- and extratextual principles of narration. In doing this the authors nevertheless identify with the disciplines of literature, sociology and history, which are marked by a multiplicity of theoretical and methodological approaches themselves. Without opposing multidisciplinary to disciplinary research, a transgression of traditional boundaries enables various contacts, creative shifts and displacements of concepts, understandings and methods. Multidisciplinarity means to travel, to move between different discursive fields, a practice that requires curiosity and openness, but also patience and desire to deal with and make use of different readings.

By accentuating differences and varieties both within the West and within the East as well as between them, we want to underline the research on Russian women's autobiographical texts as a field of discussion, creative communication, as a movement across different readings, and as an area of changing positions and understandings.

Part I
Auto/biography

Biographies of Elizaveta Kul'man and Representations of Female Poetic Genius

Hilde Hoogenboom

When Elizaveta Kul'man died in 1825 at age 17 from tuberculosis, she left behind over a thousand pages of poetry in German, Russian, and Italian, some tales, and hundreds of letters to her German tutor, Karl Friedrich Grossheinrich in German, French, English, Spanish, and Greek with commentary on her poems.[1] Grossheinrich (1782–1860) tirelessly promoted Kul'man's legacy because while she wrote for eventual publication, she never published in her lifetime. In 1833, he succeeded with the Russian Academy's publication of her collected works and a biography of her life, by the new state censor Aleksandr Nikitenko. This biography appeared at least nine times through 1847 in journals and editions of her collected works – two in Russian, three in German published in Russia (with Grossheinrich's foreword), and three in Italian.[2] In 1844, in Germany, Grossheinrich published his biography of Kul'man with extensive quotations from her letters together with her collected works in German, which went into eight editions through 1857.[3] Grossheinrich's biography appeared twice in Russian translation in 1849, but despite the added authenticity of Kul'man's own letters, it was Nikitenko's version of Kul'man's life that caught on in Russia.[4]

They differ greatly in their visions of the shape and significance of Kul'man's life and work, not least because Grossheinrich clearly wrote his biography of Kul'man in self-defense against Nikitenko's implicit charge that he harmed Kul'man's genius with his (German) pedantry, a view uniformly repeated by such later biographers as Nekrasova and Valueva-Munt.[5] Although Nikitenko speaks highly of Grossheinrich (1839, v-vi), the two distinct portraits in many ways express the different aesthetic agendas of Nikitenko and Grossheinrich, one Romantic, the other Enlightenment, respectively, which surface in discussions of the relative merits of training Kul'man in translations of classics as opposed to original poetry (1839, xi). Therefore, these biographies also function as intellectual autobiographies of the two men, as for example, Lydia Chukovskaya wrote a biography of Anna Akhmatova that is nevertheless very much about Chukovskaya. Finally, Kul'man herself was an active, self-conscious autobiographer in her letters to Grossheinrich and in her poetry. As the numerous Russian and foreign editions over a quarter century might indicate, Kul'man's is the first, most substantial, and influential auto/biography of a nineteenth-century Russian woman writer.

This rich nexus of biographical and autobiographical material presents several intersecting auto/biographical puzzles about the relationship between the subject and writer and between autobiography and biography for Russian women writers in the 1830s that continued to resonate through the end of the nineteenth century. The central problem is a subset of these interrelationships, what Boris Tomashevsky calls the "literary biography," by which he means the biographies that writers create through their writings and oral culture.[6] He argues that at certain periods in literary history, especially Romanticism, the literary biography as distinct from the actual facts of a person's life becomes a significant literary fact and functions as part of the writer's oeuvre, which then must include biographies, letters, and memoirs (49). Building on this Formalist approach, Yuri Lotman likewise puts aside the actual biographical information, but argues with Tomashevsky that literary biography is more than the author's conscious choice of a mask.[7]

In a complex scenario, Lotman explains how the need for literary biography arose in Russia only in the late eighteenth century when individual's right to be a writer came into question because of specific cultural and historical factors (I:369). Through the mid-nineteenth century, most writers, men and women, belonged to the aristocracy. The aristocracy derived its class identity from state service, until Catherine the Great reconfirmed Peter III's "Manifesto on the Freedom of the Nobility" in the 1767 Commission, and finally in the 1785 Charter of the Nobility, she freed the elite from mandatory service at court. The Russian elite, however, continued to live by this ideal and transformed actual into moral service to Russia through education, self-improvement, estate management, and generally acting as Russians' moral compass. Once writers turned professional, their claim to authority and truth no longer automatically derived from their other, real professions, generally in religious or government service. In Lotman's view, the right to authorship depends on the amount of choice a writer is seen to have in that he writes and in what he writes: less choice confers greater authority (as for example when God speaks through you), and more choice requires evidence of one's claim to be a writer (I:369). By the nineteenth century, still adhering to the service ethic of their class, authors now depended on their character for the right to write. Lotman argues that the *ad hominum* attacks of literary quarrels (especially in the eighteenth century) were symptoms of the need to have a biography, which became more acute when writers had to justify themselves professionally (I:370). The peculiar public stakes for Russian writers are evident in for example Dostoevskii's famous 1880 Pushkin speech or Turgenev's 1876 letter to Flaubert, on the occasion of George Sand's funeral, when despite feeling suitably foolish, he claims to have the right to offer condolences in the name of the Russian public.[8]

Lotman and Tomashevsky limit their discussion to men's literary biographies, but at the same time nineteenth-century Russian women writers were engaged in an equally literary process, that of inventing a recognizable literary identity as women writers. In *The Madwoman in the Attic*, Gilbert and Gubar define this problem of newness in English literature as "anxiety of authorship," which they contrast with the "anxiety of influence", or the problem of an existing tradition for men writers.[9] But Russian literary culture developed later than European literature – the titles of Nikolai Karamzin's essays speak to this point: "What Does an Author Need?" (1793) and "Why is There so Little Writing Talent in Russia" (1802).[10] In contrast to Europe, in Russia, men as well as women writers experienced anxiety of authorship more or less together, but with an important difference based on a combination of class and gender.

In her discussion of nineteenth-century French women writers, Nancy Miller notes the problem of imagining a public identity for women, an identity that in Russia was bound with one's class.[11] While the ideal of court service for noblemen, actual or its moral complement, would seem to exclude a public identity for women; nevertheless, several important women did exemplify male service and also wrote: Empress Catherine the Great, Princess Ekaterina Dashkova, and Nadezhda Durova. Dashkova participated alongside Catherine in the 1762 coup in the uniform of the Preobrazhensky regiment and later in 1783 was appointed by Catherine to be Director of the St. Petersburg Academy of Sciences and was the founder and President of the Russian Academy. A cavalry officer in the War of 1812, for which she was awarded the Cross of St. George, Durova lived as Aleksandrov, a man in dress and language. (In contrast, the influential memoirs and letters of the Decembrist wives reflect alternative service, as Russia's moral conscience in exile.) More or less court memoirs, their central concern is access to the ruler. Catherine's official memoir ends with "... ", as she bends the Empress Elizabeth's ear to her idea that Peter III is unfit to rule; it is organized around her limited access to Elizabeth. Though primarily a military memoir, Durova's emotional descriptions of two meetings with Aleksander I, whose name she took in, I think, a symbolic marriage, are as touching as the scenes Dashkova relates of her in bed with Catherine. Both depict marriages with power, or direct access to the ruler. These scenarios of women's access to power in Russia challenge the critical commonplace of feminist theorizing about women's auto/biographies in America and Europe that because women have existed primarily in the private sphere, moving into the public sphere triggered their anxiety about the right to write.[12]

These scenes suggest why the introduction to the first edition of Kul'man's Russian poems include letters that testify to favors bestowed on her by the Russian Empress Elizaveta Alekseevna and the posthumous gifts of the Empress and Grand Duchess Elena Pavlovna to Grossheinrich and their gift of her tombstone. Of all nineteenth-century Russian women writers, Kul'man alone acquired Russia's most powerful benefactress, with the exception of Nadezhda Sokhanskaya.

As if to denote her new public being (a writer), Kul'man speaks of herself in the third person in the following extract from a letter:

> Elisaveta Kul'man, who in her youth lost her father, puts herself on the same level as any poor person, for the quite simple reason that she has nothing and exists by the kindness of strangers; but Elisaveta Kul'man, to whom the Russian Empress gave a necklace as a sign of the excellence of her developing talent, and who received the honorable name of woman writer from the two great men of Germany [Goethe and Jean-Paul Richter] after they read her first compositions — this Elisaveta Kul'man cannot sell her poetry.[13]

Although keen to publish, once she receives her higher authorization from Goethe, her disdain for selling her work echoes the dilemma among established men poets about professionalization and money when one belongs to a class that derives its identity not from earning a living, but performing service – even though Kul'man is not an aristocrat and realizes she will have to work as a teacher.[14] This is evidence of literary biography at work.

Lotman posits that the more active the writer's biography, especially for Romantic poets, the less important the biographer's biography, but this inversely proportional relationship does not hold for Kul'man, or for such other relatively famous personalities as Elena Gan, Karolina Pavlova, Evdokiya Rostopchina, and Evgeniya Tur. These women actively created their literary biographies, sometimes under the guise of proclaimed passivity, but like Nikitenko's biography, the biographies written by their biographers – such critics and sometimes writers as Kireevskii, Belinskii, Druzhinin, Turgenev, and Pisarev – remained the most influential. Women's activity as literary biographers underscored their anxiety about their right to authorship. What did men's activity as women's biographers reveal, aside from men's parallel anxiety of authorship, which they could and did assuage at women's expense?[15]

The relative status of Kul'man and her biographers, all in marginal positions, is complex and difficult to judge, but she complemented their class identities in various ways. Of all the arts, poetry did not lower the writer's status, and could even raise it to the level of state service, as the Empress's awards for Kul'man's translations show.[16] Both Nikitenko, a serf who gained his freedom and worked his way up to state censor and professor, and Grossheinrich, an extremely talented linguist and tutor for the Apraksin family who arrived in St. Petersburg from Germany around 1805 at age 23, were outsiders to Russian literary culture. Relative to each other, Nikitenko was an insider, which is why Grossheinrich appealed to him initially to write the preface and biography to the Russian Academy edition. Lotman notes that one way Nikitenko defined his outsider status was linguistically, through his lack of perfect French, which gave away his class origins and as he put it, could have "freed one for some time, if not forever, from the necessity of manifesting other more important rights to the public's attention and good-will."[17] Grossheinrich knew fourteen languages, but after twenty years in Russia, he still preferred that Kul'man worked for him in German. In what may have been an expression of linguistic envy, through their biographies, both laid claim to a brilliant linguist – the first Russian woman to master ancient Greek, according to one epitaph on her tombstone – who knew German and Russian perfectly, plus nine other languages.

The symbolism of Kul'man's tombstone for her public identity extends beyond its importance as an Imperial gift and record of her national linguistic significance.[18] Engravings of Kul'man, her simple house, and of her tombstone, where she lies on her side in a death pose on a bed mounted on a pedestal with inscriptions mainly about death in ten languages, accompany Russian and foreign editions and amplify her biography. Lotman notes that it was standard to include portraits for collections by writers once they were dead (I:370), but it is hard to find any portraits of nineteenth-century Russian women writers until the turn of the nineteenth century.[19] Thus Kul'man was accorded special (male) status as a poet.

The type of literary biography that best describes Kul'man is what Tomashevsky calls the Romantic dying poet: "young, unable to overcome the adversities of life, perishing in poverty, the fame he merited coming too late"(49). Nikitenko creates a tragic Romantic poet by focusing on her brief life and death, while deemphasizing her poetry, and concludes with a verbal picture of her tombstone. In contrast, Grossheinrich underscores her prodigious, voracious intellect, and, rather than end with plot of her life (her death, which he compares in Classic fashion to the premature death of Achilles), concludes with her work: pages of her letters about future projects. It speaks of the larger picture that Grossheinrich is interested in the inscriptions on her tombstone, listing them all in the original and in translation, while Nikitenko focuses on the image of the dying girl.

It is most curious that Nikitenko had greater influence in shaping Kul'man's public identity than she herself as expressed through her poetry and the ample published selections from her letters in Grossheinrich's biography. Nikitenko's portrait of a tragic girl Romantic poet proved more plausible than the confident, intellectual Kul'man of her letters, and therefore more acceptable, to such admirers of Kul'man as Kyukhel'beker, Timofeev, Gan, Belinskii, Nekrasova, and Valueva-Munt.[20] In Kyukhel'beker's diary, there is an obvious transition from one view based on Kul'man's poetry to another after reading Nikitenko. The poet first responds to her as a poet, the best Russian woman poet he has ever read, and then imagines her as a wholesome rather than sinful female muse:

> How sad that I did not know her! Without a doubt, I would have fallen in love with her, but this love would have been as beneficial to me as my little passions for trite society creatures were harmful, in that there was not in them that which my too generous imagination had given them (228).

Nikitenko makes her poet's life more authentic by contrasting it with a fake poetic genius, the Byronic hero, the most well-known poet's literary biography, and then by maintaining that Kul'man's talent was natural, not an artificial mask (1839, iii). He compares her to a real genius when he argues that Kul'man freed herself creatively (from her tutor, he implies) when she read biographies of great artists, saw the works of Michelangelo, and transformed, decided to write great poetry in the last year of her life (1839, xi). Lastly, he appeals to a higher, even ultimate authority for truth, God and his chosen people, proclaiming that

> Elizaveta Kul'man belonged to these chosen people. We have seen above that her first childhood years were marked by signs of a decisive poetic talent, and all her life was nothing other than a sacrifice dedicated to the higher promised lands of Art (1839, xi).

In fact, Nikitenko's exalted biography of Kul'man came to provide arguably the first apparently real life Russian source for such later critical and fictional representations of Russian women writers as Elena Gan in Belinskii's 1843 essay on women writers and Gan's poet heroine's death in her 1842 tale "The Futile Gift".

The multiple texts and genres – biography, autobiography, letters, and portraits – at work in Kul'man's literary biography require, I think, an interpretive strategy that Nancy Miller calls reading between the lines. Because of the difficulty of imagining women's public identities, Miller argues for breaking down genre hierarchies and reading women's intratexts, or their fiction with their autobiographies, diaries, letters, and other non-canonical genres (64). In her great biography *George Sand, sa vie a ses oeuvres* (1899–1926), Wladimir Karénine (pseudonym for the Russian woman writer Varvara Komarova) encountered precisely this problem in dealing with Sand's biography and correspondence. More recently and along similar lines, Carolyn Heilbrun contends that "there is a wholly different voice in the letters on the one hand and the autobiographical narratives on the other."[21] These feminist approaches parallel Virginia's Woolf's prediction that, in a "mixture of biography and autobiography, of fact and fiction," lay the future of biography.[22] Grossheinrich and Nikitenko promoted Kul'man's work, personality, and life together as a whole, in what Ganzburg terms the "aesthetic and ethical significance of the image of Elizaveta Kul'man"(150). The argument between Nikitenko and Grossheinrich about the relationship between Kul'man's life and work extended to her posthumous critics, and reflected the broader critical quarrels over what a woman writer should be. Critics relentlessly read women's writing autobiographically, deducing the writer's personality from her heroines and themes, especially love. At the same time, like Gan, women writers included autobiographical information, in a process similar to the one Tomashevsky describes for men writers. In addition, like men, these women writers were also engaged in the struggle to establish their authority or qualifications to be writers by emphasizing qualities similar to those Lotman lists for men writers: "sincerity," "honesty," and "self-education aimed as intellectual and spiritual enlightenment"(I:369, 372).

In the first scholarly discussion of nineteenth-century Russian women writers, Beletskii, rightly, I think, added Kul'man herself to the list of promoters of her biography:

> The literary significance of Elizaveta Kul'man is all in this cult, which she brought on herself: in Russia, this was the first woman for which people had such high literary expectations: she shone briefly like a falling star, but in memory remained as an ideal that persistently required realization.[23]

Kul'man was an autobiographer because she contributed substantially to her biographies through her letters, which Grossheinrich quotes at great length. In the letters and recounted conversations between them, it becomes apparent that together they were everywhere conscious and calculating of the effect she and her work would produce on readers when published. Both were aware of the difference between Kul'man in life, as a poet, and as a woman writer. She wrote:

> I have such a high idea about the significance of poetry, that I rarely permit myself to lower my style and make it agree with our daily life. On the other hand, I wouldn't want to show myself as other than I really am. I am not as serious as I appear in my works, or at least, not always that serious.... And consequently, humor should appear in my poetry so that Elisaveta Kul'man does not pass for being a gloomy, unsociable, or a stubborn creature.[24]

Moreover, in an article that gives an overview of the letters, Lyove concludes that over three quarters are about her work, while the rest are personal. It is important to realize that as Kul'man wrote her poems, at the same time she wrote the letters explaining the poems, especially what she found interesting about how she had done something. Thus the poems and letters are parallel works constituting a kind of autobiography of the classical type that Bakhtin, in "Forms of Time and Chronotope in the Novel", calls "works 'on one's own writings'" by for example Cicero and Galen.[25] According to Bakhtin, the public for these works are a circle of readers, which Kul'man had for her poems and especially her tales, and this was the public on which she practiced her literary persona, just as she did in her letters with her tutor. Grossheinrich in fact amply describes what an accomplished performer of her work Kul'man becomes.

The biographies of Kul'man evolved in three stages, from rather unformed to highly elaborate, and then for the rest of the nineteenth century, a simplified version based on Nikitenko's taken root. The biographical process begins with Grossheinrich's letters written to interest the Russian Academy in publishing her works and in 1833, an unsigned introduction to their first edition. This introduction is most probably not by Grossheinrich even though the concluding paragraph of this foreword contains ideas found elsewhere in his writings.[26] The foreword emphasizes an aspect of Kul'man that is absent in Nikitenko's and Grossheinrich's biographies, including her letters, namely her faith in God. As to the shape of her life and work, the foreword is mostly about her family background and emphasize the usefulness of her poetry, first to provide some income for her poor family and second to serve as an example to inspire young people with an appreciation for literature – the very point Grossheinrich makes in his letters to the Russian Academy, which therefore substantially shaped this first published biography of Kul'man.

Nikitenko wrote his 1835 biographical ode to Kul'man's genius the year before he published his doctoral dissertation, "On Creative Power in Poetry, or on Poetic Genius", which consists solely of abstractions in the style of the title, without any mention of Kul'man; the only poets he even names, and only once, are Goethe and Shakespeare.[27] In addition to giving Kul'man's biography the themes of his intellectual preoccupations, Nikitenko read his own life into her's when he emphasized the beneficial aspect of the poverty in which she lived, her habit of working hard, and of her life in nature on Vasilievskii Ostrov, where she was an outsider to literary business in the capitol. An outsider himself from Siberia, Nikitenko was born a serf and thanks to benefactors, got the opportunity to work hard to get an education and once in St. Petersburg, make his way up in the bureaucracy to state censor. In a letter he wrote, "Elizaveta Kul'man is me."[28]

To shape his biography of Kul'man, as his model narrative Grossheinrich chose for himself the voice of the tutor of Rousseaus Emile. Like Nikitenko, he emphasizes Kul'man's life in nature, and then extends the metaphor of nature when he educates her naturally, as Rousseau advocates: without forcing her interests, he lets her choose which language she wants to learn next and explains the methods he has devised to make learning less burdensome. He includes touching little stories of their presents and pranks at birthdays, which I think serve to make Grossheinrich a more youthful companion, able to enjoy the same things that please Elizaveta, which Rousseau considers essential for a "solid attachment" with his pupil.[29] As further evidence of this affectionate bond, Grossheinrich recounts moments when Elizaveta acknowledges her debt to and feeling for him. But of course, he, Emile, is a she, and Grossheinrich's model for Elizaveta is not Rousseau's Sophie.

The identity that Grossheinrich and Kul'man choose for her is Korinna, the Greek woman poet who according to legend defeated Pindar in poetry competitions. Grossheinrich proposes to Kul'man that she create a fake body of poetry supposedly by Korinna, who left only a literary biography and no poetry (though fragments have been found since then), in the same way as MacPherson had faked Ossian's poetry. As he put it,

> you can give Korinna your own character, your thoughts, your means of action, only of course, transporting yourself to the times, land, and situation of Korinna (95: 18).

The opening of the Korinna poems (57–121) begins with the setting for Korinna's birth: "Not far from the foliage, In which I was born, Is a jasmine brush"(57). This happens to coincide with the story Kul'man was told about her own birth:

> And so once it happened that she wanted to know where she came from. And since she put this question to her mother in front of the owner of the house, who loved Elizaveta greatly, he took her by the hand to his garden, which took up a large part of the courtyard, and pointing to two jasmine bushes, growing in the shade of the Italian linden trees, he said: Do you see, my darling, these two jasmine bushes? Well, once a crane flew here with a red basket in it's beak, in which you lay, and put you down on the grass; then your daddy and mommy came, saw you and took you home. (Grossheinrich 94: 75)

Grossheinrich went into such detail about the story of Kul'man's birth because here, life was imitating art. Tomashevsky notes that the writer emphasizes certain aspects of his or her life to fit an imagined literary biography, which suggests a two-way process where not only does the life (of course) create the biography, but the reverse happens, and the biography suggests certain events that should be emphasized in the life (49). In an even clearer example, like Korinna's competitions with Pindar, Grossheinrich sort of enters Kul'man in a competition when he boasts to acquaintances that she can write a better poem about

Sappho than Lamartine. With great gusto, Kul'man enters into the spirit of the thing and describes how she sets about writing something entirely different from the nine poems by other poets: "...I dug up all my learning, bringing up events which not one of my predecessors noted"(68). The account of this successful competition, for like Korinna, she wins, takes up three pages.

Just as Korinna's biography shaped the life that Kul'man chose for herself as a poet, Kul'man's literary biography shaped those of fictional women writers. This is most clearly apparent in Elena Gan's "The Futile Gift", where Kul'man is invoked as the dying young poet Aniuta hears that her work has been published in St. Petersburg. This story is generally read autobiographically because Gan herself died soon afterwards at the relatively young age of 28. But a few scholars – Catriona Kelly, Irina Savkina, and myself – argue against the general tendency to read Gan autobiographically, a practice Gan certainly encouraged. For example, the heroine of "The Ideal" is married to a husband much like what we know about Gan's husband. Clearly, like Kul'man, Gan was intensely preoccupied with her literary biography.

In 1861, 1886, and 1892, later biographers put forth Nikitenko's version and hence we find traces of her literary biography in other works about women writers in the second half of the nineteenth century.[30] Both biographers adoringly depict Kul'man's love for nature: she talks with a jasmine tree as if it were a doll, looks at the moon and writes about it as a living being, and talks with a willow tree. Kul'man's portrait, a drawing of her grave and of her house all have wisps of shrubs and trees. Yet, paradoxically, Kul'man lived in St. Petersburg on Vasilevskii Ostrov, which might be comparable to living in Harlem during the previous century in Manhattan; that is, the outskirts of town. The motif of a girl's (and future writer's) intense relationship with nature reappears in Gan's "The Futile Gift", in Narskaia's 1860 story "A Desperate Measure", about Masha, who becomes a writer to provide for her children, and in Soboleva's 1866 tale, "Polia's Story", about a girl's pure upbringing in nature with a good tutor. Like Kul'man, Polia is a gifted storyteller.

It is ironic that Kul'man (like Grossheinrich) thought of herself as a classicist, but she is remembered very much as a Romantic. She enjoyed the occasional literary prank of including Romantic subject matter in her poems – what she called "forbidden goods" – as long as it was done smoothly (74–5). In any case, the combination of her life and work is anything but smooth; in many ways, the result contradicts Tomashevsky's idea that the literary biography makes sense of the work, because for Kul'man, despite the Korinna cycle, they remain very much separate. If we recall Heilbrun's observation about the radical difference between the private and public personnas of women writers, then it becomes clear that Kul'man is following a female paradigm for literary biography.

Notes

[1] Elizaveta Borisovna Kul'man, 'Pis'ma K.V. Grossheinrich', RGALI, f. 245, op. 1, d. 12 (German), d. 13 (German), d. 14 (French), d. 15 (Spanish), d. 16 (Greek), d. 17 (German), d. 18 (*Iliad*), d. 19 (*Odyssey*); 'Pis'ma K.V. Grossheinrich', GBL, f. 622, op. I, d. 20, (62 letters in English and Italian). For an overview of these letters in preparation for an edition that was never published, see E. Lyove, 'Pervaya v Rossii neofilologichka', *Zapiski neofilologicheskogo obshchestva pri Petrogradskomu Universitetu*, v. VIII (1915): 211–57. In conversation, Fainshtein notes that her letters are lost because the letters in archives are selections from her letters in Grossheinrich's handwriting, which is most curious. On Kul'man, see M. Sh. Fainshtein, *Pisatel'nitsy pushkinskoi pory*, Leningrad 1989, 23.

Research for this article was supported by a grant from the International Research & Exchanges Board, with fund provided by the US Department of State (Title VIII program) and the National Endowment for the Humanities. None of these organizations is responsible for the views expressed.

[2]A.V. Nikitenko, 'Zhizneopisanie devitsy Elisavety Kul'man', *Biblioteka dlya chteniya* v. VIII, I (1835):39–85. Elizaveta Kul'man, *Piiticheskie opyty*, St. Petersburg, 1833; *Polnoe sobranie Russkikh, Nemetskikh i Italiianskikh Stikhotvorenii, Piiticheskie opyty*, 2 ed., St. Petersburg, 1839. Elisabeth Kulmann, *Sämmtliche Gedichte (Avec sa biographie)*, 4 vols., St. Petersburg, 1835; *Sämmtliche Gedichte*. In 4 Theilen, 2 ed., St. Petersburg, 1839; *Saggi poetici di Elisabetta Kulmann*, S. Petersburg, 1839; *Saggi poetici con la vita (par Alex. Nikitenko) dell'autrice*, 3 ed., Milano, 1847.

For a full description, including previously unpublished archival material, of the publication history of editions, biographies, and critical reception, see G.I. Ganzburg, 'K istorii izdaniya i vospriyatiya sochinenii Elizavety Kul'man', *Russkaya literatura*, 1(1990):148–55. My gratitude to Mikhail Fainshtein, Grigory Ganzburg, and Irene Gramlich, Grossheinrich's great grand niece, for bibliographical information.

[3]Elisabeth Kulmann, *Sämmtliche Gedichte*. 2 ed., Leipzig, 1844; 3 ed., Leipzig, 1844; 4 ed., 1846; 6 ed., Frankfurt am Main, 1851; 7 ed., Frankfurt am Main, 1853; 8 ed., Frankfurt am Main, 1857.

[4]K.V. Grossheinrich, 'Elisaveta Kul'man i ee stikhotvoreniya', *Biblioteka dlya chteniya* 94 (1849): 69–117, 95 (1849):1–34, 95(1849): 61–96; St. Petersburg, 1849.

[5] E.S. Nekrasova, 'Elizaveta Kul'man (1808–25)', *Istoricheskii vestnik* 26.12 (1886): 551–79. After a very negative portrait of Grossheinrich, she concludes that "instead of an original creative power, there now stood an amazing machine"(575). A.P. Valueva-Munt, *Ne ot mira sego*, St. Petersburg, 1892. She laments that, "As an eleven-year-old girl, Liza already wrote graceful poetry; but under the influence of Grossheinrich, a passionate admirer of the classical world, she did mostly translations and imitations of classical models"(18).

[6]Boris Tomashevsky, 'Literature and Biography', in Ladislav Matejka and Krystyna Pomorska (eds.), *Readings in Russian Poetics: Formalist and Structuralist Views*. (MIT Press, 1971), 47–55.

[7] Yu. M Lotman, 'Literaturnaya biografiya v istoriko-kul'turnom kontekste (K tipologicheskomu sootnosheniyu teksta i lichnosti avtora', in *Izbrannye stat'i*, 3 vols. (Aleksandra, 1992), I:372.
[8] "Je sais que vous êtes allé à Nohant pur l'enterrement – et moi qui voulais envoyer un télégramme de condoléance au nom du public russe, j'ai été retenu par une sorte de modestie ridicule.... Le public russe a été un de ceux sur lequel Mme Sand a eu le plus d'influence – it il fallair le dire, pardieu – et j'en avais le droit – après tout." I.S. Turgenev, 6/18 June 1876, *Polnoe sobranie sochinenii i pisem*, 11:272.
[9] Sandra M. Gilbert and Susan Gubar, *The Madwoman in the Attic: The Woman Writer and the Nineteenth-Century Literary Imagination.* (Yale University Press, 1979), 48–9.
[10] *Selected Prose of N.M. Karamzin*, Trans. And Intro. By Henry M. Nebel, (Evanston, 1969).
[11] Nancy Miller, *Subject to Change: Reading Feminist Writing.* (Columbia University Press, 1988), p. 60.
[12] The titles of works on women's autobiographies tend to connect them to private life. Estelle Jelinek (ed.), *Women's Autobiography: Essays in Criticism.* (Indiana University Press, 1980); Sidonie Smith, *A Poetics of Women's Autobiography: Marginality and the Fictions of Self-Representation.* (Indiana University Press, 1987). Shari Benstock (ed.) *The Private Self: Theory and Practice of Women's Autobiographical Writings.* (The University of North Carolina Press, 1988); Felicity A. Nussbaum, *The Autobiographical Subject: Gender and Ideology in Eighteenth-Century England.* (Johns Hopkins University Press, 1989).
[13] Grossheinrich, 'Elisaveta Kul'man i ee stikhotvoreniya', (1849), 95: 87.
[14] Grossheinrich, 'Elisaveta Kul'man i ee stikhotvoreniya', (1849), 95: 32.
[15] For example, on Turgenev's fraught literary relationship with Evgeniya Tur, see Jane Costlow, 'Speaking the Sorrow of Women: Turgenev's 'Neschastnaia' and Evgeniia Tur's 'Antonina'', *Slavic Review* 50.2 (summer 1991) 328–35.
[16] Lotman, 'Literaturnaya biografiya v istoriko-kul'turnom kontekste', I:372–3.
[17] A. V. Nikitenko, *Dnevnik.* 3 vols. (Moscow, 1955) I:11, cited by Yuri M. Lotman, 'Russkaya literatura na frantsuzkom yazyke', in *Izbrannye stat'i*, 3 vols. (Aleksandra, 1992), II:351.
[18] Kul'man was first buried in the old Smolensk Cemetary, where Pushkin's nanny is buried; in 1931 she was moved to the Lazarev Cemetary, and in 1938, reinterred in the Tikhvin Cemetary near the great writers of the nineteenth century. Letter October 26, 1998 from the city of Saint Petersburg to Irene Gramlich.
[19] On turn-of-the-century portraits of living women writers, see Beth Holmgren, 'Gendering the Icon: Marketing Women Writers in Fin-de-Siècle Russia', in Helena Goscilo and Beth Holmgren (eds.), *Russia, Women, Culture.* (Indiana University Press, 1996), 321–46.
[20] V.K. Kyukhel'beker, *Dnevnik*, ed. by V.I. Orlov and Sl. Khmel'nitskii, 1929, 227–8; 'Elisaveta Kul'man,', *Izbrannye proisvedeniya v dvukh tomakh*, ed. by N. V. Koroleva, 2 vols. (Moscow–Leningrad, 1967) I:281-4. A.V. Timofeev, 'Elizaveta Kul'man, 1835', *Opyty* (St. Petersburg, 1857) 169–262. V.G. Belinskii, rev. of

Piiticheskie opyty Elisavety Kul'man v trekh chastyakh, in *Polnoe sobranie sochinenii*, 13 vols. (Moscow, 1953–9) 4:570-1; rev. of *Elisaveta Kul'man* by Timofeev, *Pss* 2:76–82. On plausibility, see David Bromwich, 'The Uses of Biography', *The Yale Review* 73.2(1984):161–76.

[21] Carolyn Heilbrun, *Writing a Woman's Life.* (Ballantine Books, 1988), 24.

[22] Virginia Woolf, 'The New Biography', *Collected Essays*, 4 vols. (Harcourt, Brace & World, Inc., 1967), 4:235.

[23] A.I. Beletskii, 'Epizod iz russkogo romantizma', Kharkov, 1919; IRLI, fond R. 1, op. 2, No. 44.

[24] Grossheinrich 95 (1849): 92.

[25] Mikhail Bakhtin, 'Forms of Time and Chronotope in the Novel', in Michael Holquist (ed.) (trans. by Caryl Emerson and Michael Holquist), *The Dialogic Imagination.* (University of Texas Press, 1981), 139.

[26] See Ganzburg's full transcriptions of Grossheinrich's letters, in which he gives some biographical data. The foreword concludes with a phrase Grossheinrich repeats in two letters, probably both written in 1841, that one should not require perfection of such a young writer. It also takes up the issue of rhyme, which he fully develops in the 1849 biography.

[27] A.V. Nikitenko, *O tvoriashchei sile v poezii, ili o poeticheskom genii*, St. Petersburg, 1836, 41.

[28] Reported to me by Mikhail Fainshtein.

[29] Jean-Jacques Rousseau, *Emile or On Education*, trans. Allan Bloom, (Basic Books, 1979), 51.

[30] M.D. Khmyrov, 'Russkie pisatel'nitsy proshlogo vremeni: Anna Bunina, Mariya Pospelova I Elisaveta Kul'man', *Razsvet* 12 (1861:213–28, 257–74); Nekrasova, 'Elizaveta Kul'man (1808–25)', and Valueva-Munt, *Ne ot mira sego.*

Autobiographical Poetry, or Poetic Autobiography?

K. Pavlova's 1847 Invective Epistle "We Are Contemporaries, Countess"*

Romy Taylor

There was plenty to disagree about in mid-nineteenth-century Russia: tensions were running high between Slavophiles and Westernizers, as well as between civic critics and "art-for-art's-sake" proponents, to name but a few factions. Furthermore, Russia's two leading women poets of the time, Karolina Pavlova (1807–1893) and Evdokiya Rostopchina (1811–1858) had never enjoyed friendly relations to begin with. So it might come as no surprise that the two rivals should exchange an invective epistle or two in the 1840's. One such epistle, Pavlova's 1847 "My sovremennitsy, grafinya" ("We Are Contemporaries, Countess"), explores well-known oppositions such as those between Moscow and St. Petersburg, Russia and the West, patriarchal values and freethinking feminism. But even more appears to have been at stake in the mêlée of the real lives of those involved. Private scandal (Rostopchina's affairs and alleged out-of-wedlock daughters), public scandal (an allegory on Poland that enraged Nicholas I), and scandal at the cross-section of private and public (vying for the attention of Polish poet Adam Mickiewicz) are all reflected in Pavlova's epistle.

Yet, where the poem's autobiographical claims may be tenuous at best, the poem's poetic innovations may have been overlooked: the poem covers new ground in areas such as lexicon and voicing. The poem's sharp wit and invective tone might have been considered unacceptably bold stances for a woman author, if not for the implication that this poem, like Pavlova's other verse, had already received her husband's stamp of approval, rendering the poem digestible to a wide range of readers, including Rostopchina herself.

Pavlova deals with the two women's similarities in the first two stanzas, leaving the remaining five stanzas to develop a somewhat exaggerated rendition of their differences. Pavlova chastises Rostopchina for her licentious lifestyle, which is pitted against the more sedate example of Pavlova herself, who claims to stay home and mind her husband:

> Мы современницы, графиня,
> Мы обе дочери Москвы;
> Тех юных дней, сует рабыня,
> Ведь не забыли же и Вы!
>
> Нас Байрона живила слава
> И Пушкина изустный стих;
> Да, лет одних почти мы, право,
> Зато призваний не одних.
>
> Вы в Петербурге, в шумной доле,
> Себе живете без преград,
> Вы переноситесь по воле
> Из края в край, из града в град;
>
> Красавица и жорж-зандистка,
> Вам петь не для Москвы-реки,
> И вам, свободная артистка,
> Никто не вычеркнул строки.
>
> Мой быт иной: живу я дома,
> В пределе тесном и родном,
> Мне и чужбина незнакома,
> И Петербург мне незнаком.

По всем столицам разных нации
Досель не прогулялась я;
Не требую эманципации
И самовольного житья;

Люблю Москвы я мир и стужу,
В тиши свершаю скромный труд,
И отдаю я просто мужу
Свои стихи на строгий суд.

[We are contemporaries, Countess,
Both daughters of Moscow;
After all, even you, vanity's slave, can't
Have forgotten those youthful days!

Byron's glory propelled us forward,
As did Pushkin's verse, heard straight from his lips;
Yes, it's true we're approximately the same age,
Yet our callings are quite different.

You live noisily in Petersburg,
Nothing cramps your free lifestyle,
Your travel as you please,
From land to land, from city to city;

Beauty and George-Sandist,
It's not your lot to sing for Moscow-river,
And no one has crossed out your poetry lines,
Since you are a liberated female artist.

My life is different: I live at home,
In close-quartered and familiar bounds,
I know neither foreign lands
Nor Petersburg.

I have not yet strolled
In all the capitol cities of different nations;
I don't require emancipation
Or an autonomous lifestyle;

I love the peace and frost of Moscow,
I carry out my humble work in quiet,
And I simply present my verse
To my husband, for his stern judgment.][1]

This poem has been quoted by many memoirists describing the Pavlovs. However, the qualities that kept these lines in the forefront of memoirists' minds were more likely the poem's clever and light-spirited jabs, and innovative lexicon, rather than its value as biographical and autobiographical fact. Twentieth-century readers have likewise generally ignored the epistle's formal innovations, or poetic value, and have instead emphasized its biographical and autobiographical claims. For example, the poem was quoted in a 1970 biography of Pavlova's husband, the minor writer and publisher Nikolai Pavlov (1804–1864). The biographer, V.P. Vil'chinskii, cites variant stanzas to bolster his description of the Pavlovs' married life:

> …Karolina Karlovna [Pavlova] placed high value on the poetic taste of Pavlov, who was the *primary judge* of her verse. Here is how she describes this in an epistle to Countess Rostopchina:
>
> Не тот мой жребий. Не для света,
> Не для молвы я рождена,
> И вдохновения поэта
> Таит покорная жена.
>
> Люблю Москвы я мир и стужу,
> В тиши свершаю скромный труд,
> И отдаю я просто мужу
> Мои стихи на грозный суд.[2]

[That is not my fate. Not for society,
Nor for fame was I born,
And a poet's inspiration
Is hidden by a submissive wife.

I love the peace and frost of Moscow,
In quiete I fulfill my humble work,
And I simply give my husband
My verse, for his terrible judgment.]

The poem's final claim, that Pavlov sternly crosses out his wife's lines, seems tongue-in-cheek enough to arouse suspicion of its basis in biographical fact. Indeed, the poem's general tendency toward hyperbole should, perhaps, prompt a re-examininination of even its more innocuous claims. For example, Rostopchina's reputation as a "beauty" has been accepted unquestioningly; Pavlova, on the other hand, is usually considered to have been more poet than beauty. Yet, to compare portraits of Rostopchina and Pavlova, one would be hard-pressed to say which was the beauty, and which was "bony, theatrical, masculine" (as Pavlova was described). In fact, in the late 1820's, Pavlova (then, Jaenisch) inspired unreciprocated passion in two suitors to such a degree that their lives were shattered by her rejection (one more than the other).[3] Rostopchina's beauty, in contrast, was considered overrated by some of her closest acquaintances (her face was greasy, her features too large, her figure too small).[4] The most convincing explanation seems to be that personality played a larger role in perceived attractiveness than did actual physical features. Rostopchina was admired in the 1830's not simply for her beauty, but for her tact, charm, and warmth; Pavlova was disliked, in the 1840's, not for her old-fashioned dresses, but for heartlessness and egotism, with which nearly all memoirists charge her.

For example, N.V. Berg described Pavlova as "standoffish, haughty" ("choporn[aya], nadut[aya]").[5] Pavlova's presence at salon gatherings could be problematic, according to Elagina's letters, since she was apt to loudly declaim verse, for hours at a time, in foreign languages such as Polish and German.[6] According to Boris Chicherin, Pavlova "posed" as an ideal wife and tender mother[7], and the Pavlovs' son Ippolit certainly had little good to say about his mother in his bitter reminiscences.[8] Such descriptions call into question the poem's claim that Pavlova renders her "humble work" in "quiet" ("V tishi svershayu skromnyi trud"): little seems to have been humble, or quiet, about Pavlova.

Her husband, for his part, emerges in memoir accounts as no more of a "strict judge" than she emerges as a submissive wife. In fact, Pavlov the "judge" displayed rapt and respectful attention during readings of his wife's poetry.[9] Khomyakov was of the opinion that Pavlov was intimidated by his wife's increasing literary fame.[10] Yet, intimidated or not, Pavlov lobbied tirelessly for his wife, writing countless letters recommending her work and copying her poems for informal distribution.

All in all, it seems hardly likely that Pavlova submitted her verse to anyone's judgment, including her husband's, given that she might more accurately have described her husband as "fawning scribe" than "strict judge". What motivated Pavlova's representation of herself, and why was Rostopchina chosen to serve as her antithesis? The "why" of choosing Rostopchina has been explained by several scholars: Rostopchina was "the negative foil for woman writers," according to Hilde Hoogenboom, and challenging Rostopchina as Moscow's foremost woman poet may have been a way for Pavlova to gain entry into the male tradition, according to Olga Peters Hasty.[11]

But what prompted Pavlova to write this epistle when she did, in 1847?

A brief survey of the two poets' literary careers may suggest an answer. Rostopchina's earliest publications, in the early 1830's, had been met with acclaim and instant popularity. By 1841, when her first collection of poetry was published, she had been called "Russia's premier poet" on several occasions.[12] Her social success was equally phenomenal, from imperial balls to elite literary drawing rooms.[13]

In contrast, Pavlova's literary fortunes remained modest until her family's 1836 inheritance and her 1837 marriage. By the early 1840's, she was hosting one of the most prominent literary salons in Moscow, known for substance rather than glitter: poetry, history, philosophy, foreign luminaries (e.g. Liszt), all topped off by a glorious dinner, personally supervised by her husband Pavlov, a famed gourmet. When, in 1841, the more established Rostopchina published two poems about visiting Moscow, it was only natural that the up-and-coming Moscow poet Pavlova would write a response: in her 1841 poem "Gr[afine] Rostopchinoi," Pavlova gently chastises her rival for slighting her hometown.

Apparently, Pavlova's 1847 epistle was likewise written as a reaction to Rostopchina's newest publications. It seems hardly a coincidence that Pavlova wrote her epistle (in January, 1847) while all Moscow was embroiled in scandalous "uproar and gossip". The cause of the scandal was a new ballad by Rostopchina, published anonymously (but with hints as to the author's identity) in a December, 1846 edition of the newspaper *Severnaya pchela*.[14] Rostopchina's poem, a political allegory entitled "Nasil'nyi brak" ("A Forced Marriage"), set a knight-baron (Russia) against his unhappy wife, married against her will (Poland). Rostopchina composed the allegory while travelling through Poland,[15] and might never have published such a controversial poem, had Gogol' not been delighted with it when they met later in Rome. Gogol' urged Rostopchina to send the poem to St. Petersburg: "They won't understand it, and they'll publish it... You don't know how stupid our censorship is..."[16]

Gogol' proved right about the censors, but underestimated the czar. While the Rostopchins were still in Europe, "Nasil'nyi brak" was wreaking its own brand of havoc in Russia. Copies of the publication were recalled, but this measure only increased the poem's worth, and schoolchildren and poets across Russia committed the poem to memory. Less sympathetic readers responded with their own ballads, replicating the allegorical setting but focusing sympathy, instead, with the husband (Russia).[17]

It seems that Pavlova's 1847 epistle is also an answer, of sorts, to Rostopchina's allegory. In fact, the variant stanzas share lexicon with Rostopchina's poem. In Pavlova's lines

И вдохновения поэта
Таит покорная жена.
[And a poet's inspiration
Is hidden by a submissive wife.
(Underscoring here and elsewhere, mine)]

she claims to have the submissive qualities that the errant wife in Rostopchina's allegory lacks, according to the husband's complaints:

Все не покорна мне она,
Моя мятежная жена!... [lines 9–10]
[She continues to refuse to submit me,
My rebellious wife!...]

Теперь внемлите непокорной...[line 38]
[Now look at her, unsubmissive,...]

Таить от всех ее должна... [line 79]
[She should hide [her fate] from everyone...]

Finally, while Pavlova claims to submit her verse to her husband's strict judgment, the piteous baron in Rostopchina's allegory must ask his servants to judge whether he, or his wife, is in the right:

Pavlova:
И отдаю я просто мужу
Свои стихи на строгий суд. [lines 27–8]
[And I simply present my verse
To my husband, for his stern judgment.]

> vs. Rostopchina:
> Судите, кто меж нами прав?
> Язык мой строг, но не лукав! [lines 36–7]
> [Judge which of us is right!
> My tongue is strict, but not wily!]

Yet Pavlova's response differed from the others, because instead of replicating the allegorical setting, Pavlova instead treats the allegory's face-value theme: a dispute between husband and rebellious wife. In Pavlova's poem, the "wife" is modeled by the emancipated Rostopchina, who has now dispatched with patriarchal authority once and for all. The poem's tension is provided by her counter-example, a woman managing to humbly scratch out poetry without disturbing the harmony of patriarchal relations, modeled by Pavlova herself.

Much emphasis in Pavlova's epistle is placed on a woman's freedom to write.This continues themes in Rostopchina's allegory, where the rebellious wife (Poland) complains that she has no freedom of expression. Pavlova's lines 15 and 16

> И вам, свободная артистка,
> Никто не вычеркнул строки
> [And no one has crossed out your poetry lines,
> Since you are a liberated female artist.]

insinuate that someone *should have* crossed out Rostopchina's lines, such as those conveying pro-Polish sentiments in "Nasil'nyi brak."

Yet perhaps a Polish factor of another nature was also at work. Rostopchina's allegory was known to have been dedicated to the Polish poet Adam Mickiewicz ("Posvyashchaetsya myslenno Mitskevichu"), then in exile in Paris. Publication of Mickiewicz's poetry, or even mention of his name, had been forbidden in Russia since 1834,[18] so Rostopchina's allegory appeared in print without the Mickiewicz dedication. But given the widespread popularity of the allegory, it is likely that Pavlova knew of it from more than the published source, and thus knew of this dedication.

By the 1840's, Mickiewicz had become an important "ghost" in Pavlova's life, having been her Polish tutor and, in a manner of speaking, her fiancé, in the late 1820's.[19] Pavlova's writing, her salon, and even her husband may have helped her gradually overcome her obsession with Mickiewicz. However, Rostopchina's dedication of her allegory to Mickiewicz may have been jarring. Even if Pavlova had relegated Mickiewicz to memory, Rostopchina was now infringing upon that memory – and upon Pavlova's idealization of herself as "Mickiewicz's fiancée." On the appearance of Rostopchina's allegory in print, a rumor that Rostopchina had taken a new lover, "a Polonophile", spread through Moscow.[20] Although the rumor was probably groundless, it is certainly likely that Moscow's gossips postulated Mickiewicz as a candidate.[21]

Pavlova's epistle was most likely never sent to Rostopchina, and it remained unpublished until 1899.[22] Who, then, was its intended audience? Rostopchina, for one: she probably had more than one occasion to hear the poem. Pavlova and her salon circle probably enjoyed a good chuckle at Rostopchina's expense when the poem was read aloud, and perhaps Pavlova, in writing this epistle, was consoling herself for having landed with the short end of the stick in all those areas where she reproaches Rostopchina. But the "husband-judge" Pavlov himself, his wife's erstwhile scribe, agent, and maitre d', was probably the main intended reader. The Pavlovs may have felt a common bond when united against Rostopchina, and perhaps when Pavlov saw his marriage in this poem's terms, he felt less upstaged by his wife. Most importantly, the poem makes a reference to one of Pavlov's own early poems, an 1823 dedication to an unidentified female addressee:

> К ***, при посвящении ей перевод трагедии "Мария Стуарт"
> Когда мой перевод, не славе обреченный,
> Возьмешь досуга в час к себе на строгий суд,
> Быть может, кинув взор на сей листок забвенный,
> С улыбкой примешь ты мой первый, скромный труд…[23]
>
> [To ***, While Dedicating to Her a Translation of the Tragedy "Maria Stuart"
> When my translation, ill-fated for fame,
> You take, in an hour of leisure, for your strict judgment,
> Perhaps, casting your glance on this forgotten page,
> You will accept with a smile my first, humble work…]

The Pavlovs held no monopoly on the rhyme "sud/trud," nor was it uncommon to find requests to judge one's humble work in Golden Age poetry. Salon hostesses, in particular, were expected to judge poetry introduced at their salons.[24] The *words* "sud" and "trud" are also found in Pushkin's work: Evgenii Onegin submits himself to Tatyana's judgment in Canto 4 ("Sebya na sud vam otdayu," 4:XII), and judges himself in Canto 6. The *rhyme* "sud/trud" appears in Pushkin's 1830 sonnet, "Poetu." However, the coincidence between Pavlov's 1823 "na strogii sud/moi skromnyi trud" and his wife's 1847 "skromnyi trud/na strogii sud" is nevertheless striking.

Perhaps this coincidence signals that the poem's claims are to be taken literally? In other words, Pavlova had indeed submitted a poem with a different rhyme ending to her husband's judgment, but Pavlov, acting as domestic censor, struck out those lines and substituted his own rhymes, composed years earlier. If this scenario seems farfetched, a more likely one might be that Pavlova manipulated her poem to create this impression. An observer who knew her husband's poetry well (such as Pavlov himself) would leave the poem convinced that the poem's claims had been proven within the text of the poem itself, since one of Pavlov's rhymes "now" graced the ending. With this gesture, Pavlova beefs up the poem's rhetoric at the same time as she flaunts her own poetic pyrotechnics. She writes her poem, *and* submits it to her husband's judgment, or has her cake, and eats it too.

While Pavlova's contemporaries complained that she was difficult to bear in person, her poetry found listeners in many circles. This dichotomy seems to have inspired a dual response from Rostopchina to the 1847 epistle. On one level, the petty feud continued.[25] On another level, however, Rostopchina proved herself to be open to a dialogue of a different sort. In 1840, Rostopchina had written,

> Каждый женский стих
> Волнует сердце мне...
> ("Как должны писать женщины")
>
> [Every line written by a woman
> moves my heart...
> ("How Women Ought to Write")]

Indeed, the "zhenskii stikh" under discussion, Pavlova's 1847 epistle, evokes a surprising response in Rostopchina's poetry. In 1857, Rostopchina re-published a two-volume collection of her verse, prefaced by a new dedication.[26] The opening stanza relies heavily on forms and lexicon from Pushkin, especially his 1828 "Poltava" dedication and Tatyana's letter to Onegin.

But at the center of Rostopchina's dedication, just before Rostopchina declares herself a poet (line 19: "dushi poeta..."), it is not Pushkin, but Pavlova, who is echoed, especially the claim that the author submits her "humble work" to a "judge" ("skromnyi trud / sud"):

Кто втаине был мне вдохновеньем,
Кто был мне цель, совет и суд, –
Я приношу с благоговеньем
В последний раз мой скромный труд!

[Who was secretly my inspiration,
Who was my purpose, counsel and judge, –
I bring with veneration,
For the last time, my humble work!]
(lines 13–16)

This repeating rhyme "skromnyi trud / sud" evidences a broader pattern among poems written by women in nineteenth-century Russia. First, a man's encouragement should have inspired the woman to set pen to paper. Rostopchina's "Nasil'nyi brak" claims inspiration from Mickiewicz, Pavlova's 1847 epistle — from Pushkin and Byron, and Rostopchina's 1857 dedication, from a lover, probably Andrei Karamzin (son of the poet and historian).

Equally important was the expectation that a man should have read, judged, and approved a woman's poem before its publication or distribution. This is what ostensibly happened with Pavlova's 1847 epistle, and (in spirit) with Rostopchina's 1857 dedication (Andrei Karamzin had died several years earlier). In fact, this is also what happened when Gogol' encouraged Rostopchina to publish her allegory. Pavlova's claim that her "humble work" has been submitted to a "judge" seems to have been a particularly effective way to fulfill this expectation, which may be why Rostopchina avails herself of the same rhetorical device and rhyme. Rostopchina's dedication follows the forms and lexicon of Pushkin's tradition, but it is Pavlova's *trud/sud* rhetorical device which helps Rostopchina appropriate these forms for her own voice.

A few years after Pavlova had composed her invective epistle against the emancipated George-Sandist, Rostopchina, the "rules of the game" established therein had become obsolete. By the early 1850's, Pavlova had more to worry about than rival poets: the Pavlovs' marriage was breaking up, fueled by Pavlov's gambling and the awkward pregnancy of Pavlova's unmarried cousin and ward (who subsequently became Pavlov's common-law wife). Pavlova left Moscow in 1854, now herself an independent woman in the vein of George Sand, gracing foreign capitals, taking lovers, and writing verse far from any husband-judge's oversight. Rostopchina, on the other hand, was now quietly residing in Moscow. Surely the extremely complicated real-life biographies of each poet can explain this reversal of fortune and role. However, if we imagine for a moment that art supersedes realia in motivating the unfolding of a poet's biography, we might wonder whether the tension of the exaggerated opposition set up in Pavlova's epistle became too much to bear, and trading places provided the only solution.

Rostopchina and Pavlova faced the tricky task of defining themselves and their poetry vis-à-vis male poets. According to Stephanie Sandler, Rostopchina's 1838 poem "Chernovaya kniga Pushkina" had "ask[ed] implicitly whether the Pushkin tradition in Russian literature was and is a male tradition."[27] Olga Hasty writes: "...the woman poet found herself in an impossible situation: to avow her gender was to foster a feminine poetic tradition distinct, and thus easily excluded, from the male tradition; yet to disavow her gender was to concur implicitly with the disparagement of a woman's capacity to write poetry."[28] But the dialogue between Pavlova and Rostopchina reveals ways that these issues were resolved. In the 1840's and 1850's, a woman in Russia could freely write poetry; this poetry was better digested, however, when accompanied by self-denigration. Yes, the Pushkin tradition is predominantly male. But women gradually appropriate verse composition as their own, while minimizing the perceived transgression by referring to male instigation, judgment, and approval of their verse.

Pavlova had few female friends and did not nourish any young women poets with the warmth of her heart; she was certainly no feminist's feminist. Yet, her 1847 epistle, thoroughly enjoyable on its own terms, inspired a dialogue with Rostopchina and helped found a women's authorial tradition in nineteenth-century Russian poetry, fostering an atmosphere in which "mute Psyches" of the Silver Age and later were sure to find their voices.

Notes

* I would like to thank Hilde Hoogenboom, Jenifer Presto, Irina Savkina, especially my advisor Sarah Pratt, for their very helpful comments on this paper.

[1] Karolina Pavlova, *Polnoe sobranie stikhotvorenii*, Biblioteka poeta, Bol'shaya seriya, 2nd ed. (Moscow–Leningrad: Sovetskii pisatel', 1964), pp. 134–5. Translations throughout are mine.

[2] V.P. Vil'chinskii, *N.F. Pavlov: zhizn' i tvorchestvo* (Leningrad: Nauka, 1970), pp. 104–5. Italics mine.

[3] The two were Cyprian Daszkiewicz, in compulsory internal exile from Poland; and N.M. Yazykov (1803–1846), the poet. Daszkiewicz apparently committed suicide over his unrequited love for Jaenisch: see Mickiewicz's correspondence in Adam Mickiewicz, *Dziela* (Czytelnik, 1955), vol. XIV. For discussion of the letters, see Jean-Charles Gille-Maisani, *Adam Mickiewicz: poete national de la Pologne. Etude psychoanalytique et caracterologique* (Bellarmin, 1988), pp. 235–245. Yazykov was less open about his feelings for Jaenisch, but Rapgof suggests their epistolary relationship (which tended to be lengthier and warmer on Yazykov's side) was based on unrequited love on Yazykov's side: Boris Rapgof, *K. Pavlova: Materialy dlya izucheniya zhizni i tvorchestva* (Petrograd: Trirema, 1916). Yazykov wrote epistles to Pavlova throughout their lives, and himself never married.

[4] 1836 entry of S. N. Karamzina, cited in E.P. Rostopchina, *Talisman* (Moskovskii rabochii, 1987), p. 270.

[5] N.V. Berg, 'Posmertnye zapiski', *Russkaya starina* (1891): 229–279, p. 263.

[6] Lina Bernstein, 'Avdot'ia Petrovna Elagina and her Contribution to Russian Letters,' *Slavic and East European Journal,* 40.2 (1996): 215–35, p. 226.

[7] B.N. Chicherin, 'Vospominaniya', *Russkoe obshchestvo 40–50-x godov XIX v.*, Part II, S.L. Chernov (ed.) (Moskovskii universitet, 1991), p. 10.

[8] I.N. Pavlov, 'Vospominaniya', *Russkoe obozrenie* 4.38 (1896): 887–895.

[9] Berg, *Posmertnye zapiski*, p. 264 (fo. 5 above).

[10] In an 1841 letter, Khomyakov wrote:
"Недавно Павлова читала прекрасную балладу свою 'Старуха'. Павлов перед ней пасует. Скоро ее стихи будут читаться больше его повестей. Он, кажется, боится этого."
["Recently Pavlova read her first-rate ballad, 'The Old Woman', Pavlov is playing second fiddle to her. Soon her verse will be read more than his short stories. It seems that he is afraid of this."] In I.S. Zil'bershtein (ed. and intro.), *A.S. Pushkin i ego literaturnoe okruzhenie: Portrety i risunki* (Moscow: Gosudarstvennyi literaturnyi muzei, 1938), p. 50.

[11] Hilde Hoogenboom, 'A Two-Part Invention: The Russian Woman Writer and her Heroines from 1860 to 1917', *unpublished PhD dissertation* (Columbia University, 1996), p. 90; Olga Peters Hasty, 'Dvukh solov'ev poedinok', AAASS Convention, Boston, Nov. 1996.

[12] For example, P.A. Pletnev wrote in an 1840 letter: "Она [Ростопчина], без сомнения, первый поэт теперь на Руси." ["Without a doubt, [Rostopchina] is the premier poet in Russia today."] Letter to Ia.K. Grot, Dec. 10, 1840, in Rostopchina, *Talisman* (fo. 4 above), p. 276.

[13] In the 1840's, however, Rostopchina's personal life became acutely complicated, while literary styles and critics' expectations were changing drastically. By the time Rostopchina returned her full attention to literature, in the late 1840's, she was already hopelessly out of touch with literary fashion, as well as with her own muse. In fact, Rostopchina's early popularity brought detrimental results over the long term: she had never learned to revise or edit her poetry, nor had she sought out friends' or colleagues' suggestions before publication. What was uneven, yet inspired, in the 1830's, remained uneven in the 1840's and 1850's, but without inspiration. Rostopchina's novelty as a woman writer, speaking in a woman's voice and noted for her beauty and social grace, wore off as she aged.

[14] 'Nasil'nyi brak', *Severnaya pchela* 17 Dec. 1846: 1155–1156; A.V. Nikitenko, 'Dnevnik', *Russkaya starina* 65.2 (1890): 371–406, p. 371.

[15] N.V. Berg, 'Grafinya Rostopchina v Moskve (Otryvok iz vospominanii)', *Istoricheskii vestni*k 51.3 (1893): 691–708, pp. 692–4.

[16] Louis Pedrotti, 'The Scandal of Countess Rostopchina's Polish-Russian Allegory', *Slavic and East European Journal*, 30.2 (1986): 196–214, pp. 196–7.

[17] V.S. Kiselev-Sergenin, 'Po staromu sledu: o ballade E. Rostopchinoi *Nasil'nyi brak*', *Russkaya literatura: Istoriko-literaturnyi zhurnal*, 3 (1995): 137–152. The essay on Rostopchina in *Poety 1840–1850-x godov* lists three poems disagreeing with Rostopchina's allegory (A.S. Golitsyn, 'Sud vassalov' or 'Otvet odnogo iz vassalov baronu i ego zhene'; N.V. Kukol'nik, 'Otvet vassalov baronu'; E.P. Rudykovskii, 'Ty prav vo vsem, nash povelitel'…'). Listed in defense of Rostopchina's allegory is an anonymous response, 'Otvet starogo vassala'. 'Rostopchina', *Poety 1840–1850-x godov*, Biblioteka poeta: Bol'shaia seriia, 2nd ed. (Leningrad: Sovetskii pisatel', 1972: 63–128), p. 65.

[18] In Russia, Mickiewicz had been widely published and read in the late 1820's and early 1830's, until the 1834 ban. Despite this ban, Pushkin, Berg and others found ways to publish Mickiewicz anonymously. The ban on Mickiewicz was lifted only after the death of Nicholas I.

[19] Pavlova was certain that Mickiewicz had asked for her hand in marriage on November 10, 1827. The subject had certainly been broached: Mickiewicz's 1828 correspondence (to his friend Cyprian Daszkiewicz, who was, at the same time, hopelessly smitten with Pavlova [Jaenisch], himself) reveals that Mickiewicz was sure neither of what was promised, nor of what he wanted. Mickiewicz wrote:

"Je lui ai seulement demande si elle songe a se marier, sans me mettre le moins du monde en avant… *Je n'ai fait aucune promesse.* C'est elle qui laissa entendre qu'il n'y a pas de chance que nous nous voyions, et elle a encore mentionne des obstacles, sur lesquels je ne l'ai pas questionnee et dont elle a fait un secret…"

["I asked her only whether she had thought of marriage, without putting myself at a disadvantage in advance… *I never made any promise.* It was she who gave me to

understand that we could no longer see one another, and then she again mentioned obstacles, about which I did not question her, and which she has kept a secret..."] Gille-Maisani, cited in fo. 3 above, p. 239; italics in original.
The obstacles most likely involved an inheritance the Jaenisch family was to receive, on the condition that Mickiewicz did not marry into the family. It seems that Mickiewicz never learned the entire story: he repeatedly asked Daszkiewicz to find out how large Jaenisch's fortune actually was. In early 1829, Mickiewicz seemed to have made up his mind to marry Jaenisch:
"Dis a [Jaenisch] que j'attends Golitsyne pour trouver un poste ici ou aller a l'etranger. *Dans un cas comme dans l'autre*, je serai a Moscou et *l'epouserai*, ou bien je me fiancerai et donnerai rendez-vous a Dresde. Tu peux lui montrer ces lignes. Dis-lui qu'elle renonce a ses reveries nocturnes et qu'elle soit in bonne sante, car je n'aime pas les malades." (Gille-Maisani, 241; italics in original)
["Tell [Jaenisch] that I am waiting for Golitsyn to find me a position here or to go abroad. *In either case*, I will be in Moscow and *will marry her*, or will become engaged to her and meet her in Dresden. You can show her these lines. Tell her to renounce her nocturnal reveries, and to be in good health, because I don't like sick people."]
However, when Mickiewicz came to Moscow, rather than marrying Jaenisch, he offered her his friendship in place of his love.
[20] Kiselev-Sergenin, 'Po staromu sledu' (cited in fo. 17 above), p. 137.
[21] Rostopchina had met Mickiewicz, in Moscow, as a girl: she describes this meeting in a letter to E. Malevskaya, March 17, 1852: Evdokiya Rostopchina, *Stikhotvoreniya. Proza. Pis'ma* (Moscow: Sovetskaya Rossiya, 1986), p. 358. During the years of the Rostopchins' stay in Europe (1845–7), no mention of any meeting between Rostopchina and Mickiewicz is made in Mickiewicz's biographical chronicle, *Kronika zycia i tworszosci*. Yet, Rostopchina and Mickiewicz were living in the same cities and had common acquaintances. In addition, Rostopchina shared Mickiewicz's interest in mysticism: she used the pseudonym "Yasnovidyashchaya" (The Clairvoyant) and was a popular host of seances. Mickiewicz was living predominantly in Paris, but made trips to Switzerland and Italy, including several visits to Gogol', during this time: B.F. Stakheev, *Mitskevich i progressivnaya russkaya obschestvennost'* (Moscow: Gos. izd-o kul'turno-prosvetitel'noi literatury, 1955), p. 52.
[22] Pavlova's 1841 epistle to Rostopchina, however, was published in Pavlova's lifetime (but after Rostopchina's death) in Pavlova's 1863 poetry collection.
[23] N.F. Pavlov, *Sochineniya: Tri povesti. Novye povesti. Stikhotvoreniya. Stat'i* (Moscow: Sovetskaya Rossiya, 1985), p. 205.
[24] Lina Bernstein, 'Women on the Verge of a New Language: Russian Salon Hostesses in the First Half of the Nineteenth Century', in H. Goscilo et al. (ed.), *Russia, Women, Culture* (Indiana UP, 1996), 209–24.
[25] Zakrevskii, the governor-general of Moscow, was displeased with the anonymous epigram "Ty ne molod, i ne glup..." Rostopchina was suspected to be the author; to vindicate herself, she took measures to find out the true author, who turned out to be Pavlov. There were no repercussions until 1853, when Pavlova sent her father to complain to the same Zakrevskii that Pavlov was gambling away her family's fortune.

This complaint gave Zakrevskii the perfect chance to avenge himself for Pavlov's epigram, in the resulting search, arrest and six-month exile of Pavlov. A year later, Rostopchina satirized Pavlova's spat with her former friend I.I. Panaev, in the poem 'Pesnia po povodu perepiski uchenogo muzha s ne menee uchenoi zhenoiu' (Rostopchina, Stikhotvoreniya…, cited in fo. 21 above, pp. 370–3). Despite these events, Pavlov maintained cordial relations with Rostopchina: he occasionally frequented Rostopchina's Saturday salons in Moscow (Berg, 'Grafinya', 702), and when he read the caricature of himself in Rostopchina's *Dom sumasshedshikh* (1858), he was reported to have laughed heartily without taking offense (N.V. Sushkov's letter to Rostopchina, *Dom sumasshedshikh: shutka-satira* (Moscow, 1858), pp. 707–9).

[26] V.S. Kiselev-Sergenin, 'Taina Grafini E.P. Rostopchinoi', *Neva* 9 (1994): 267–284, p. 268.

[27] Stephanie Sandler, 'The Law, the Body, and the Book: Three Poems on the Death of Pushkin' *Canadian-American Slavic Studies*, 23.3 (1989): 281–311, p. 299. Indeed, when Rostopchina published her poem, 'Chernovaya kniga Pushkina', she preceded it with Zhukovskii's letter to her, as if supplying proof positive that the transgression was pre-authorized. In the poem itself, Rostopchina likewise makes concessions to gender restrictions:

Но не исполнить мне такого назначенья,
Но не достигнуть мне желанной вышины!
Не все источники живого песнопенья,
Не все предметы мне доступны и даны:
Я женщина! .. во мне и мысль и вдохновенье
Смиренной скромностью быть скованы должны!

[But I won't be able to fulfill such a task,
I won't reach the desired height!
Not all sources of vital song,
Nor all subjects, are accessible and given to me:
I am a woman! .. In me, thought and inspiration
Should be reconciled with humble discretion!]

[28] Hasty, cited in fo. 11 above, p. 2.

К вопросу о типологии женской автобиографии

Ольга Демидова

Автор исследования обращается к женской автобиографии в рамках проекта "Русская история глазами женщин", сосредоточиваясь, в основном, на периоде рубежа 19–20 веков и последующих десятилетий. Таким образом, хронологические рамки исследования оказываются достаточно широкими; событийные рамки включают в себя все наиболее значимые коллизии европейской и российской истории от Первой мировой войны и событий 1917 года до последующей эмиграции, межвоенных десятилетий и Второй мировой войны. Материалом для исследования послужили как опубликованные тексты известных авторов, так и малоизвестные и/или архивные тексты, подготовленные/готовящиеся мною к публикации.

Авторы архивных текстов – эмигрантки, пережившие все ужасы российской революции и гражданской войны и волею судьбы оказавшиеся за пределами России[1]. Время создания текстов – от 1917 до конца 1960-х, т. е. они были написаны как под непосредственным впечатлением от событий, так и по памяти по прошествии довольно длительного времени; в последнем случае возможно говорить о неизбежных аберрациях, взаимных наложениях различных хронологических пластов и т.п.

Социальные, возрастные, культурные характеристики авторов текстов весьма разнообразны: это представительницы как минимум трех поколений, всех сословий, многих профессий (писательницы, художницы, актрисы, деятельницы образования, сестры милосердия и пр.). На этом основании естественно предположить, что авторский идентитет будет конструироваться по-разному в различных текстах в зависимости от того, в каких социокультурных границах находится автор и каких ролей придерживается, каким конвенциям следует, какие табу боится или, наоборот, стремится нарушить. В связи с этим значительный интерес представляет вопрос о типологии ролей, конвенций и табу, актуализированных в текстах, т.е. в конечном счете вопрос об автоконцепции женской личности в рамках чужого дискурса (подробнее об этом см. далее).

Любому исследователю, имеющему дело с большими массивами текстов, приходится сталкиваться с необходимостью их систематизации (классификации), на первый взгляд, столь мало приложимой к произведениям автодокументальных жанров. Однако систематизация в данном случае является скорее методическим приемом, поскольку позволяет рассмотреть группы текстов, объединенных по различным признакам, и выявить сходство и различия авторской позиции и принципов конструирования авторского идентитета. Кроме того, она позволяет с большей определенностью говорить о типологических характеристиках автобиографических текстов. Ниже предложены некоторые из возможных вариантов классификации, основанные на наиболее очевидных и общих для всех рассматриваемых текстов признаках. На мой взгляд, они приложимы к произведениям как женского, так и мужского пера, однако ни в коей мере не претендуют на универсальность и вполне допускают – при необходимости – возможность иных классификаций в зависимости от задач того или иного исследования.

Одним из традиционных вопросов, требующих разрешения при работе с автобиографическими текстами, является вопрос о "чистоте жанра". Рассмотренные с этой точки зрения, тексты подразделяются на:

а) собственно автобиографии, с данным автором жанровым определением;

б) мемуары;

в) дневники;

г) письма.

Необходимо отметить, что дневники и мемуары рассматриваются мною именно как литературные произведения документально-психологической прозы, и, таким образом, к ним вполне приложимо утверждение о взаимовлиянии литературных текстов и представлений о полоролевых различиях[2]. Совершенно очевидно, что оба жанра документируют меняющиеся представления о мужском и женском, изменяясь при этом сами, а иногда и способствуя изменению литературных моделей женского и мужского[3].

Основываясь на предложенной Л. Гинзбург классификации произведений психологической прозы[4], я отношу все указанные тексты (мемуары, дневники, письма) к автобиографическим[5], исходя из определения автобиографии как описания своей жизни, основанного на работе памяти и сосредоточенного на психологических переживаниях, мыслях и чувствах автора. С этой точки зрения, и дневникам, и мемуарам, несомненно, присущи автобиографические черты (вообще вопрос о возможности "чистой" автобиографии заслуживает, на мой взгляд, специальной дискуссии[6]). И в дневниках, и в мемуарах фиксируются события частной жизни автора на фоне общественной и культурной жизни, нередко сопровождаемые самоописанием и самооценкой. Дневник позволяет проследить все стадии нелегкой работы автора по самопознанию[7] и познанию мира, определению своего места в нем, самоидентификации. Мемуар в большей или меньшей степени предоставляет те же возможности, но внимание автора направлено не на происходящее в данный момент, а отодвинуто во времени. Дневниковую запись, таким образом, можно рассматривать как "автобиографию момента" или "точечную автобиографию"; мемуар – как "автобиографию в ретроспективе" (термины мои – О. Д.). Однако нередко и дневниковые записи приобретают ретроспективный, мемуарный характер, когда запись делается по прошествии значительного времени, т. е представляется возможным говорить не столько о ”чистоте”, сколько о пограничности и взаимопроникновении жанров, причем не только на содержательном, но и на сугубо формальном, структурном уровне. Авторы автобиографий нередко включают в свои тексты дневниковые записи, адресованные им или написанные ими письма, свои и чужие воспоминания об описываемых событиях (см., например, *Курсив мой* Н. Берберовой). Кроме того, в соответствии с русской культурной традицией авторы (как женщины, так и мужчины) вообще нечасто дают своим несомненно автобиографическим текстам жанровое определение ”автобиография”.

Возможно, наиболее спорным покажется попытка поместить письма в указанный ряд автобиографических текстов. Однако к письмам приложимы все вышеописанные характеристики; более того, представляется возможным выделить письмо-автобиографию (деловую или интимную, причем нередко даже в сугубо деловое письмо-анкету авторы вносят сведения не только фактографического характера[8]), письмо-дневник, письмо-мемуар; существуют письма, объединяющие признаки всех названных видов. Достаточно вспомнить известные всем письма М. Цветаевой и З. Гиппиус, письма Евг. Пастернак Б. Пастернаку[9]; из не ставших пока достоянием исследователей – письма А. Даманской В. Миролюбову и А. Горнфельду, Н. Берберовой В. и Б. Зайцевым[10] и др.

Инвариантом жанровой классификации, тесно связанным с нею, можно считать классификацию женских автобиографических текстов по хронологии и широте охвата событий. Хронологические рамки текстов могут быть самыми разнообразными: от развернутых жизнеописаний до фрагментарных зарисовок отдельных событий, которые можно рассматривать как ”наброски плана” или ”материалы” для более полной автобиографии. В некоторых случаях подобные фрагменты публиковались автором задолго до того, как вошли в законченный текст мемуарно-автобиографического характера.

Другой вариант классификации представляет собой классификация по степени общественно-культурной ”значимости” автора и участия в описываемых событиях, в рамках которой разграничиваются:

а) автобиографии политических и общественных деятелей;

б) автобиографии деятелей культуры (писательниц, артисток, художниц и пр. как первого, так и второго, третьего и т.п. ряда);

в) автобиографии, авторы которых не принимали активного участия в общественной, политической, художественной жизни, являясь лишь наблюдателями и "протоколистами". Последние – наиболее многочисленны и менее всего изучены; они находятся в позиции многоуровневой маргинальности, и к ним в силу этого реже всего обращаются как читатели, так и исследователи. Между тем, тексты подобного рода позволяют судить о том, какими способами репрезентирует себя, в каких социокультурных границах находится и каким литературным образцам следует обычная, "среднестатистическая" женщина, пишущая автобиографию в 20 столетии, в отличие от автора предшествующих эпох, если таковые отличия имеются[11].

Можно утверждать, что тексты первых двух типов, по преимуществу, построены по схеме "я и события", тогда как тексты третьего типа основываются на установке "события глазами автора" (хотя возможны исключения, особенно в текстах второго типа[12]). Следует также принимать во внимание, что в тексте любого из указанных типов отбор материала неизменно производится автором и, таким образом, является своего рода косвенной характеристикой. Большее внимание уделяется именно тем событиям, степень участия в которых автор оценивает как весьма значительную, и эти события, как правило, описаны более детально и более эмоционально; таким образом автор количественно и качественно маркирует описываемое как *свое* в рамках чужого дискурса.

И, наконец, женские автобиографические тексты можно классифицировать по степени выдержанности "установки на достоверность", как правило, постулируемой автором. Подобная установка присуща любому автодокументальному тексту, по определению стремящемуся предельно точно воссоздать реальность, однако следует учитывать и то обстоятельство, что автобиография – жанр по определению же субъективный, хотя и представляется возможным говорить о большей или меньшей субъективности текста, о стремлении (выявленном или не выявленном) автора к объективности, об установке на "точность" описаний и характеристик и т.п., т.е. об автобиографии как реконструкции и/или деконструкции действительности[13]. Субъективность в данном случае может быть двоякого рода: как осознанное и нередко постулируемое стремление к точности факта и как неосознанное, но явно выраженное стремление не выйти за рамки господствующего дискурса ("своего" для мужчин и "чужого" для женщин).

Значительный интерес также представляет сравнительный анализ в этом аспекте мужских и женских автобиографических текстов, что, на мой взгляд, является одним из продуктивных направлений гендерноориентированного исследования автобиографии. Например, сравнение текстов того и другого рода, посвященных описанию событий 1917 и последующих лет, участниками которых были авторы, делает очевидным принципиальное идеологическое различие мужской и женской автобиографии. Мужчины, даже в жанрово маркированных текстах, в подробностях воссоздают прежде всего внешние события, т. е. тяготеют к жанру сухой исторической хроники, отводя ссбс роль фиксирующего происходящее наблюдателя. Женщины, по преимуществу, стремятся воссоздать эмоционально-нравственную историю, свою и своего поколения, сопровождая описание происходящего этическими оценками. У мужчин вызывают неприятие действия отдельных личностей и политических партий, у женщин – нарушение или отсутствие нравственных законов. Иными словами, мужчины руководствуются установкой на событийную достоверность, женщины – на достоверность переживаний и нравственного императива, даже если в некоторых случаях их точка зрения противоречит сложившимся стереотипам[14]. Так, одна из авторов, сравнивая русскую революцию с французской, отдает предпочтение "кровожадному животному Марату" и "озверевшей толпе, которая хватает и тащит на гильотину людей", поскольку эта толпа все же "идейна". В России же "пьяной, безобразной толпой солдат" и "дикой толпой крестьян" руководят люди, "которым политика помогает ничего не делать и красть, <...> благо все теперь происходит безнаказанно"[15].

В военных автобиографических текстах, описывая события гражданской войны, мужчины представляют их как последовательность военных действий, удачных или неудачных в силу разного рода обстоятельств; оценке подлежат эти обстоятельства, военное искусство, опытность полководца и т.п. В женских текстах война представлена как изначально бессмысленное и безнравственное братоубийственное действо, бесцельно уносящее тысячи жизней, хотя борьба с большевиками признается необходимой.

При изучении женских автобиографических текстов (как, впрочем, и мужских) возникает целый ряд вопросов, связанных с личностью автора[16]; однако все они, на мой взгляд, так или иначе приводят к вопросу о степени авторского умолчания. Все рассматриваемые мною тексты написаны в рамках чужого дискурса, с соблюдением определенных норм письма, обусловленных не менее определенными нормами восприятия полов, и с учетом жестких границ допустимого и табуированного в саморепрезентации. Роли, в которых выступают авторы, – традиционные женские роли спутницы жизни, жены, матери, хранительницы очага (Т. Манухина, Ф. Беннигсен, Ю. Кутырина, Н. Щербачева и др.), дочери (Е. Лакьер, А. Линден), бабушки (Е. Сущинская), сестры и/или сестры милосердия (В. Шелепина), одинокой женщины, самостоятельно зарабатывающей на жизнь (А. Даманская, А. Петрункевич), ученицы (Г. Кузнецова, И. Одоевцева, В. Романович, в определенном смысле – Н. Берберова). Следует отметить, что закрепление за автором одной какой-либо роли достаточно условно: как правило, в рамках одного текста совмещаются несколько ролей. Иногда роль принимается автором как данность, в некоторых случаях намеренно педалируется, реже автор подчеркнуто отталкивается от нее, постулируя свое стремление освободиться от навязанных рамок. Однако в любом случае роль предполагает наличие определенных табу, запретных тем, которых следует избегать, даже если это противоречит фактам реальной биографии автора (т. е. можно утверждать, что в данном случае жизнь оказывается менее табуированной, чем литература).

Классический случай – дневник Г. Кузнецовой[17], ни единым словом не упоминающий об истинных отношениях автора с И. Буниным. На страницах дневника Кузнецова предстает перед читателем как начинающая писательница, ученица Мастера, живущая в его доме и делящая с ним и его женой трудности эмигрантского быта, т.е. выступает во вполне допустимых для молодой женщины ролях приемной дочери, помощницы и ученицы. И если о полноте отношений с Буниным проницательный читатель может при желании догадаться, причина ухода ученицы из дома учителя так и остается неизвестной – на нее нет даже намека.

Одоевцева в первой части своих мемуаров создает вполне прозрачный миф о своей платонической дружбе с Гумилевым, во второй – о счастливом браке с Г. Ивановым[18]. Даманская умалчивает о своей семейной драме и многочисленных увлечениях[19], Романович – о своей деятельности во время гражданской войны[20], Шелепина – о том, что сестрам милосердия приходилось выполнять не только свои сугубо профессиональные обязанности[21]. Все перечисленное – результат известных запретов, связанных с постулируемыми патриархатным обществом ”женской стыдливостью” и ”типично женской” полоролевой ориентацией: женщинам по определению ”не полагалось” быть излишне откровенными в описании интимных подробностей, равно как и открыто говорить о принадлежности к определенным профессиям, к которым относилась и профессия агента разведки[22].

И даже Берберова, по собственному признанию, этой стыдливостью не обладавшая, оказывается ”не в силах открыть о себе все”[23]. Правда, она делает оговорку: коль скоро ”бацилла” откровенности была открыта до нее, нет смысла открывать ее заново[24]. Тем не менее, у внимательного читателя *Курсива* возникает ряд вполне закономерных вопросов, а сопоставительный анализ текста Берберовой с ее художественной прозой и с текстами других авторов, писавших о ней, дает основания предполагать, что умолчания в *Курсиве* – того же порядка, что и недомолвки в вышеперечисленных текстах. С одной стороны, Берберова как будто выходит далеко за рамки дозволенного, вполне откровенно рассказывая о своем стремлении одновременно ”освободиться” и ”спрятаться”, укрыться за мужской одеждой, о своих отношениях с близкой подругой или о преодолении собственных страхов. С другой, целые этапы ее жизни, необычайно важные для становления личности, словно ”проваливаются” куда-то, образуя многочисленные лакуны в повествовании, при этом за рамками текста остаются собственно любовные переживания автора, ее интимный опыт[25].

Впрочем, *Курсив мой* можно рассматривать и как пример своего рода мифотворчества в рамках автобиографического текста. На первый взгляд, Берберова реконструирует историю своего времени и поколения и свою собственную историю, преследуя вполне определенную цель: рассказать о себе правду, какой бы она ни была. Однако при внимательном прочтении текста нетрудно убедиться в том, что Берберова создает миф о себе как об Иной, отличной от всех остальных, ни на кого не похожей Личности. И этой задаче подчинено все в *Курсиве:* автор производит тщательный отбор материала, оставляя лишь то, что способствует созданию мифа об "инакости" Нины Берберовой, и с удивительной последовательностью выстраивает этот ряд, конструируя его из мини-мифем (детство, отношения с родителями и подругами, годы жизни с Ходасевичем и пр.). Следует отметить, что даже жанровое определение "Автобиография" подчеркивает эту "инакость"[26]. При этом за рамками повествования остается все, что могло бы свидетельствовать о другой, не вписывающейся в творимый миф, стороне личности автора.

Разумеется, далеко не все авторы настолько сознательно и последовательно творят миф о себе, однако определенная степень "мифотворчества" свойственна любому автобиографическому тексту как таковому. Автор творит миф, ориентируясь, как было указано выше, на бытующие в культуре полоролевые стереотипы. В силу этого любой автобиографический текст изобилует умолчаниями и недоговоренностями, во всех без исключения есть немало "темных" мест и "провалов". Что происходит с тем жизненным материалом, который остается "за текстом"? Оказывается ли он безнадежно утраченным, отброшенным автором как ненужный? Скорее всего, да, если речь идет о не-литераторе. В этом случае биографические лакуны либо вообще невозможно восстановить, либо для их восстановления требуется большая исследовательская работа, которая далеко не всегда увенчивается успехом[27]. Что же касается умолчаний в писательских автобиографических текстах, их возможно "расшифровать", обратившись к художественному творчеству автора[28], как правило, позволяющему разгадать загадки автобиографического текста. "Дешифрующее чтение" подобного рода – еще один из продуктивных способов исследования женских автобиографических текстов (как и автобиографий вообще), убедительно доказывающий, что автобиография представляет собой значительно более табуированный и более "таинственный" жанр, чем художественная проза[29].

Список архивных текстов, изданных или готовящиеся к публикации, на которых основана статья

1. Вера Романович, "Воспоминания. Письма к Е. Л.Миллер" в *Новый журнал*, № 195 (1994), сс. 281–298.
2. Татьяна Манухина, "Путешествие из Петербурга в Париж в 1921 году", в Ольга Демидова (ред.-сост.), *Путешествие из Петербурга в Париж. Воспоминания русских писательниц о первых годах советской власти (1917–1924)* (Wilhelmshorst,1996), сс. 157–202.
3. Александра Петрункевич, "Некоторые главы из ненаписанной книги "Как это было". Воспоминания одной русской за 1917–1922 год", в *Путешествие из Петербурга в Париж*, сс. 215–241.
4. Юлия Кутырина, "Октябрьские дни в Москве. (Из моего дневника)", в *Путешествие из Петербурга в Париж*, сс. 203–214.
5. Надежда Щербачева, "Воспоминания", в *Звезда: Ежемесячный литературно-художественный и общественно-политический независимый журнал*, № 2 (1996), сс. 96–113.
6. "В мире скорбны будете..." Из семейного дневника А. П. и Ф. В.Беннигсенов", в *Звезда*, № 12 (1995), сс.165–176.
7. Ванда Линден, *Воспоминания.* – The Bakhmeteff Archive. Mss Linden V.
8. Александра Линден (сестра мужа В. Линден*), Воспоминания и дневник 1917–24гг.* – The Bakhmeteff Archive. Mss Linden A.
9. Елена Лакьер, *Дневник.* – The Bakhmeteff Archive. Mss Lakier.
10. София Сущинская (бабушка Лакьер), *Бегство из Одессы в Севастополь и эвакуация в Египет.* – The Bakhmeteff Archive. Mss Sushinskaiia.
11. Августа Даманская, *Письма В. Миролюбову* – ОР ИРЛИ. Ф.185. Оп.1. Ед. хр.472.
12. Августа Даманская, *Письма А. Г. Горнфельду* – ОР РНБ. Ф.211. Ед.хр.1306.
13. Августа Даманская, "На экране моей памяти", в *Лица. Биографический альманах.* Вып. 7 (Спб.:Феникс, 1996), сс. 112–160; *Новый журнал*, № 198/199, 202, 203/204, (Нью-Йорк, 1996), сс. 273–315, 152–188, 198–258.
14. Нина Берберова, *Письма Вере и Борису Зайцевым 1940-х – 1950-х гг.* – The Bakhmeteff Archive. Mss Zaitzev.
15. Зинаида Журавская, Письма А. Даманской 1920-х – 1930-х гг., в Ольга Демидова (ред.), Женский вопрос в контексте национальной культуры. Вып. 3, Ч. 1, Спб., 1999, сс. 130–151.

Ссылки

[1] См. прилагаемый список архивных текстов, использованных при подготовке доклада.
[2] Подробнее об этом см.: Ina Schabert, "Gender als Kategorie einer neuen Literaturgeschichtsschreibung", in Hadumod von Bussman und Renate Hof (eds.), *Genus. Zur Geschlechterdifferenz in der Kulturwissenschaften* (Alfred Kroener Verlag Stuttgart, 1995), SS.163–204; рус. перевод: Ина Шаберт, "Гендер как категория новой истории литературы", в Элизабет Шоре и Каролин Хайдер (ред), *Пол, гендер, культура* (М.: РГГУ, 1999), сс. 109–130.
[3] Примерами последнего можно считать дневники Зинаиды Гиппиус и *Курсив мой* Нины Берберовой, о которых речь ниже.
[4] Л. Я.Гинзбург, *О психологической прозе* (Л.:Советский писатель, 1971).
[5] О близости жанров мемуара, дневника и автобиографии см., например: Т. М. Колядич, *Воспоминания писателей. Проблемы поэтики жанра* (М.:МГПУ, 1998); А. Г. Тартаковский, *Русская мемуаристика XVIII–первой половины XIXв. От рукописи к книге* (М.:Наука, 1991).
[6] Близость жанров автобиографии и мемуаров неизменно оговаривается в толковых, литературных и энциклопедических словарях. Кроме того, подтверждение этому можно найти и у авторов автобиографий, см., напр, утверждение Берберовой: "Автобиография – рассказ о себе, воспоминания – рассказ о других. Впрочем, случается, что и воспоминания косвенно больше говорят о самом авторе, чем о людях, о которых он вспоминает". – Нина Берберова, *Курсив мой. Автобиография* (М.:Согласие,1996), с. 29.
[7] Ср. название автобиографии Николая Бердяева – *Самопознание* и дневника Юлии Кутыриной – *Исповедь моей души* (текст дневника опубл. мною в: *Путешествие из Петербурга в Париж. Воспоминания русских писательниц о первых годах советской власти (1917–1924).* Wilhelmshort:Frank Goepfert Verlag,1996).
[8] См., напр., ответы на анкету С.Венгерова. – ИРЛИ. Отдел рукописей. Ф.377.
[9] См.: Существованья ткань сквозная. Борис Пастернак. *Переписка с Евгенией Пастернак. Дополненная письмами к Е. Б.Пастернаку и его воспоминаниями* (М.:Новое литературное обозрение, 1998).
[10] Готовятся мною к публикации.
Даманская Августа Филипповна (1875–1959) – прозаик, переводчица, журналистка; подробнее о ней см. вступит. статью к ее мемуарам. Публикация, вступит. статья и комментарий О. Демидовой, в *Лица. Биографический альманах.* Вып.7 (Спб.:Феникс, 1996), сс. 112–119.
Миролюбов Виктор Сергеевич (1860–1939) – издатель, редактор, журналист.
Горнфельд Аркадий Георгиевич (1867–1941) – литературовед, критик; их обоих Даманская считала своими учителями в литературе.
[11] О круге вопросов, связанных с женской автобиографией 19 в., см., напр.: Ирина Савкина, "Чужое – мое сокровище": Женские мемуары как автобиография

("Воспоминания" С.В.Капнист-Скалон)" в *Гендерные исследования*, № 2 (М.: Человек и карьера, 1999), сс. 178–208.
[12] См. нашу статью "Aliens in the Hostile World" в: *New Gender Consciousness in Language and History of the Modern Age* (Zuerich – в печати).
[13] Гинзбург говорит об установке на подлинность, ср.: "Особое качество документальной литературы – в той установке на подлинность, ощущение которой не покидает читателя, но которая далеко не всегда равна фактической точности" (Л.Я. Гинзбург, *О психологической прозе,* с. 10).
[14] Сказанное, разумеется, не означает, что этические оценки отсутствуют в мужских автобиографиях; речь в данном случае идет о "среднестатистической" тенденции, делающейся очевидной при анализе больших массивов автобиографических текстов.
[15] "В мире скорбны будете..." Из семейного дневника А. П. и Ф. В. Беннигсенов. Публ. О.Демидовой, в *Звезда*: *Ежемесячный литературно-художественный и общественно-политический независимый журнал*, № 12 (1995), с. 170. Цитируемый текст – довольно редкий пример парного семейного дневника, в котором приводится параллельное описание одних и тех же событий 1918–1920гг., сделанное мужем и женой.
[16] См. об этом, в частн., указ. соч. И.Савкиной.
[17] Галина Кузнецова, *Грасский дневник* (М.:Московский рабочий, 1995).
[18] Ирина Одоевцева, "На берегах Невы", в Ирина Одоевцева, *Избранное* (М.:Согласие, 1998).сс.235–328; 382–472; 483–528; 550–557;Ирина Одоевцева, "На берегах Сены" в Ирина Одоевцева, *Избранное*, сс. 571, 635–638; 645; 696–708; 713–740; 745–789.
[19] Понадобился год архивных разысканий, чтобы лишь частично восстановить историю замужества Даманской и ее разъезда с мужем; тайны рождения ее сына раскрыть не удалось.
[20] Основываясь на косвенных признаках, можно утверждать, что она некоторое время выполняла задания английской разведки.
[21] Заслуживает внимания тот факт, что не все из перечисленных текстов предназначались для публикации; т.е., даже создавая текст для предельно узкого (напр., семейного) круга читателей или предназначая его для закрытого архивного хранения, авторы не решались нарушить существовавший стереотип саморепрезентации.
[22] Интересно отметить, что табу профессионального характера оказались менее живучими, чем т.наз."запреты нравственного порядка".
[23] Нина Берберова, *Курсив мой*, с.505.
[24] Там же.
[25] См., напр., намеренно фрагментарное описание Wanderjahre. – Нина Берберова, *Курсив мой,* сс. 133–135.
[26] Подробнее об этом см.: Ольга Демидова, "Автобиография как сотворение мифа: "Курсив мой" Нины Берберовой" в*: Sciences and Humanities: Современное гуманитарное знание как синтез наук. Материалы международной научной конференции* (Санкт-Петербург, 2–3 декабря 1999). (Спб., 1999). С.64–65.

[27] Исследование такого рода необходимо при восстановлении биографии автора и имеет лишь опосредованное отношение к исследованию автобиографии как таковой.
[28] Блестящий пример подобного "дешифрования" – статья Д.Томсона "Мужское Я в творчестве Зинаиды Гиппиус: литературный прием или психологическая потребность?" в *Преображение: Русский феминистский журнал.* № 4 (1996), сс.138–149. См. также нашу статью "В поисках идентичности: "Мыс Бурь" и "Курсив мой" Нины Берберовой" (готовится к печати).
[29] Ср. парадоксальное, на первый взгляд, утверждение Берберовой: "Первая часть современных автобиографий – раскрытие себя. Вторая – очень часто – писать обратное тому, что было, в борьбе с самим собой, если еще продолжается борьба. И третья – умышленное усложнение авторами писаний о себе". – Нина Берберова, *Курсив мой,* с.505.

The Authorised Version:

The Auto/Biographies of Vera Panova

Catriona Kelly

This paper is not intended as a substantive contribution to research on the writings of Vera Panova (1903–1975). Rather, it uses Panova's work to raise a number of broad issues of interest to the study of Russian women's autobiography in general. The first is the question of the relationship between different kinds of life-writing, autobiography and biography, the memoir of self versus the memoir of another, or "the Other". Recent writing on autobiography has taken this as a discrete literary or para-literary genre, an alternative and specific version of fiction distinguished by its pretensions to authenticity, its assurances or insinuations that there exists a real-life "fabula" of which this account is the "syuzhet"; analysis has catalogued the rhetorical conventions that are associated with this mission of persuasion. Additionally, to a modernist or post-modernist sensibility, autobiography has been of interest for its expression of interiority, its commemoration of the experiences, doubts, and hesitations of a self which may be atomised and ephemeral, but which is still in some way tangibly present.[1] The lives written about do not have to be outwardly remarkable, but they do have to be memorably inward, to recall mental vicissitudes and evanescent sensations exquisitely different from those of any other writing subject. One sub-branch of this kind of life-writing is the "portrait of the artist", as exemplified by Joyce, by Nabokov's *Speak, Memory*, by Bruce Chatwin's *What am I Doing Here* or by Tsvetaeva's autobiographical essays; another is the sort of self-conscious personal history manifested not only in Simone de Beauvoir's *Mémoires d'une jeune fille rangée* but also in Nina Berberova's *Kursiv moi* (a text that deserves the kind of extended study that has been given to, for example, Nadezhda Mandelstam, Lidiya Chukovskaya or Evgeniya Ginzburg).

There are, however, many autobiographies which do not offer such tantalising vistas of apparent self-revelation as the texts just mentioned, and which are not even salvaged by their status as testimonials of the times in which the writer lived (the capacity in which autobiography has usually been valued by social and political historians).[2] Rather, they are biographies in the first person, official histories of achievement that happen to be written in the first person. Records of exceptionality, texts of this kind are at the same time impersonal, rendering individual history in a manner that draws heavily upon formula. An example of this kind of text is the revolutionary autobiography: the life histories composed by 1920s Soviet workers about how they came to Communism in the years of revolution: here moments such as the first reading of Lenin's *Who is to Blame?* or *Marxism and Empiriocriticism* were obligatory perepeteias in the narrative.[3] Another is the life of the Soviet artist, which had its own kind of equally restrictive conventions. As an unusually frank autobiographer in this genre, the comic actor Igor' Il'insky, recollected, when composing his memoirs in the late 1950s, he was warned by well-wishers, "They won't print a book of the sort you have in mind! You're a People's Artist of the USSR. You ought to be an example for Soviet youth. But you've narrated one or two scenes from your life which are exemplary in a bad way. They'll throw those out and only leave in what's good."[4] As a matter of fact, Il'insky got his way, and the memoir includes some surprisingly (in the context) discreditable episodes, for example the account of a flaming row with his father when Il'insky was an adolescent; but the fact that the book was published at the height of the Khrushchev Thaw was surely of significance here. By and large, memoirs of Soviet artists, including writers, were tedious chronicles of books written, lectures delivered, famous figures encountered, interspersed with sage thoughts – a combination of *tvorcheskii put'* (a stereotypical presentation of the "creative path") with advice on how to live life to the supposedly naive reader.[5]

The first two volumes of the canonical anthology *Sovetskie pisateli: avtobiografii* (Soviet Writers: Autobiographies), which contain around 120 life histories, provide many examples of this kind of third-person biography.[6] As the introduction ominously puts it: "A vital sense of duty to the nation provokes an impelling need in writers to test themselves. This is perhaps whence originates the desire to experience one's life's path once more and to scrutinise it, to generalise from experience, to *pass on that experience to younger generations*."[7] The principle of *sotsial'nyi zakaz* (the "social command" or "commission", i.e. the demand that written texts should respond to topical political and social questions and be ideologically correct) applied as much to autobiography as to any other genre of Soviet literary or para-literary activity. What this in practice meant was that autobiographies, like novels and newspaper articles, were often directly commissioned by Soviet publishing-houses, which supposedly acted as agents for the will of the Soviet masses (many of the autobiographies in *Sovetskie pisateli* were indeed written to order in this way). As the phrasing in the quotation suggests, an externally imposed "duty" was supposed to dictate a "desire" to communicate via a mediating sense of "need". And the "need" to which the writer responded, as one of the authors in *Sovetskie pisateli* makes clear, was nothing less than the prestige of the entire nation: "One's biography equals the forty hero cities of the Soviet Union."[8] No wonder, then, that on the one hand, many of the autobiographies began with the formulation, "Pisat' o sebe trudno" (Writing about oneself is hard), and that, on the other, the "self" that emerged had little of the uncertainty that is associated with modernist autobiographical writing in the West, and which, indeed, characterises such key Russian modernist texts as Blok's *Vozmezdie* (Retribution) or Akhmatova's *Poema bez geroya* (Poem without a Hero).

To be sure, manifestations of self-doubt, such as irony and humour, were not altogether absent from the narratives collected by Brainina and Nikitina, some of which took at least a mildly critical view of the pomposity to be found in the standard writer's life. The dramatist and prose writer Boris Lavrenyov, for example, stated, with refreshing openness, "I can't stand it when writers carry themselves round like precious vases of some kind and don't talk like human beings, but rather, let forth weighty statements and prophetic utterances".[9] Naughtily parodying the genre requirements of the official autobiography, he announced at the beginning that, "in order to avoid misunderstandings", he wanted to make clear that his ancestors included "no district supervisors, high-ranking officers in the Tsarist secret police, military procurators or ministers of internal affairs".[10] And Yury Smolich rather wistfully recalled the autobiography that he had supplied when requested for one as a young man: "Born 1900. Date of death will follow when relevant."[11] Generally, though, uncertainty was remarkable by its absence: "self-criticism", where present, was not allowed to threaten the life history's status as exemplary text, but instead figured in the form of accounts of difficulties overcome. The typical life-history in the book consisted of a list of literary projects, meetings with other famous writers (including, if at all possible, Gorky), prizes received, and official positions held (right up to the Board of the Union of Writers or the Supreme Soviet), with, in between, truisms – "The only weapon available to a writer when he writes a novel is the word" – landing as heavily as human cannonballs.[12] Sometimes, to be sure, surprisingly interesting details were supplied about a writer's early childhood, but personal information entirely disappeared once the appearance of his or her first book had been recorded, according to the principle articulated by Samuil Galkin: "For a writer the most important part of his autobiography is his books."[13]

It would be comforting to record that the autobiographies by Soviet women in the book modified this pattern in any significant way. However, the mere handful of female writers included in the two original volumes of *Sovetskie pisateli* (all of five, namely Inber, Karavaeva, Seifullina, Forsh, and Shaginyan), limited personal information to childhood events as well. And indeed, Anna Karavaeva went further than this in her striving to accommodate the official template of writerly autobiography. Only the most general details about her family were mentioned: the reader was told, "My relations and friends were honest and hard-working people, but their horizons were narrow and petit-bourgeois".[14] This underlined the author's heroic *podvig* in turning herself, by constant self-education, into a major Soviet writer, as well as a witness of historic events essential to the nation's reshaping, including the Russo-Japanese War, the 1905 Revolution, the ("unsatisfactory") February Revolution, the Treaty of Brest (which provoked in her "a joyful sense of relief and triumph"), and the Second World War. Every possible sense of personal engagement with these events was played down: no distinction was drawn between those witnessed at first hand (for instance, the industry drive of the first months of wartime) and those simply read about in the newspaper (for instance, the Beilis case). And, just as individual comment was effaced by hearsay and cliché, so the complex, and potentially extremely interesting, processes by which Karavaeva maintained her position as an officially honoured Soviet writer while ideological lines changed were evoked in frustratingly evasive language. Of the rewriting of her early novel *Lesozavod* (The Saw Mill), which went through a "post-Socialist Realist" redaction to bring it into conformity with the linguistic constraints set out in the 1934 Congress of Soviet Writers, she observed, "Over the years I had come to the conclusion that the folkloric decorations [of the original version] weighed the novel down and therefore later [the timing is not made more precise!] they were removed [by whom?] without regret."[15] Once again, externally imposed "duty" and "need", and internal "desire", were made to be in perfect harmony.

Narratives of this kind have had a rather limited appeal for Western analysts of autobiographical discourse, including those of feminist inclinations: the temptation to treat them as manifestations of false consciousness has been hard to resist. For instance, Barbara Engel and Anastasiya Posadskaya, in their *A Revolution of their Own*, record a tussle with one of their informants, Sofiya Pavlova, who was eager to provide them with a life history of just this kind:

> Pavlova's interview reflected her continuing loyalty to the system to which she had devoted her life. She seemed reluctant to criticize any Soviet actions, refusing to discuss the outlawing of abortion in 1936 and downplaying the fact that her beloved second husband perished during the terror of the 1930s. Only Posadskaya's persistent questioning led Pavlova to acknowledge the harmful consequences to her son, who was born after his father's arrest and because of the new family code of 1936, was registered as having no father, that is, as illegitimate. Likewise, only as a result of Posadskaya's insistent questioning did Pavlova acknowledge that women's access to the higher reaches of the party might have been limited. [...]

> The first time Posadskaya interviewed her, Pavlova talked about her childhood, about her first and second marriages, her difficult move to Moscow, the births of her children, and her hardships during the war years. But then she had second thoughts. In her own opinion, her political work – her work for the party, in international organisations and the like – was what really mattered about her life, even though nobody was interested in it at present.[16]

The passage here can be taken as a schematic polarisation of two different views of "what really mattered" about Pavlova's life: party work versus private life. In the view of Engel and Posadskaya, Pavlova's privileging of the first and omission of the latter was a peculiar and regrettable form of behaviour, something bordering on self-censorship. In a kind of therapeutic attempt to restore wholeness and unity to their informant's life-history, they attempted to fill up the gaps left by Pavlova, persuading her to dwell on the stretches of her life that she wished to excise. As they state, in the account printed in their book "we have included both her personal history and that of her political work" (p. 51).

I do not cite this instance in order to accuse Engel and Posadskaya of unethical or suspect behaviour. The composite version of Pavlova's life that they have put together is without doubt broader and more valuable as source material for historians (as well as more interesting) than the history of party work that she might have produced in fidelity to the Soviet dogma that "there is no such thing as a personal life" (*lichnogo net*) – to quote a line from Fyodor Gladkov's paradigmatic production novel, *Cement*. However, I think there are some problems with always reading "official" Soviet first person narratives as though they were inadequate and insufficient, of invariably following the instructions given by Véronique Garros, Natalia Korenevskaya, and Thomas Lahusen in the introduction to their collection of 1930s memoirs, *Intimacy and Terror*: "The reader might also explore what the diaries *do not tell.*"[17] This is partly because reading for omissions makes the hiatuses and silences of Soviet diaries take on a false particularity, as though "telling all" were an effortless activity in other societies, and as though the genre conventions of autobiography, in fact one of the more nationally idiosyncratic genres, translated effortlessly from society to society. But it is also, and more importantly, because emphasis on information that is concealed or played down distracts attention from the actual ways of telling in Soviet official autobiographies. It would, after all, be equally interesting to consider what stories these memoirs *are* in fact narrating, as Hilde Hoogenboom has so effectively done in the case of Vera Figner's autobiography, or as Beth Holmgren did in her study of Nadezhda Mandelstam and Lidiya Chukovskaya.[18] This is what I shall attempt in the following brief sketch of a selection of published memoirs composed by and about Vera Panova.[19]

It is important to make clear at the beginning that my purpose is not to reverse the decline in Panova's reputation that has set in since her death, and to discover previously unsuspected independence of mind and literary originality in her work. She was the subject of respectful reviews in Soviet literary journals during her lifetime, and of an adulatory – and impeccably tedious – official biography; she was accorded the signal honour of a multi-volume *Sobranie sochinenii* (collected works) and of a volume of memoirs by friends and relations.[20] But the popularity of her work has faded, and it has proved hard to recuperate her from oblivion. Adele Barker gives her only a lukewarm commendation in the article that she wrote for the *Dictionary of Russian Women Writers*:

> Panova's works are characterized by their traditional style, free of literary experimentation. The moral standards she advocates have less relation to the Socialist canon than to traditional old-fashioned morality. The darker Dostoevskian sides of human behavior are foreign to her, as is exploration into the complexities of human behavior. Her characters, both male and female, tend to be good and decent people who go astray only to return to the right path in their lives afterward. Panova has won a place in Soviet letters not only for the empathy she felt for her characters but for her sincerity as a writer during times when it was difficult to write both sincerely and well.[21]

To be fair, the unadventurousness of Panova's prose is less striking when it is related to the possibilities available to official writers working in the Stalin years: the *in medias res* opening of *Vremena goda* (The Seasons), published in 1954, as well as the text's emphasis on *byt* (everyday life), created something of a furore when the novel was first published. But, like many Soviet writers, she rose at best to the level of a competent realist in the late nineteenth- or early twentieth-century manner. There is nothing in her writing, technically speaking, to indicate that *Ulysses* was ever published, or indeed that the work of, say, Babel, Bulgakov, Olesha or the 1920s Olga Forsh ever existed. Even the work that has brought her most enduring fame, the children's stories that she produced in the 1950s, now seems ideologically overburdened. In the novella *Seryozha*, for example, the child's-eye perspective very effectively employed in much of the novel is rather clumsily suspended in places so that the reader can overhear conversations between his mother and stepfather about moral matters. When Seryozha addresses a bossy and interfering neighbour as "you stupid fool" (*durak*), for instance, his mother is horrified, but his stepfather responds with, "There's no pedagogical teaching according to which you can take exception to a boy calling a fool a fool."[22]

Equally, there are plenty of standard Soviet motifs in Panova's memoirs. In the essays published in the collection *Zametki literatora* (A Writer's Observations, 1972), for instance, memories are centred on the writer's intellectual development, and in particular, on a bookcase, "its lower shelves taken up by various work-tools and rolled-up blueprints. On the upper shelves stood various books, among them Pushkin, Gogol', and Turgenev – my first [intellectual] food, the real legacy I got from my father."[23] In fact, these books were quite literally a "legacy", since Panova's father had drowned while she was still a small girl. But a critic of psychoanalytical inclinations would look in vain for any indication of trauma resulting from this. According to a standard Soviet – and indeed, as Andrew Wachtel has shown, Russian[24] – typology, childhood is represented by Panova as a time of untroubled joy and a storehouse of memories for the budding writer. And the collection contains the expected sprinkling of ruminations on the *tvorcheskii put'* and upon the literary process, complete with obligatory platitudes about Pushkin – "He embraced the whole world in his soul, both the West and the East".[25] And in Panova's more substantial memoir, *O moei zhizni, knigakh i chitatelyakh* (On My Life, Books, and Readers, 1980), personal detail disappears from view (as, according to the canons of Soviet life-history, it should) once the writer is established, to be replaced by accounts of dealing with publishing houses, meeting well-known Soviet writers, and, eventually, receiving the letters from readers that were a standard tribute to the Soviet writer.[26] For anyone interested in autobiography as self-revelation, there is a good deal too much of "books and readers", and far too little of Panova's "life" in *O moei zhizni, knigakh i chitatelyakh.*

As I have already emphasised, the main concern of this paper is not to deal with what is left out of Panova's autobiographies, but it is important to grasp that the documents were produced at the end of the writer's life, in the late 1960s and early 1970s, under the relatively severe censorship that was imposed after the fall of Khrushchev. There is naturally no trace in them of the Panova who emerges from Sergei Dovlatov's collection of aphorisms *Solo na Undervude* (Solo for an Underwood Typewriter), published in America – a woman of forceful opinions and acerbic turn of phrase; nor does one gather from them the extraordinary role that (as recalled by Andrei Bitov) Panova played as one of the few women who had the status of a major literary patron, someone constantly appealed to as the writer of character references and the sponsor of manuscripts being sent to Soviet publishers.[27] Equally naturally, the memoirs gloss over the fate of Panova's second husband, Boris Vakhtin (father of the writer of the same name, Panova's elder son), who was arrested in 1935 and was later to die in a labour camp. And since *O moei zhizni* stops short in 1946, it includes no account of Panova's third marriage, or of her dreadful last years, both of which are dealt with in detail in a riveting memoir by Serafima Yur'eva. Yur'eva, Panova's last secretary, was employed as an amanuensis after a stroke in 1967 had left the writer hemiplegically paralysed and nearly blind, so that she was forced to have the compositions that she could still manage to create taken down in dictation. Yur'eva's memoirs record a Panova in whom despotism was rather pathetically combined with physical helplessness. For instance, when Panova made a fuss about what she was going to wear for an interview with a film director who was hoping to make a cinematic version of her novel *Sentimental'nyi roman* (Sentimental Novel), Yur'eva contrived out-bully her:

> I know better than you what dress I should wear in order to receive a film director! And smack! down goes her fist on the arm of her chair. At this point I – now at the point of absolute desperation – also smacked my hand down on the table. Pull yourself together! Or else you'll put paid to the chances of *Sentimental'nyi roman* getting filmed, don't you see?[28]

Yur'eva also records details of Panova's third marriage that make the last years of Lev and Sof'ya Tolstoi seem tranquil and harmonious. Panova's third husband, David Ryvkin (who wrote under the pen-name David Dar) was a frustrated and unproductive minor writer and bon viveur who liked to surround himself with a coterie of young men to whom he played mentor, and perhaps more. Panova referred to Dar's friends as his "boy wives" (*mal'chiki-zheny*), while Dar himself complained to Yur'eva that "all our [married] life she's hated them [i.e. his young male friends], she's simply been jealous of them."[29] The marriage finally broke down completely in recriminations, arguments about who was the better writer and entitled to become sole owner of the couple's copy of Dal's classic dictionary of the Russian language, and, after Dar's departure to new accommodation, a stream of scornful letters from Panova to their joint acquaintances about the appalling behaviour of her former husband.

All of this makes Yur'eva's account a fascinating, repellent, and apparently authentic document of life in the late Soviet cultural elite, a text where even the comments *en passant* have a peculiar force (as in the revelation that Boris Vakhtin the son met his end aged 51, "suddenly and while holding the telephone receiver" (p. 13). The text is also interesting for Yur'eva's own standpoint as narrator, at once championing the cause of Panova and openly manipulating her for her own good (as when she arranged for the editor of a publishing house to visit and be reassured that Panova had not lost her wits after her stroke, pp. 99–100), and asserting both her indomitability and her frailty (as manifested, for example, in unsparing quotation from Panova's 1967 diary, in which the most recurrent theme was an impatient longing for death ("Idi bystrei, Vremya! – "Skoree begi, vremya" – "Tol'ko smert' pomozhet", p. 19).

Compared with this, Panova's own memoirs are disappointing indeed: the narrative tone is thoroughly bland, the content undemanding. They seem the living illustrations of a poem by Ol'ga Berggol'ts that was a favourite of Panova's: "Net, ne iz knizhek nashikh skudnykh/podob'ya nishchenskoi sumy,/uznaete o tom kak trudno/kak nevozhmozhno zhili my." [No, not from our books, skinny/as a beggar's purse/will you discover how hard, how impossibly hard our lives were.][30] Yet the question of what Panova's official memoirs *do* communicate (apart from the fact that it was difficult to speak directly) still remains interesting. AsYur'eva's memoirs reveal, to include even as much personal detail in one's memoirs as was made available in *O moei zhizni* was to mount a challenge to the canons of official Soviet autobiography:

> Panova found it easy to write about her life; she did it without looking over her shoulder, with the sense that she was leaving behind a memoir for those dear to her, for her relations. What had happened had happened: it was nothing to do with any stranger.
>
> But she needed money. She had no other recent work, nor did she look likely to produce any. She couldn't keep on republishing old stuff *ad infinitum*. So Dar decided to get her notes ready for publication. But if she was going to publish it, she had to rewrite it. Panova resisted. She got low. She didn't want to write any more. With enormous difficulty, Dar talked her round [...] In her present condition it wasn't so simple for her to resurrect the internal editor and censor that she'd 'exiled'. She had no success in producing the kind of thing that it was permitted to publish.
>
> Only his respect for Panova as a person and for her literary reputation stopped the chief editor from rejecting the typescript once and for all. He asked her to cut various sections out altogether, and to write up some new ones: on her books and her writers. 'The radiant vision of my life' was one of these; at first, it was supposed to disappear entirely. They allowed her to say that her second husband had come to a tragic end. That was all. *After a violent battle she was allowed to leave in the love and family theme.*[31]

Incidentally interesting because it lays bare the importance of money as a stimulus to publication for Soviet writers (a motivation absolutely never addressed in Soviet sources dating from after the foundation of the Union of Soviet Writers in 1932, and meant for the public eye), this stretch of Yur'eva's memoir is of more immediate relevance to my theme here because it indicates just how inflammatory to official Soviet taste Panova's apparently rather guarded text was. Though the form of one section of the autobiography, the "visionary" chapter, caused problems, the main stumbling block was the content. Panova was considered to have been revealing more than she should have done by allowing *any* personal material into the depiction of her adult life.

That said, writing *O moei zhizni* was not simply a matter of playing cat-and-mouse with the dictates of official taste. Surrendering privacy was not an unproblematic action for Panova herself, as her difficulty in reworking *O moei zhizni* indicates. She was in real life, according to the account of Andrei Bitov, among others, someone who protected her private territory fiercely, receiving those on official business in a positively queenly manner (she used her sitting room as a kind of domestic equivalent to the Soviet official's office, *priemnaya*). And the representation of her autobiographical self in the manner that she wanted was something to which reticence was essential, given that, as her younger son Yury Vakhtin made clear in his extremely interesting memoir of her, she had self-consciously remade her personality. She initiated her assault on the literary metropolis of Leningrad in the late 1930s disadvantaged in a whole variety of ways. She came from the provinces (and from the cultural backwater of Rostov-on-Don, which, as she herself recorded in *O moei zhizni*, did not even have a picture gallery when she was a child and young woman). She had begun her career as a journalist for the children's press, writing pot-boiling articles and stories for pioneer newspapers (for example *Yunye Lenintsy*) in Rostov, emphatically not a prestigious activity; her life took a further turn for the worse after Boris Vakhtin senior's arrest, after which she, the mother of three small children, was forced to take rented accommodation way out in the countryside and to work as a typist on a collective farm. Yet, for all that, she maintained a steely determination and a commitment to self betterment. "That our mother had managed to raise herself to an 'elevated' situation was absolutely obvious to us children, and that sense was absolutely not undermined by the external circumstances of our lives – the fact that we didn't have a place of our own to live in, or that our mother had the humble occupation of a typist."[32]

What makes Panova's memoirs interesting is precisely this vehement commitment on Panova's own part to *kul'turnost'*, the search for a cultivated life. Only Panova's obsession with *kul'turnost'* can explain why her memoirs open with a scene depicting a reprimand meted out by her father to the cat for bad manners. The apparently trivial episode is in fact heavy with significance, displaying an interesting and revealing tension between a certainty that good table manners are important to civilised life, and a perception that conformity equals "lack of initiative":

> [The cat] is sitting next to my father, pretending he has nothing in mind. But he does not manage to keep it up for long. Now he has

> stretched out his paw and laid it on the table. In the middle of the table stands a big dish of braised beef — the delicious-smelling steam rises high above the dish. At the end of the meal, my mother will cut off a slice of beef and put it in Zaika's own bowl, but Zaika would much prefer to stretch out for the beef himself and stick his claws into the scented, juicy meat, and that is why he is stretching out his paw. But now my father's sharp command rings out: 'Zaika!' and the cat immediately retracts his paw and sits serenely on the chair, paws in line — the embodiment of politeness and lack of initiative.[33]

The fact that Panova's representation of herself was intended to display loyalty to *kul'turnost'* in the sense of a wide range of civilised (and in some ways contradictory) values is brought out also by another apparently inconsequential reference, this time to the family's desperation to acquire appropriate furniture in the 1920s, a desperation that Panova sees as deriving not from materialism, but from a sense that the intelligentsia had a duty to live in a cultured way (p. 81).

In what it does reveal as well as in what it does not, *O moei zhizni* is a characteristic document of Soviet middle-class consciousness, an expression of the views of those who were more at home in the 1930s and 1940s than in the 1920s, and who sought to combine a "masculine" commitment to moral fibre and discipline with a "feminine" interest in domestic possessions and refined behaviour. A governing motif in Panova's recollections, including the unpublished ones that she passed on to Yur'eva, was the amused sardonicism she directed at the hardline ideologies of the 1920s, especially as embodied in the beliefs of her unnamed first husband. This man, in Panova's account, insisted his daughter was wrapped up in a scarlet cloth (the colour of the Soviet flag) from the moment she came into the world, and named Alya not Natasha because the latter was a "bourgeois name".[34] Extremely conscious of her public image, Panova offered, in her memoirs, insights into a culture where writers were public figures, used, like officials, as clearing-houses for complaints, worries, and petitions.[35] But she also provided suggestive material about the Soviet intelligentsia's negotiation of the divide between the private and the public.[36] The published version of *O moei zhizni* was only to a limited extent under Panova's control: an earlier memoir written for her family had had to be reworked in order to make it acceptable for publication by adding material on "books and readers". And Panova had to fight to keep in even as much personal material as remains in the final version. Yet at the same time, as her son, Yury, pointed out, the official tone of the memoirs was to some extent a matter resolved by Panova herself: "She wrote the book for adults, and the emphases in it are placed differently than they were for us [i.e. in the stories she told to her children]."[37] Panova may have pushed back the boundaries of what could and could not be uttered by a prominent Soviet writer when depicting his or her life for the general public, but at the same time she illustrated just how important to her those boundaries were.

The boundaries remained in place for many of those who remembered her as well. As Yur'eva pointed out, this was true even of the anthology of recollections published after the relaxation of Soviet censorship, in 1988: "The 32 authors of the book in its 447 pages cheerfully omit *the human being*: we have Panova the social activist, the writer, and even the mother to some extent. Her family life, loves, attachments, the sufferings she endured, so dreadful they almost make one feel insane to think about them and all the tragedy of the end of her life, which probably played a significant role in her sudden death, were veiled in silence."[38] But perhaps Panova herself would have preferred to be remembered without "sufferings" and "tragedy", given that the "family life" that she fought to retain *O moei zhizni* was itself stereotypical: a glowing tribute to her father as civilising force, and to the virtues of Boris Vakhtin as husband and father to her children. The passages dealing with Vakhtin in the book were less a plausible account of an intimate relationship between two independent and assertive adults than a "sentimental memoir" (*Sentimental'nye vospominaniya*, to play on the title of one of her novels), of a supposedly ideal family life. Panova, though by all accounts a remarkable woman, could not find a way of confronting her own most idiosyncratic features – her bad temper and determination not to be ground down – except by representing these as part of a nationwide striving for self-transformation through *kul'turnost'*. But, whatever their demerits if judged by the canons of modernism or post-modernism, the memoirs none the less remain valuable as an authentic reflection of mid-twentieth-century Soviet intelligentsia selfhood, and above all of the nostalgia for *byt* that was at least as significant a facet of identity after 1953 as was the self-denying ascetism more often associated, by "official" and "unofficial" sources alike, with intelligentsia values. Moreover, the complicated publication history of *O moei zhizni*, and the writer's struggle to combine family history and official biography in the book, point to the fact that the phrase "pisat' o sebe trudno" was more than a cliché. Expected simultaneously to stress the *zakono-mernost'*, normality, of their biographies and the exceptionality of these, Soviet writers did indeed find the composition of autobiography at least as hard as they found the composition of fiction that conformed with the supposedly inflexible, but in fact constantly shifting, canons of Socialist Realism.[39]

Notes

[1] See, for example, Sidonie Smith, *A Poetics of Women's Autobiography: Marginality and the Fictions of Self-Representation* (Bloomington, Indiana, 1987); Rebecca M. Pauly, *Le Berceau et la bibliothèque: le paradoxe de l'écriture autobiographique* (Saratoga, California, 1989); Michael Sheringham, *French Autobiography: Devices and Desires* (Oxford, 1991); Mariella Günter, *Anatomie des Anti-Subjekts: zur Subversion autobiographischen Schreibens bei Siegfried Kracauer, Walter Benjamin und Carl Einstein* (Würzburg, 1996); Alexander Frederik Zweers, *The Narratology of the Autobiography: An Analysis of the Literary Devices Employed in Ivan Bunin's "The Life of Arsen'ev"* (New York, 1997).

[2] On the life story as testimonial, see e.g. Jehanne Gheith, 'Introduction' to *The Memoirs of Princess Dashkova: Russia in the Age of Catherine the Great* (Durham, NC, 1995), pp. 1–26, esp. pp. 16–17; and Sheila Fitzpatrick's introduction to eadem and Yuri Slezkine (eds.), *In the Shadow of Revolution: Life Stories of Russian Women from 1917 to the Second World War* (Princeton, 2000).

[3] For a discussion of late examples of this genre, see Marianne Liljeström's contribution to this volume.

[4] Igor' Il'insky, *Sam o sebe* (Moscow: VTO, 1961), p. 6.

[5] Of course, this genre is not limited to Soviet autobiography. A typical Tsarist official autobiography, that of Pavel Ignat'ev, last Imperial Minister of Education, has been described as 'unreadable [...] because [it] so meticulously excluded the personal' (Michael Ignatieff, *The Russian Album* (London, 1987), p. 14). And academic autobiographies in Britain, Germany, and the Netherlands (such rule-proving exceptions as those of the louche historian Richard Cobb aside), can equally well be classified as 'biographies in the first person'. On the other hand, the memoirs of American self-made men such as Conrad Hilton (a copy of which is still made available to guests in the chain of hotels which he founded) have the self-hagiographising style of the lives of Soviet revolutionaries.

[6] B. Ya. Brainina and E. F. Nikitina (eds.), *Sovetskie pisateli: avtobiografii* (2 vols.; Moscow, 1959). This collection was eventually extended by 3 further volumes, published in 1966, 1972, and 1988, and including a rather higher proportion of life-histories by women, but the essential formula of *tvorcheskii put'* plus important encounters and sententious ruminations remained little altered.

[7] Ibid., vol. 1, p. 3 (Introduction): emphasis mine.

[8] 'Tvoya avtobiografiya – sorok pobednosnykh gorodov tvoei strany', S. Galkin, ibid., vol. 1, p. 287.

[9] Ibid., vol. 1, p. 622.

[10] Ibid., vol. 1, p. 614.

[11] 'Rodilsya v 1900. O dne smerti soobshchu dopolnitel'no'. Ibid., vol. 2, p. 378.

[12] B. Gorbatov, ibid., vol. 1, p. 318.

[13] Ibid., vol. 1, p. 287.

[14] Ibid., vol. 1, p. 513.

[15] Ibid., vol. 1, p. 522. A slightly different reason for the changes to *Dvor* is given on p. 523, this time ideological.
[16] B. A. Engel and A. Posadskaya-Vanderbeck (eds.), *A Revolution of their Own: Voices of Women in Soviet History*, trans. S. Hoisington (Boulder, Colorado, 1998), pp. 50–51.
[17] See V. Garros, N. Korenevskaya, and T. Lahusen (eds.), *Intimacy and Terror: Soviet Diaries of the 1930s* (New York, 1995), p. xvii. Emphasis original.
[18] See H. Hoogenboom, 'Vera Figner and Revolutionary Autobiographies: The Influence of Gender on Genre', in L. Edmondson (ed.), *Women in Russia and Ukraine* (Cambridge, 1996), pp. 78–93; B. Holmgren, *Women's Work in Stalin's Time: On Lidiia Chukovskaia and Nadezhda Mandelstam* (Bloomington, Indiana, 1993). For a study of Soviet selfhood that adopts a rather similar approach to the one adopted here (but uses as its basis an autobiographical text by a male worker), see J. Hellbeck, 'Fashioning the Stalinist Soul: the Diary of Stepan Podlubnyi, 1931–9', in S. Fitzpatrick (ed.), *Stalinism: New Directions* (London, 2000), 77–116.
[19] In the discussion after my paper was presented at the 'Models of Self' conference, some participants commented that it would have been interesting to include a treatment of unpublished archival memoirs by Panova here. However, since my concern is not what Panova *might* have said in public had censorship circumstances been different, but with how she in fact did present herself to the world as an official Soviet writer under censorship conditions, her 'private' self-descriptions are of at best marginal relevance to the analysis here.
[20] A. A. Ninov, *Vera Panova: Zhizn', tvorchestvo, sovremenniki* (Leningrad, 1980).
[21] M. Ledkovsky, C. Rosenthal, and M. Zirin, *Dictionary of Russian Women Writers* (Greenwood, Connecticut, 1994), p. 484; I was not much more complimentary myself in my *History of Russian Women's Writing*.
[22] V. Panova, *Serezha, Valya, Volodya, Evdokiya* (Leningrad, 1961), p. 49.
[23] V. Panova, *Zametki literatora* (Leningrad, 1972), p. 8.
[24] See *The Battle for Childhood: Creation of a Russian Myth* (Stanford, 1990).
[25] *Zametki literatora*, p. 55.
[26] *O moei zhizni, knigakh i chitatelyakh* (2 vols.; Moscow, 1980).
[27] S. Dovlatov, *Zapisnye knizhki* (St Petersburg, 1992), p. 22; A. Bitov, 'Vera Fedorovna', in A. A. Ninov, N. A. Ozernova and V. A. Oskotsky (eds.), *Vospominaniya o Vere Panovoi: Sbornik* (Moscow, 1988), pp. 409–14.
[28] Serafima Yur'eva, *Vera Panova: Stranitsy zhizni* (Tenafly, 1993), p. 87.
[29] Yur'eva, *Vera Panova*, p. 68.
[30] On Panova's liking for the poem, see Vakhtin, 'Glazami mladshego syna', in Ninov, Ozernova, and Oskotsky (eds.), *Vospominaniya*, p. 52.
[31] Yur'eva, *Vera Panova*, pp. 21–2. My emphasis.
[32] Yu. Vakhtin, 'Glazami mladshego syna', in Ninov, Ozernova, and Oskotsky (eds.), *Vospominaniya o Vere Panovoi*, p. 44.
[33] Panova, *O moei zhizni*, p. 4. On the importance of 'strength of will' to Soviet identity, see my article, '"The Education of the Will": Advice Literature, *Zakal*, and Manliness in Early Twentieth-Century Russian Culture', in B. Clements, R. Friedman and D. Healey (eds.), *Masculinity in Russian Culture* (publication forthcoming).

[34] On the red cloth, see Yur'eva; on the names, *O moei zhizni*, p. 128. No doubt Panova's husband liked the name Alya because of a folk-etymological association with *alyi* (scarlet).
[35] The first letter she ever received from a reader was one from a group of 'women workers, white-collar workers, and housewives' *(rabotnitsy, sluzhashchie, i domokhozyaiki)* asking for her help in tracking down muslin for their embroidery circle. (See *O moei zhizni*, p. 332).
[36] On this issue as a general aspect of women's memoirs in Russia, see Gheith, 'Introduction' in *The Memoirs of Princess Dashkova*, p. 3; and Barbara Heldt, *Terrible Perfection: Women in Russian Literature* (Bloomington, Indiana, 1987), 68–76.
[37] See Yu. Vakhtin, 'Glazami mladshego syna' in Ninov, Ozernova, and Oskotsky (eds.), *Vospominaniya*, p. 45.
[38] Yur'eva, *Vera Panova*, p. 109.
[39] For a pioneering discussion of this aspect of official Soviet writing, see D. Shepherd, *Beyond Metafiction: Self-Consciousness in Soviet Literature* (Oxford, 1992).

The Remarkable Revolutionary Woman:

Rituality and Performativity in Soviet Women's Autobiographical Texts From the 1970s.

Marianne Liljeström

In 1975, an anthology entitled *Bez nikh my ne pobedili by* and containing short autobiographical texts written by Soviet women was published.[1] The anthology belongs to a specific Soviet autobiographical genre, which could – according to a notion introduced by N.K. Krupskaya in 1934 – be characterised as "collective memoirs" or "sources of mass origin".[2] According to V.S. Golubtsov, the main purpose and plot of the women's *sborniki* is to tell stories about how Soviet women became equal members of society.[3] In his view, the purpose of all anthologies is, by telling the events of the past, to help the Soviet people in its struggle for building communism. At the same time, the texts are meant to mediate to the younger generations "the richest possible experiences of those warriors, who created Soviet power".[4] In this manner, Golubtsov defines both the pragmatic political purpose and the ideological-educational tasks of these texts. Faithful to the Soviet discourse on gender equality, the women writers are seen to construct themselves solely as dedicated revolutionaries, committed to the higher political Cause. From this perspective, the texts can be read as testimonial narratives.

In testimonial texts individuality is presented as an identity which is formed as a continuation of the collective. Individuality and identity are not necessarily the same, but the identity in question is constructed as that part of the individuality, which is worth writing about. Hence, the testimonial text becomes a site for construction of identity: the writer is represented as an inseparable part of the whole, which in the Soviet context gives her story a remarkably "depersonalised" character with a metanarrative of the collective's struggle to win political ground and aims. As such, the testimonial texts become stories of heroic and exemplary lives.[5] All autobiographical stories can, of course, in some sense be considered testimonial: sometimes the writers just embrace the illusion of singularity, that is, the illusion of total uniqueness by rising above others. There is, however, an obvious conflict embedded here: to write herself as a part of the collective, the writer must form her own self or identity as a speaking self, which again by definition is separate from the collective. No matter how much she manifests her "I" as a part of the "us", or using Violette Leduc's expression "Mon cas n'est pas unique", she must in part "deny" the collective, within which or in relation to which her own narrated self is formed. Thus, even in connection to testimonial texts one could use Paul John Eakin's definition of autobiography as a "self-conscious consciousness of the self".[6] In testimonial texts, the hegemonic and exclusive consciousness of the self is a constantly expanding political consciousness. The master plot in these texts is this ongoing growth, without which there would be no narrative.

In this article, I read the texts by using the concepts of rituality and performativity. The concept of rituality is used to refer to those narrated practices which, in my reading, are constructed as socially and culturally the most significant ones. In the autobiographical texts, these practices appear, at the same time, as most conventionalised and most arbitrary. I will investigate whether this paradox can be interpreted as creating space for reflections on the position of the writing subjects. Rituality has, however, a performative dimension, which cannot be reduced to mere rules or rubrics.[7] The citation of the Law of the Same brings authority to the writing female subject. The female "I" emerges, thus, through the calling of the subject to a certain place in the discourse of equality. However, to "iterate" the ritual in a "new" context, means also a change in the ritual itself – in repetition, difference is brought along.

I will read the texts through the following key themes: firstly, the higher Cause and class struggle; secondly, expanding consciousness; thirdly, political correctness; fourthly, educating, supporting comradeship; fifthly, successful career; sixthly, the heroic, brave, self-sacrificing and modest revolutionary; seventhly, "the woman question" and the dutiful daughters; and eighthly, the absence of private life. I read the following texts: *Puti–dorogi* by L.E. Karaseva, *Kto – kogo?* by M.O. Levkovits and *Stranitsy let perebiraya...* by T.A. Kukharenko. Karaseva's story takes place between World War I and the end of 1938. She writes about the victory of the Bolsheviks in Uralsk, and about her becoming a zhenotdel activist. Levkovits tells a more detailed story about her work as a zhenotdel leader in Kiev in 1922–1924. Kukharenko's story, again, is a chronological narrative about her career as a woman scientist, starting in 1928 and ending at the time of her writing the text in 1973.

The higher Cause and class struggle

The women writers construct their identities by positioning themselves within the Bolshevik revolutionary struggle and the construction of socialism. It is this active participation as dedicated revolutionaries in political party work that is also the condition for their writing and their texts being published. I understand context both as certain material conditions which enable their narrated revolutionary identities and their practical activities and as something textually constructed. In their stories the interconnectedness between identities and activities is exposed as a chain of causality: the identity makes the activities possible, and the growth of experience strengthens the identity. In the texts I have chosen to study, different – quite personalised – contexts can be traced. Firstly, context is constructed as an ongoing historical, revolutionary struggle: Karaseva worked during the First World War as a teacher in the village of Ilek (in Uralskii region), which was situated on the steppes between Orenburg and Uralskii. These steppes were historical places where Emelyan Pugachev had roused the peasants against the tsarist autocracy. This location made Karaseva interested in revolutionary history, she read a great deal and dreamt about giving her strength to the struggle for the people's cause.[8] The February revolution in 1917 was therefore warmly welcomed by her: "what joy and enthusiasm did not the fall of the tsarist dictatorship awake!".[9] Secondly, context is constructed as a certain new, Soviet-style school-commune, which, in the case of Kukharenko, forms "together with the new socialist life style the consciousness and psyche of the young woman".[10]

Thirdly, context in Levkovits' story, which begins in May 1922 with her arrival in Kiev, is twofold. On the one hand, there is NEP, the economical, social and political situation of the party, a time when "the young Soviet state faced enormous problems".[11] Levkovits describes these problems and "some kind of new beat of the pulse in the city" in detail: privately owned stores were selling "everything – confectioner's products and jewellery, women's hats and other things that belonged to the female toilet, watches, bicycles, clothes and shoes. There were both music and ordinary restaurants. Privately owned dining rooms tempted with aromas from long ago forgotten entrees".[12] She states that "NEP was not supposed to bring fashion products, but things that people really needed, such as soap, china, boots, printed calico, scythes, sickles, wheels etc. Lenin had so rightly said, that in this struggle the question of 'who – whom' (*kto – kogo*) is going to be decided". On the other hand, Levkovits frames her story also with an ideological-political context: Lenin's advice concerning party work among women, his emphasis on "the enormous meaning of the participation of women in the building of socialism" which he had declared to Klara Zetkin as the basis for finding "the path to women" (*iskat' dorogy k zhenshchinam*). In Lenin's view the party had found this "path" through the women's sections of the party committees. "In the ranks of the enthusiastic work of the party among women I also appeared", Levkovits writes.[13]

In spite of the difference in emphasis, there is for the three texts a common context, which consists of the revolutionary Cause including the overall purpose of strengthening Soviet power and the necessity to involve masses of working women in construction of the socialist society. This context is narrated as a "conjunctural testimoniality", i.e. the time and place of the stories.[14]

Expanding consciousness

Serving the Cause requires a performativity of an expanding and constantly growing political consciousness, a capability of acting according to the "correct" political line. The texts are written in accordance with this requirement. Political consciousness serves to strengthen revolutionary identity, and vice versa. Both Karaseva's and Levkovits' narratives represent some special moments in this evolution: the stories form what Katerina Clark has called "politicized variants of the Bildungsroman".[15] The narratives tell about various developmental "stages" of their political consciousness and portray them as processes of carrying out constantly more demanding tasks given by authoritative party organs. The party's trust in them is a sign of their growing consciousness. In Karaseva's case this is illustrated by the successful completion of the revolutionary tasks she is ordered to do: from taking a report to the brigade head quarters during the period of counter revolution in Uralsk, while the chapaevists were preparing to storm the city, and going on reconnaissance in order to find out the situation of the enemy, to being appointed as the only worker for a party district paper and later as a worker in the agitation and propaganda commission of the Central Committee. Levkovits' story starts with her fifth journey to Kiev and in her words, "every time I was enriched with even greater revolutionary experience".[16] She had a mandate from the Central Committee of the CP Ukraine as head of the zhenotdel of the Kievan district committee. Levkovits had already achieved a high political consciousness. The plot, featuring specific challenges she is confronted with in her strivings to perform the assigned tasks, is constructed as sign and proof of this consciousness.

Kukharenko's story is different in this respect. In her narrative the consciousness is reached during the years in the school-commune and as a result of the hardships she went through during her years of study. The hardships form the background for her constantly developing scientific career – the acquired consciousness as a state of mind and identity frames her narrative, it enables her to write about her career as a success. Her "politically correct consciousness" was to work hard in her own scientific field. And all this she learnt in the school-commune: She tells how she, together with her brother, came to the school in 1924. As thin and pale city children, they made a sharp contrast to the strong, tanned, swift, barefooted kids they were surrounded by. However, soon they were like the other kids. Every child had a goal, and they worked hard in all areas of the school's daily activities. Through punishment they became "materially responsible persons".[17] The teachers did everything to develop their gifts. In the school, she became a member of the pioneer organisation, "and immediately the pioneer discipline, political meetings, marches, literary readings, singing songs at the camp fire, became the most important part of my life". She left the school with the knowledge that she would not be afraid of any work and not let any kind of hardship in life put her down.[18]

As conscious revolutionaries the narrators contrast themselves with descriptions of other "politically not yet fully mature chapaevist heroes" as in Karaseva's case[19] or the party district committee workers "who devalued the political work among women" as in Levkovits' case.[20] Through this construction they appear as extraordinary and outstanding women communists and a woman scientist.

Political correctness

The writers present the "highest" state of political consciousness as the realisation of the "correct" party line. *Stikhinost'* in any form is eliminated, and in accordance with the attained consciousness the narrators construct their stories as "documents" or reports about controlled and disciplined political activities, guided by famous, older and more experienced party leaders.

Karaseva's and Levkovits' narratives position them as representatives of the "correct" general party line. This also includes a conviction that party work among women is necessary. Karaseva produces her "correct" position in the form of the mandatory, ritualistic appraisal of the absent Lenin, who is, however, made present in the text through some red Cossack soldiers, who had heard Lenin give speeches, and who tell that Lenin's "only worry was to create a happy life for the working people".[21] Karaseva also tells about a telegram sent by Lenin to M.V. Frunze participating in the defence of the city of Uralsk and about her speeches to the peasant women about Lenin's advice in solving the woman question. Having arrived in Kiev,

Levkovits is in the midst of a local struggle between the general party line and several sections of the opposition (Trotskists, Workers' Opposition and "secret oppositions"). She constructs herself as very energetic, the reason why she quickly gains the confidence of the local party secretary, who informs her about the situation: "I talk with you openly, because I'm convinced that the Central Committee sent us a defender of the general party line", the secretary says. The negligence she detects in her area of work are explained by the inner party struggle. Her political correctness also gets proven through the "lecture" on the woman question she spontaneously delivers for "doubting" local party officials.[22]

Kukharenko's political correctness is expressed by the exemplary role, the vanguard position, she ascribes to students from the working class: "The 'student-party-thousanders' (*studenty-parttysyachniki)* were steady and serious people. And for many, study was not easy, but demanded enormous work. Following their example, other students developed an interest in workers' meetings".[23] As a member of the upwardly mobile social group of the Soviet intelligentsia, Kukharenko states her political reliability by emphasising that from 1946 until 1961 she functioned as a member of the party bureau of the institute where she worked, and that for many years she also ran a seminar on dialectical materialism at the factories "Red October" and "Red Proletarian".[24]

The positions the women writers ascribe themselves in their texts are thus decisive for how they describe their political correctness and reliability. Simultaneously, "correctness" and reliability are constructed as responsible and authoritative positions. However, in all narratives, the ideologically rhetorical and phraseological ways of expression are present.

Educating, supporting comradeship

The women writers are guided and supported in their activities by older, more experienced, well-known communist leaders and scientists, the overwhelming majority of whom are men. The texts are filled with names of famous communists and, in part, the stories are constructed as meetings with these venerable and adored persons. In some sense their narratives are stories about these worshipped leaders, the myths of the revolutionary heroes become further consolidated in their texts. The meetings with them strengthen the women even more in their firm conviction of doing the right thing. In spite of always being in a terrible hurry, the heroic party leaders give them valuable advice, guide them further on their chosen paths, and thank them in a very patronising way for the work they have done. "With the most lively interest", Karaseva tells us, "Krupskaya asked how the peasants live, and how the teachers work. She was interested in everything. I, who tried to tell the most important things, listened with great attention to her advice".[25] Karaseva ends her story with the following words:

> While remembering N.K. Krupskaya, K.I. Nikolaeva and other women communists who in a self-sacrificing manner served the cause of the party, the cause of socialism, I want to say that my whole life I strove to follow their example.[26]

For Levkovits the adored comrades are named as the party secretary in Kiev N. Tkachev, a member of the Central Committee of the CP of Ukraine, G.I. Petrovskii, and, of course, Krupskaya, Zetkin, Nikolaeva, Stasova etc. whom she meets in a section at the XXIII party congress. Kukharenko praises the pedagogues and the older comrades in the school-commune. They gave the children their heart and became their friends: "Believing in their example, we learned to look at the world as marvellous".[27] Kukharenko's text is filled with names of famous scientists who tutored her in her academic career.

By telling about their experiences of and contacts with these famous and adored leaders the memoirists construct themselves as extraordinary and special. At the same time as the myths about the leaders are strengthened, the narrators also construct these famous persons as a means of emphasising their own importance and their meaningful identities as dedicated revolutionaries.

Successful career

The memoirists all have a successful career. This is also the reason why their stories are published in the anthology in the first place. Karaseva and Levkovits become party officials: throughout their narratives they advance from lower positions at higher. Proving themselves as reliable and trustworthy communists, they are rewarded with even more responsible tasks, the fulfilment of which they describe as both a challenge and an honour. Their brave, dedicated, persistent and consistent work assign them positions of influence over important questions within the party organisations. One example is Levkovits' struggle to improve the situation for women at the "Bolshevik" factory: In the text she wonders why budget resources have not been used to improve the women's situation. The answer was: nobody cared, and she states:

> But now it is going to change… And we are not going to rest before everything is in order. But, of course, we need your support. The question is not solved, and Tkachev smiled for the first time. Eventually the party bureau voted for her suggestions and she writes: Wings were growing on me.[28]

The construction of oneself as invaluable for the fulfilment of assigned tasks is made in the name of the Cause and the collective: "An enormous joy and pride filled my heart, because my election to the party congress meant above all acknowledgement of the importance and value of zhenotdel work", writes Levkovits, and continuing to construct her own meaningfulness and importance, she writes: "I was sad to leave the work among working and peasant women in Kiev. For two and a half years the valuable and hard work to liberate women in the district took a big step forward, but there was still a lot to do…".[29]

The hardships Kukharenko went through to get were she was when writing her story is the most notable trait in her story of a successful career. Simultaneously, she explains her success, showing a great deal of self-awareness:

> With energy, love for work and persistence, which were awakened by the importance of this work, I was capable of developing within a fairly short time a satisfying method… This was a step forward in the research on coal. The method is still used in many countries… The tenth five-year-plan is in the process of realisation… And it is joyful to say that in this general work of our people there is also my modest part… The last days of 1973. I just came back from Minsk, where I was an opponent on a dissertation. On my table there are many congratulations, letters and postcards from earlier postgraduate students, colleagues from the Soviet Union and from abroad.[30]

In order to situate themselves as extraordinary and important women, and thus to make themselves visible and authorise their narratives, the narrators elevate themselves above the collective.

The heroic, brave, self-sacrificing and modest revolutionary

An important part of the stories is the construction of the dedicated, hard working revolutionary with apparently gender-neutral characteristics. This is the revolutionary Human Being whose generic traits, according to Kukharenko, are "love for work, a quest for knowledge, a civic world vision, pureness of thoughts and a communist world view ".[31] The revolutionary hero is constructed as extremely hard working and does not necessarily need to eat: "often we took only one dinner for several people to the dormitory, and it also happened that we did not eat at all". The hero does not care about his looks or dress ("we put on whatever we had"). The hero never gets tired in the struggle for the Cause: in order to explain party politics in the villages "we walked about 20 kilometres every day"[32] and the dedicated party secretary hardly sleeps at all: "Can we get hold of him still in the raikom, I asked Anya Shor. Absolutely. He never leaves before 12 o'clock at night".[33] The revolutionary hero performs a fearlessness of death, he is very brave. Karaseva confronts death and shows an extreme courage in taking the report mentioned earlier to the brigade head quarters and going on reconnaissance. In the midst of success, the hero, however, also shows an astonishing modesty and even shyness: "I remember that I was especially embarrassed by the big bouquet of flowers sent by the Komsomol organisation", writes Kukharenko.[34]

The range of exemplary revolutionaries is, however, broadened in the narratives: "Women wrote not a few heroic pages in the chronicles of the revolutionary struggle".[35] The enumeration of names – a typical feature especially in Karaseva's and Levkovits' stories, as in general in Soviet women's autobiographical texts from the 1960s and 1970s – increases the amount of women connected to the otherwise so gender-neutral revolutionary image. Karaseva and Levkovits also construct a female revolutionary genealogy by mentioning some women comrades who had been killed. Karaseva remembers a peasant's daughter who took the name of Ivan Penkov and joined the Red Army, and who died in the struggle for Uralsk. This "Ivan" had shown enormous courage by running against the enemy and shouting: "We are going to win, brothers, comrades!". The soldiers followed her and the enemy groups were destroyed.[36] Levkovits tells about an occasion on the road to a peasant village where she sees a big white rock on which two words were written: Marusya Boguslavka. The answer to the existence of this block was, according to her, given by the people's epic from the 16th century. The Turks were capturing people from the village and Marusya was very courageous during the fight. By standing silent at the memorial for a while, Levkovits, together with her women companions, showed respect to this "great heroine of the Ukrainian people". At that moment she thought about other contemporary heroines, communist girls, who were killed by the kulaks.[37]

In spite of the assumed gender-neutral traits of the revolutionary Human Being, the descriptions of his appearance are presented in gendered codes. The revolutionary man has "strong hands" (Karaseva about Chapaev), is "tall with a typical worker's facial structure" and "low voice" (Levkovits about Tkachev), is "stocky and strongly modest" (Levkovits about Petrovskii, who "was not beaten by the tsarist secret police, not by penal servitude in Sibiria, not by exile in Yakutsk").[38] The revolutionary woman is constructed both on the basis of these "generic", morphologically male traits and with different female epithets:

> She stood out among others because of her sharp, lively intellect, her great organisational capacities, she was a wonderful speaker. I clearly remember her look: short hair falls down on her high forehead, she jerks it; brown, beautiful, shining eyes, she smiles when she talks with people. She was dressed simply… she was totally and wholly consumed by work.[39]

The older women communist leaders show motherly affection and warmth: "N.K. (Krupskaya) looked at the picture with a smile and asked me to read the poems. I read. For a long moment she looked at me, then stood up and kissed me on my head".[40] According to Karaseva, K.I. Nikolaeva was a "wonderful communist, a human being of great heart and wit… a wonderful person, direct, stern, just…The behaviour of K.I. Nikolaeva stayed as an example of high spiritual burning, great love for the people and work". She met Nikolaeva for the first time in 1924: "When I went to her, she looked at me attentively and said: It is time, comrade, to change your training suit and leather jacket from the civil war to female clothing... I did not keep silent and answered: I am now a student and I wear what I have...".[41] I interpret this quote to explain that in peaceful times of socialist construction, women do not have to look like men anymore, they can, in their appearance and dress, become female again. Femininity is constructed as both normalcy and luxury. Karaseva, however, expresses both revolutionary modesty and the poverty of her student years. Femininity is, thus, considered both as naturalness and desired appearance, and as vanity.

"The woman question" and the dutiful daughters

The Leninist understanding of the woman question plays an important role in Karaseva's and Levkovits' narratives. They both create their careers as activists in the party's work among women, and they both construct an image of the working and peasant woman as an objective for their self-sacrifice and hard work. The women are very poor, they live under extremely harsh conditions surrounded by dirt and decay, they lack the basic necessities of life: "Then we came to the village. And what a situation!...The women were very thin, they were washing clothes with a washing board and they made food in an open oven".[42]

"The majority of peasant women knew hardly anything about their new rights and obligations given to them by the October revolution",[43] and the party had to go to them and explain to them their new situation. Working women are constructed as ignorant and, therefore, in great need of the party's enlightening work. It follows "naturally" from their exploited situation and poverty that working women are supportive of Soviet power: their spontaneously affirmative, but hidden attitude must simply be awakened. Lack of consciousness may at first result in resistance, but if the zhenotdel workers are good and persistent enough, the women are going to realise that their interests are defended by the party. Levkovits writes about on instance where her own role in getting the women to realise their interests is constructed as decisive:

> Another woman, looking somewhere to the side, said: we already had meetings, but nothing good came out of them...But at six o'clock working women came to the meeting. Everybody waited to hear what the representative from the party district committee was going to say...Well, comrades, I started, you are having a hard time...Many of these shortages can be eliminated right now, and we will absolutely do that. But also you are guilty for some of them. Power is in the hands of the working class, that is, in your own hands... Now your own comrades are presiding over the institutions, the ones you elected, and they are not masters but people for you to order... We suggested that they should elect a delegates' meeting of the most energetic and most free workers' wives.[44]

In addition to their own efforts – not always described in accordance with "revolutionary modesty" – quoting the Magic Words of Lenin always had an enormous influence on the poor and mostly illiterate women:

> In the light of an oil lamp peasant women listened to me with great attention. I cited Lenin's words, which invited working and peasant women to build a new life... And they all accompanied me on my way and wanted to say farewell... Following Lenin's advice, the party developed deeper and wider its work among women.[45]

The zhenotdel workers were rewarded with the women workers' confidence. Karaseva tells about her work as an editor for the magazine "Rabotnitsa" (Woman Worker):

> The editorial board was in constant contact with the female masses, and it systematically organised meetings with them...Women workers turned to their magazine also with personal questions, and they were always met with the support and help they needed.[46]

In carrying out their orders and tasks, the narrators are confronted with many obstacles and challenges. They have to fight "bearded peasants dressed in good quality fur coats"[47] who threaten their lives and wives of kulaks and tradesmen who shout: "We have nothing to do at meetings, the husband is the head of the household, he decides everything. That's not women's business". But "instinctively" poor peasant women always gave a strong blow to these "orators".[48] In addition to these expressions of class struggle, they also have to face a certain lack of understanding among party members. Levkovits tells about her "lecture" on the basics of the woman question for the Kievan party officials. Alongside the construction of herself as very dedicated and knowledgeable, she, however, does not want to upset or irritate the male audience and shows "female" modesty, attentiveness and sensitivity instead: "I saw that Laurentii and Pavel looked at each other, and I hurried to finish my 'improvised lecture'".[49] In spite of all the importance that Levkovits ascribes zhenotdel work, she also belittles it: when Laurentii praises her as "a real zhenotdel specialist", she protests: in addition to her work in the zhenotdel, she had been an editor, a public defender and a lecturer at the district party school.[50] In the text, she clearly wants to expand her credentials from being considered "only" a zhenotdel activist. Thus, she underlines the hegemonic understanding of generic party work as the "most important" and constructs herself as a helpmate of the revolution. The ascribed helpmate role of women activists is explicitly expressed by Frunze in Karaseva's text. During the counter-revolutionary period in Uralsk, she helped together with other women, in the hospital, and she was on call the day Frunze came to visit:

> When Frunze saw me, he said hello and asked: 'You are also here?' 'Well of course, we women also serve our people and do everything that is possible to speed up the victory over the enemies of the revolution', I exclaimed. 'Well done (*molodets*), young people!', Frunze said.[51]

The absence of private life

The memoirists construct their stories with an almost complete absence of any references to, not to mention events about their private and domestic life. The image of heroic revolutionaries with total dedication to public activities excludes all statements of their personal lives. Kukharenko is the only one of the narrators who implies that she has a domestic life as well. She mentions her children incidentally in a couple of subordinate clauses: In 1937 she defends her candidate dissertation,

> [a]nd after one month, I had a son, my second. This occasion, which happened to a 26 year old Komsomol-girl, mother of two children, at a time when the scientific grades in the Soviet Union had been introduced not long before, was quite an extraordinary phenomenon... The children grew and studied, and they also needed attention, to be taught a love for work and a social view of the world.[52]

By mentioning at the end of her narrative that her first son is a biophysicist and the second a geologist, and that her grandson is learning multiplication tables, Kukharenko, however, also constructs herself as a perfect mother with educated and intelligent children. Her extraordinariness is even more accentuated through her capacity to combine a very successful career with motherhood. Only as a Mother is femaleness included in the Law of the Same. The "gender-neutral" Revolutionary Woman is, however, constructed, as a rule, without home, family, personal life, children and sexuality.

The same or different

The overarching purpose and master plot of these texts is to constitute the phallic revolutionary female subject. This subject is dedicated to a higher political Cause and is thus constructed within the Law of the Male/Same of Soviet discourse on equality. The texts construct the Remarkable Revolutionary Woman. This woman differs from other ordinary women because of her "mature" political consciousness, which enables her to act on behalf of and for the sake of other women. Autobiographical writing being historically a male domain, a genre where above all "already known" or famous men write their reminiscences, positioning themselves in a *deja lu*,[53] the exceptional character of women writers is presented on the basis of an interesting asymmetrical gender paradox: an exceptional man is essentially like other men. Other men can become exceptional. Exceptional women, however, regard themselves as different from other women. In Soviet women's texts, the Remarkable Woman, on the one hand, distances herself from other women: she needs these others to construct herself as exceptional. On the other hand, representing others in accordance with the male norm, her remarkability functions as the access to the universality of the Same.

The women narrators do not write themselves into a psychological model of Woman. As remarkable women they do not construct themselves in relation to the template of a feminine woman, who – according to Sidonie Smith – always writes herself in relation to men and through a life cycle that is connected to biologically inscribed phenomena, such as childhood, maidenhood, childbirth, marriage, widowhood etc.[54] As I noted above, these dimensions are almost totally absent from the texts. Such traits as sacrifice and kindness, usually ascribed to the feminine woman, are transferred wholly to the public sphere, transformed into a dedication for the Cause and the Struggle. Hence Soviet women have only One, Common Self to write about, that is, their selves are interchangeable, and the "collectivity" constructed in the texts is uniform. In its linearity, the Cause structures the content of women's lives as the same: there is a master plot depicting a positive heroine who proceeds through different transformations – assisted by older and more experienced and politically conscious party members – and symbolically resolves the "spontaneity/ consciousness dialectic" (Clark) and reaches a higher stage of self-sacrifice and fearlessness of death. This manuscript allowed some women to speak. Hegemonic Soviet discourse of the 1960s and 1970s, and therefore also censorship as a cultural and political mechanism, produced female subject positions that were connected to power and authority. As I have shown, one can, in the texts, read many rituals, repeated activities to which power is attached. Women's gendered positions (or characteristics, activities etc.) as such do not give them authority, but the citation of the Law of the Same, the "echoing" of previously authorised activities in their writing, produce for The Remarkable Revolutionary Women certain positions of power and authority.

While emphasising all this uniformity in women's autobiographical texts, the question remains: does the "fact" that the writers are women, that the "signature" is female, make any difference for how meaning is constructed in the texts? Or are these "phallic" texts simply incorporated into the universal, and thus subsumed once again in the patriarchal logic of meaning? Given that the author is an "ideological product",[55] given that the women writers have internalised the importance of Soviet "self-fashioning" – i.e. the discovery of a usable self,[56] a way of thinking and moulding their experiences according to the ethos of the party (self-censorship) – how is it possible to take into consideration their "difference"? Is it possible to write with a female signature *and* fully subscribe to the Law of the Same?

As an acknowledged sign in hegemonic Soviet discourse, gender was produced as hierarchic and asymmetric. Hence, the identity categories men and women are socio-symbolically and culturally constructed as incommensurable. This means that in my reading specific gender qualities, ascribed to the identity categories, appear in the ways that different gendered characteristics and activities are linked together, not in the qualities themselves or in possible causes to the linkages. In this sense, gender can be understood as a position which is directly or indirectly attached to certain values, advantages, mobility etc., which constitute the preconditions of the positions of the identity categories. In my understanding, this also means that despite the fact that the citation of the Phallic Law of the Same brings certain authority to the female subjects, this citation can never be performed as the "same". The context of the citation is already different. This is also why ritualistically narrated practices momentarily are attributed an arbitrary character. In the texts, I read this arbitrariness in Levkovits' need for support from the men she just declared as totally without concern for party work among women. Or in the construction of the peasant's daughter, who, during the civil war, was forced to take a male name (Ivan Penkov) in order to join the Red Army. I also read an arbitrariness in Karaseva's way of constructing the highly adored and honoured party leader M. Frunze – People's Commissar of Military and Naval Affairs – as astonished about women participating in the defence of the revolution. This arbitrary character of narrated practices can be interpreted as fissure in the uniformity of the conventionalised rituals.

The women writers do not "simply" iterate but they "reiterate" those rituals which within Soviet hegemonic discourse are constructed as socially, politically and culturally most significant and which they themselves have internalised. However, the iterability of these practices means that they, according to Derrida, combine repetition with change.[57] If Soviet women's autobiographical texts, however, are simultaneously considered as "conjunctural testimonial" narratives, situated within a certain time and place, the female selves constructed in the texts as images could even be understood as comments on the gap between the discourse on equality and everyday practices. In this sense, the female self could be seen as a theoretical manoeuvring, not as a unifying principle. While the production of an authoritative speaking position does not have to be understood as the invention of "a personal voice for me", the question of tone remains crucial, as

Meaghan Morris has emphasised.[58] Producing a position is a problem of rhetoric, of developing enunciative strategies, precisely in relation to the cultural and social conventions that make speaking problematic or impossible for *women*.

Notes:

[1] See Marianne Liljeström, 'Regimes of Truth? Soviet Women's Autobiographical Texts and the Question of Censorship', in Markku Kankaanpuro (ed.) *Russia: More different than most.* (Kikimora Publ. 2000).
[2] V.S. Golubtsov, *Memuary kak istochnik po istorii sovetskogo obshchestva* (Moskva, 1970) p. 72.
[3] Golubtsov, *Memuary kak istochnik*, p. 31.
[4] Ibid., p. 50.
[5] For Latin American women's *testimonios*, see Doris Sommer, '"Not Just a Personal Story": Women's *Testimonios* and the Plural Self', in Bella Brodzki and Celeste Schenck (eds.) *Life/Lines: Theorizing Women's Autobiography* (Cornell University Press, 1988) pp. 107–130.
[6] Paul John Eakin, *Fictions in Autobiography: Studies in the Art of Self-invention* (Princeton University Press 1985) p. 8.
[7] See Victor Turner, 'Social Dramas and Stories About Them', in W.J.T. Mitchell (ed.) *On Narrative* (University of Chicago Press 1981) p. 155–156.
[8] L.E. Karaseva, 'Puti-dorogi', in *Bez nikh my ne pobedili by* (Moskva 1975) p. 72.
[9] Ibid.
[10] T.A. Kukharenko, 'Stranitsy let perebiraya…', in *Bez nikh my ne pobedili by* (Moskva 1975) pp. 394–395.
[11] M.O. Levkovits, 'Kto–kogo', in *Bez nikh my ne pobedili by* (Moskva 1975) p. 260.
[12] Ibid., p. 261.
[13] Ibid., p. 260.
[14] Elspeth Probyn, *Sexing the Self. Gendered Positions in Cultural Studies* (Routledge, 1993) p. 106.
[15] Katerina Clark, *The Soviet Novel. History as Ritual* (University of Chicago Press, 1981) pp. 16–17.
[16] Levkovits, p. 260.
[17] Kukharenko, p. 395.
[18] Ibid., p. 396.
[19] Karaseva, p. 74.
[20] Levkovits, p. 263.
[21] Karaseva, p. 76.
[22] Levkovits, pp. 267, 263.
[23] Kukharenko, p. 398.
[24] Ibid., p. 402.
[25] Karaseva, p. 79.
[26] Ibid., p. 83.
[27] Kukharenko, p. 396.
[28] Levkovits, pp. 266, 269.
[29] Ibid., pp. 274, 275.
[30] Kukharenko, pp. 401, 405–406.

[31] Ibid., p. 395.
[32] Ibid., pp. 397, 398.
[33] Levkovits, p. 266.
[34] Kukharenko, p. 401.
[35] Karaseva, p. 77.
[36] Ibid., p. 78.
[37] Levkovits, p. 273.
[38] Ibid., p. 271.
[39] Karaseva (about Z.A. Prishchepchik), p. 80.
[40] Ibid., p. 83.
[41] Ibid., pp. 82, 83.
[42] Levkovits, p. 264.
[43] Ibid., p. 272.
[44] Ibid., pp. 264, 265.
[45] Karaseva, pp. 79, 80.
[46] Ibid., p. 82.
[47] Ibid., p. 78.
[48] Levkovits, p. 273.
[49] Ibid., p. 263.
[50] Ibid., p. 262.
[51] Karaseva, p. 74.
[52] Kukharenko, pp. 401, 403.
[53] Nancy, K. Miller, 'Representing Others: Gender and the Subjects of Autobiography', *differences*, vol. 6, no. 1 (1994) p. 16.
[54] See Sidonie Smith, *A Poetics of Women's Autobiography: Marginality and the Fictions of Self-Representation* (Indiana University Press 1987).
[55] See Michel Foucault, 'What Is An Author?', in Paul Rabinow (ed.) *The Foucault Reader* (Penguin, 1984).
[56] See Sheila Fitzpatrick, 'Lives and Times', in Sheila Fitzpatrick and Yuri Slezkine (eds.) *In the Shadow of the Revolution: Lifestories of Russian Women. From the 1917 to the Second World War* (Princeton University Press, 2000).
[57] Jacques Derrida, 'Afterword', in his *Limited Inc.* (Evanston, 1988), p. 119.
[58] Meaghan Morris, *The Pirate's Fiancee: Feminism, Reading Postmodernism* (Verso, 1988) p. 7.

Part II
”Я – Ты – Они – Другие”

Я и *Ты* в женском дневнике

(дневники Анны Керн и Анны Олениной)

Ирина Савкина

Женские дневники – это тексты, которые до сих пор редко становились объектом научного исследования. Среди причин научного "презрения" к дневникам Фелисити А. Нуссбаум называет то, что они часто остаются неопубликованными, иногда слишком длинные, затянутые, в них недостает связности и они не воспринимаются как классические реалистические тексты.[1]

Последний аргумент играл большую роль в русском/советском литературоведении, где вопрос о каноне "Большой литературы", "настоящей литературы" всегда стоял особенно остро, и не удивительно, что автодокументальные жанры, маркированные знаком маргинальности, критика часто соединяла с женским, развивая, например, идею о том, что "дефектный" или "промежуточный", с точки зрения Канона, дневник – это тот жанр, куда может быть безболезненно канализировано женское творчество.

В определении дневника обычно выделяют такие черты, как отсутствие ретроспективного взгляда на события, то есть синхронность записи событию (в отличие от мемуаров и автобиографии), неадресованность (в отличие от письма) и непредназначенность для публичного восприятия[2]. Однако, на мой взгляд, все названные признаки и особенно – последний (неадресованность) – могут быть проблематизированы.

Адресат, имплицитный читатель – важнейший способ структурации собственного идентитета. Адресат, с моей точки зрения, есть во всех автодокументальных жанрах (в том числе и в дневнике).

Во-первых, адресация – закон любого акта письма: чтобы осуществлять этот акт, ”автор должен стать другим по отношению к себе, взглянуть на себя глазами другого”[3]. Писать – значит читать (хотя бы самому). Сам акт письма подразумевает некоторую публичность, адресованность, и в этом смысле автор всегда существует в ситуации дискурсивного принуждения.

В женских автодокументальных текстах ”конвенциональное” *Ты* особенно важно, об этом писали представительницы феминистской критики по отношению к жанру автобиографии. По мнению Домны Стантон, разорванность и двойственность пронизывает сам дискурс женского автовысказывания, которое должно одновременно быть оправдывающимся (перед лицом структурированного в тексте патриархатного читательского *Ты,* персонифицирующего запрет на писательство) и протестующим, самоосвобождающимся[4].

По-моему, вышесказанное имеет прямое отношение и к дневнику, где тоже есть подобный адресат, несмотря на то, что, как кажется на первый взгляд, дневник текст закрытый и не расчитанный на публичное прочтение. Но, как я попытаюсь показать ниже, последнее не соответствует действительности, по крайней мере в отношении русских женских дневников первой половины XIX в., в которых балансирование на границе приватности и публичности, секретности и открытости составляет важнейший момент поэтики дневникового жанра (или субжанра). Формы адресация дневника – идет ли речь о реальной или символической фигуре или о некоей неперсонифицированной ”адресованности”, ”диалогичности”, – важный момент проявления подобной пограничности, промежуточности. То есть, как мне кажется, в женском дневнике самые важные фигуры – это ”*Я*” и ”*Ты*”.

Я хотела бы рассмотреть в контекте этой проблемы два женских дневника, написанных в 20–е годы XIX века: *Дневник для отдохновения* Анны Петровны Керн и *дневник Annette* Анны Алексеевны Олениной.

Обе Анны известны в русской культуре в основном как персонажи биографии А. С. Пушкина и адресатки его лирических стихотворений, и только в этой связи упоминались и изучались их тексты. Меня эти "молчащие музы" будут интересовать как авторы и субъекты дискурса.

Дневник для отдохновения Анны Керн представляет собой подневные записи с 23 июня по 30 августа 1820 года, которые она партиями, с очередной почтой отправляла из Пскова в Лубны, где оставались ее родные и среди них – непосредственный адресат этого эпистолярного дневника, двоюродная тетка Феодосия Петровна Полторацкая[5].

Дневник Анны Алексеевны Олениной – это записи с 20 июня 1828 по 2 февраля 1835 года, занесенные в альбом, на лицевой стороне которого золотыми буквами вытесненно имя *Annette*. Однако более точно было бы сказать, что регулярные записи дневника заканчиваются в 1829 году, далее следуют по одной небольшой записи под 1830; 1831 и 1835 годом[6].

Оба дневника написаны на двух языках, по-французски и по-русски. У Керн французский текст встречается чаще, чем русский (перевод А. Л. Андерс), у Олениной – наоборот (перевод М. В. Арсентьевой).

Как уже говорилось, *Дневник для отдохновения* двадцатилетней Анны Керн – это эпистолярный дневник. Делая записи каждый день, а точнее – по несколько раз в день, Анна Петровна с очередной почтой отправляла их в Лубны Феодосье Полторацкой. В названном тексте легко обнаруживается большое влияние литературной традиции, а именно традиции сентиментального эпистолярного романа[7], где изображаются идеальные, чувствительные герой и героиня и, как правило, фигура идеального друга или идеальной подруги, кому адресуется исповедь чувствительного сердца.

Все названные выше литературные парадигмы и стереотипы существенно важны для автора *Дневника для отдохновения*. Одна из ролей, из которых автор пишет, по которым она структурирует свое *Я,* – это роль "Клариссы-Юлии-Дельфины". Реальные обстоятельства жизни перестраиваются в сюжет сентиментального романа, действующие лица которого – молодая чувствительная, страдающая героиня, идеальный возлюбленный – офицер, с которым в бытность в Лубнах была (или только намечалась) романтическая любовная история (используя язык цветов, Керн называет его в тексте Eglantine (Шиповник) или Immortelle (Бессмертник), подруга-конфидентка и посредница в диалоге влюбленнных.

Этот диалог, как часто бывает в сентиментальном романе, ведется с помощью литературы. Керн выписывает и переводит с французского (так как ее избранник не владеет иностранными языками) отрывки из читаемых ею произведений, среди которых романы Коцебу, г-жи де Пьенн, Жермены Де Сталь, Стерна, г-жи Севиньи, г-жи Бэрней (вероятно, Френсис (Фанни) Берни), упоминаются также Шиллер, *Новая Элоиза* Руссо, Лабрюйер и Озеров.

Использование чужого слова не только помогает выразить чувства с помощью готовых формул[8], но и позволяет объективировать свое *Я*, превратить его в некий персонаж, ”идеальную героиню”, с такими чертами, как чувствительность, нежность, способность к вечной любви, добродетельность и терпение. Особенно активно разрабатывается идея добродетели, которая должна помочь сохранить целостность и идеальность *Я* в реальных жизненных обстоятельствах. Последние не могут быть перестроены, но могут быть ”перемотивированы” с помощью романной парадигмы.

В соответствии с этим образом *Я* как чувствительной сентиментальной героини строятся и образы адресатов – прямого и косвенного. *Он*, к которому через посредницу-конфидентку обращены излияния чувств, – парный идеальный герой, подруга – идеальное *Ты* (”дорогой, нежный” (143), ”обожаемый” (147) друг, ”мое утешение, мое сокровище” (143) и т. п.)

В рамках этого романного сюжета о трех чувствительнейших душах, Лубны, откуда автогероиня переехала во Псков, изображаются как условное пространство – рай, где время стоит, и вечно продолжается вечная любовь. То, что происходит с ”изгнанной из рая” героиней, – это испытание, после которого последует возвращение в рай, все вернется на круги своя, история получит счастливый конец – ”наступят для нас более счастливые времена и тогда мы вместе перечитаем его” (дневник – И. С.; 143).

То есть в определенном смысле или на определенном уровне дневник строится как художественный текст с известным сюжетом и с героями, у которых есть знакомые литературные амплуа; и на этом уровне журнал Керн вписывается в жанр сентиментального дневника, где автор, как отмечает Е.Фрич, обычно отбирает для записи только прекрасные впечатления жизни[9].

Но на этот слой текста, где *Я* и *Ты* структурируются по матрицам, заданным социокультурными и литературными конвенциями, накладываются иные дискурсы, создающие ту несогласованность, фрагментарность и противоречивость *Я*, которую отмечают все пишущие о дневнике и особенно о женском.

В тексте Керн подобная противоречивость и несогласованность отличает и дневниково-эпистолярное *Ты*. Когда речь идет о диалоге с идеальным *Ты* – alter ego автора, то это практически и не диалог, а акт самокоммуникации, здесь нет признаков переписки, нет принципа перекодировки, постоянной смены точки зрения, для переписки характерных и обязательных.

Но на других уровнях текста адресат (уже реальный) выполняет иные функции. Феодосья Петровна была для Керн *своим,* близким человеком и в том смысле, что была свидетельницей ее лубенских любовных увлечений, и потому, что была членом семьи, человеком, хорошо знавшим историю ее насильственного, по воле отца и родных, брака с генералом Е. Ф. Керном.

Именно с таким адресатом – членом семейного круга, занимавшим промежуточную позицию, можно было обсуждать проблему собственной семейной жизни и отношений с мужем. В этом контакте между двумя *своими* женщинами возникает та ситуация женской "болтовни" (в отсутствие мужчин), которую Иригарэй считает местом, где может проявить себя "женский телесный язык", освободившийся от "маскарада женственности"[10].

Как видно из текста дневника, Анне Петровне не удается уложить свои отношения с мужем в "сентиментальный сюжет".

> Никакая философия на свете не может заставить меня забыть, что судьба моя связана с человеком, любить которого я не в силах и которого не могу позволить себе уважать, словом, скажу прямо – я почти его ненавижу. Каюсь, это великий грех, но кабы мне не нужно было касаться до него так близко, тогда другое дело (168)

– в этом и других подобных болезненных, напряженных высказываниях получает голос репрессированная телесность: ужас и ненависть вызывает все, связанное с близостью, телесным контактом с мужем: Анна не может без раздражения находиться с ним в одной комнате, сидеть рядом в тесной карете. Пребывание в одном пространстве с супругом вызывает негативные телесные реакции: слабость, головную боль, раздражительность, болезненность. Можно сказать, что ее тошнит генералом Керном. В страдании, в описании болезненных состояний, как замечает Иригарэй, можно видеть жестикуляцию тела женщины[11]. Испытываемое Анной нервное напряжение, болезненная эмоциональная возбудимость провоцирует ее на нарушение того "маскарадного" образа "чувствительной добродетельной женщины", который она одновременно старательно выстраивает.

В связи с темой телесного отвращения к мужу и собственных болезненных состояний в дневнике Анны Керн довольно подробно обсуждается проблема наступившей нежелательной беременности. Зародившийся ребенок воспринимается исключительно как часть Керна – и потому вызывает реакцию полного, практически физиологического отторжения, которое так сильно, что заставляет автора дневника нарушать самые заветные табу: "ежели бог даст, я рожу прежде времени (о чем ежечасно молю бога и думаю, что не грешу перед ним"(185)[12]. Она прямо говорит о ненависти к будущему ребенку (211), о нежелании иметь детей и о том, что нежность ее к первой дочери, маленькой Катеньке тоже "недовольно велика", но этого (будущего ребенка – И. С.) все небесные силы не заставят меня полюбить... " (212). Подробное описание ссор и столкновений с мужем тоже переполнено знаками "телесности" – здесь язык автора освобождается от этикетных формул сентиментального романа. "<Он> дорогой орет на меня во всю глотку" (184); "Бедная моя дочка так испугалась громких воплей этого бешеного человека, что с ней сделался понос" (186).

Дневник становится тем местом, где женщина-автор может выплеснуть "такие эмоции, как, например, интенсивное горе или гнев, которые культура, к которой она принадлежала, запрещала для публичного выражения"[13].

Но и эти "запретные" чувства выговариваются не только "про себя" – эмоциональная, на грани нервного срыва исповедь, как мы уже говорили, все же адресована – адресована другому, который воспринимается как *свой женский другой.*

Однако одновременно эта исповедь имеет и иного адресата, косвенно она обращена к отцу как виновнику создавшегося положения (в конце переписки эта переадресация выражена уже и прямо: "можете показать ему в моем дневнике те места, какие сочтете подходящими" (235). Мнение отца, воля отца, Закон Отца – это цензурующее *Ты*, перед которым дочь старается оправдаться в своем дневнике и против которого она иногда бунтует. Но, функцию цензора, представителя патриархатного порядка в некотором роде выполняет и прямой адресат, Феодосия Полторацкая, наряду с ролями идеального двойника или женски-семейного *своего* человека. Ее точка зрения довольно часто структурируется в тексте как некая позиция благоразумной, контролирующей нормы. Чем экстремальнее развиваются отношения Анны с мужем, тем чаще адресатка, папенька и все родные, пожертвовавшие ею во имя социального статуса и приличий, сливаются в одно "вы". То есть, как мне кажется, можно сделать вывод, что одна из ипостасей *Ты* в дневнике Керн – это цензурующее *Ты* – и оно представлено как возникающей на втором плане фигурой Отца, так и непосредственно женским *Ты* адресата, *тетушки*[14].

По отношению к этим *Ты, Я* текста находится в той двойственной, разорванной позиции, о которой говорят феминистские критики: женское авторское *Я* мечется между мимикрией и бунтом, между попытками структурировать свою "самость" в границах, заданных *Ты-цензором*, представляющим точку зрения социокультурной нормы, и стремлением разрушить эту тюрьму правил, репрессирующих истинные желания.

Бунтующее, освобождающееся от канонов *Я* высказывает себя в эмоциональных срывах, криках, дискурсе болезни (о которых я писала выше) или в проговорках, противоречащих тому "правильному" образу *Я*, который выстраивается на поверхности текста.

Строя образ *Я*-персонажа, автор выступает в роли писателя, через объективацию, "оперсонаживание" *Я* (с использованием чужого языка – в лингвистическом и литературном смысле) она легитимирует для самой себя существование в определенных образах – это момент самоинтерпретации и самообъяснения. Но, с другой стороны, для пишущего *Я* важен не только результат – некая версия себя и своей жизни, предложенная другим, но и процесс письма сам по себе как форма самозаявления: и освобождения, и сотворения себя.

При этом акт дневникового письма, как уже подчеркивалось, осуществляется одновременно как секретный и как публичный. Последнее проявляется в самом факте эпистолярной адресованности и в *пере*адресации текста другим через посредничество своей корреспондентки: Анета просит Феодосию Полторацкую читать избранные страницы дневника Иммортелю/Шиповнику, маменьке, отцу; на страницы дневника заглядывают и даже вставляют туда свои записи племянник мужа Павел Керн (173) и сам генерал (177).

Именно эта пограничность, балансирование на границе приватности и публичности образует то поле напряжения, в котором *Я* говорит о себе и объективируя себя, создавая *Я*-персонаж, *Я*-для-других, и выражая или сотворяя в самом процессе бунтующего письма собственную самость, *Я*-субъект.

Написанный восемью годами позже дневник Анеты Олениной не имеет эпистолярной формы, но и в нем можно видеть черты адресованности и игры на границе открытости/закрытости текста. В записях дневника встречаются фразы обращенные к самой себе, к журналу или просто к кому-то. "Да, смейтесь теперь, Анна Алексеевна, а кто вчера обрадовался..." (57); "Один ты, друг мой журнал, знаешь, что за чувства во мне, когда я слышу *его* голос" (135); "прости, журнал, души моей утешитель!" (164) и т.п.

Ты этих обращений – некое идеальное *Ты, Ты*-двойник, функция которого напоминает назначение того *господина* (или скорей *госпожи*) *Никто* (Nobody), к которому адресует свой журнал пятнадцатилетняя Фрэнсис Берни (Frances Burney). Это понятие (Nobody), как замечает Стюард Шерман, "с первых страниц се журнала выполняет двойную функцию, фигурируя и как подлинное отсутствие и как необходимое, существенно важное доверенное лицо (лучший друг и конфидент), которого Берни отождествляет с самим журналом"[15]. Интересно, что в женском дневнике структура "ни к кому не обращаюсь" заменяется на "обращаюсь к *Никому*", что маркирует самое потребность в адресованности, в диалогичности.

Однако, кроме такого символического адресата и в оленинском дневнике (как у Керн) предполагаются или называются и более конкретные читатели-адресаты, например, будущие дети.

> Я хотела, выходя замуж, жечь Журнал, но ежели то случится, то не сделаю того. Пусть все мысли мои в нем сохранятся; и ежели будут у меня дети, особливо дочери, отдам им его, пусть видят они, что страсти не ведут к щастью, а путь истиннаго благополучия есть путь благоразумия" (64).

Важно заметить, что такая адресация текста детям сразу приписывает ему некоторый сюжет, результативность; предполагается, что текст дневника может в будущем послужить дидактическим пособием.

Но кроме гипотетических будущих читателей дневник Анеты имел скорее всего читателей реальных, современных. Хоть автор и декларирует секретность своих записей, но в одном месте дневника встречаем приписку, сделанную рукой подруги (59), а на последних страницах – прямое обращение к Антонине и Лидии Блудовым, новым задушевным подругам Анны, из чего можно сделать вывод, что они все вместе перечитывали записи. Важно отметить, что все более редкое обращение к дневнику после 1830 года мотивируется в последней записи текста (2. 02. 1835) тем, что "дружба моя с милыми Блудовыми занимает все минуты, остающиеся от шумной пустой, светской жизни. *Наша переписка – настоящий журнал...*" (160, курсив мой – И. С.).

Наряду с дружественным *Ты* в разных его обличьях в дневнике Анны Олениной, есть, хоть, в отличие от журнала Керн, и не названное прямо, контролирующее, цензурующее *Ты; Ты* как воплощение социокультурных норм и конвенций; *Ты*, чей строгий взгляд почти все время влияет на тот образ *Я*, который отражается в зеркале дневника. Метафора зеркала, которая часто используется, чтобы подчеркнуть монологичность и исповедальность дневника, на самом деле очень уместна здесь как раз по обратным причинам. М. Бахтин в одной из своих ранних работ справедливо заметил, что "видение себя в зеркале – это всегда взгляд на себя глазами другого (ведь наша собственная наружность не имеет для нас цены)", и, смотря в зеркало, мы придаем лицу то выражение, которое ориентируется на такое восприятие нас другими, которое кажется нам желательным или "нормальным"[16].

Самописание, самообъективация, совершаемая в дневнике, – это выражение оценки другого и нашего отношения к этой оценке. В женском дневнике автору прежде всего приходится учитывать отношение господствующего патриархатного дискурса к ней как женщине, не как к индивиду, а как к репрезентации представлений о женственности и ее социокультурном статусе в данное время и в данном обществе[17].

Анна Оленина в своем дневнике пишет, можно сказать, из конкретной социокультурной "роли", которую навязывает общество, где она живет, девушке ее возраста и положения, – это роль невесты, барышни на выданье.

Она пересказывает чужие слова и намеки на необходимость сделать партию, фиксирует известия о чужих свадьбах, благоразумно повторяет расхожие мудрости ("я сама вижу, что мне пора замуж, я много стою родителям..." (64), говорит о необходимости закончить свою "девственную Кариеру" (82). "Кто мог бы сказать, что безпокоит меня мое состояние непристроенное, incertain..." (114). Такие слова как "я много стою родителям", "непристроенное состояние" и особенно прелестный "канцеляризм" "девственная карьера" – это *чужое слово*, внедренная внутрь авторской речи точка зрения цензурующего *Ты*.

В размышлениях автора дневника о своем будущем можно видеть чрезвычайно противоречивое смешение разных дискурсов. С одной стороны, развивается идея долга, покорности, самопожертовавания и религиозного смирения – тот набор характеристик, который православная религия и связанная с ней социокультурная традиция связывает с представлениями об идеальной женщине, христианке (см. напр., 64). С другой стороны, она примеряет на себя образ нормальной, расчетливой, благоразумной жены и хозяки – "тетушкин идеал". Для тетушки Варвары Дмитриевны она сочиняет стихи (61–63), в которых, рисуя совершенно безыллюзорный образ будущего супруга и семейной жизни, основанной на расчете и привычке, Анета объективируют нарисованный образец с помощью иронии, изображает скорее пародию на "нормальный брак", чем приемлемую для себя модель.

В то же время, из других записей можно видеть, что брак, построенный на неравенстве предъявляемых к мужчине и женщине требований, вызывает в авторе дневника несогласие и иногда бунт, временами почти феминистский (см. запись от 7 июля 1828 г.: 60).

Ситуация "девушки на выданье", из которой Анета почти все время пишет в дневнике за 1828 год, изображается ею таким образом как некая пограничная ситуация – нахождение на пороге. В этом положении она ощущает навязываемое ей общественным давлением чувство собственной несостоятельности, неполноценности, дефицитности, недоделанности "карьеры" и одновременно чувствует себя товаром, выставленным в витрине для осмотра и покупки. Но в то же время в такой ситуации *по эту сторону* черты есть возможности выбора разных *Я*, и автор как бы перебирает, примеряет на себя эти разные варианты, объективируя себя в героиню литературных текстов. В нескольких местах своего дневника Анета выступает в роли писательницы – она создает "повести" и "романы" на материале своей собственной судьбы.

Первая попытка создания такого романа о себе – в записи от 18 июля. Текст имеет название *Непоследовательность или Любовь достойна снисхождения.* Персонажи жизни выступают под своими именами, довольно известными культурному человеку: Пушкин, Глинка, Вяземский. Женских действующих лиц "всего три – героиня – это я, на втором плане – моя тетушка <...> и мадам Василевская. <...> Я говорю от третьего лица. Я опускаю ранние годы и перехожу прямо к делу" (67). Далее начинается собственно романный текст, где героиню зовут Аннет Оленина, рассказывается о ее страстной любви к не очень достойному человеку и о знакомстве с Пушкиным – что, вероятно, должно стать завязкой действия. Потом следует портрет и характеристика Пушкина, по которой можно предположить, что главный мужской персонаж создаваемого романа жизни выступает в роли демонического героя, "модного тирана".

> Бог, даровав ему Гений единственной, не наградил его привлекательною наружностью. Лице его было выразительно, конешно, но некоторая злоба и насмешливость затмевала тот ум, который виден был в голубых или, лучше сказать, стеклянных глазах его... (67–68).

К сожалению, здесь, едва успев начаться, текст романа и заканчивается, снабженный таким комментарием автора: "Я хотела написать роман, но это мне наскучило, я лучше это оставлю и просто буду вести мой Журнал" (70).

Судя по названию текста и портрету героя, Пушкин должен был выступать в этом романе в роли романтического соблазнителя, принимающего Анету за светскую невинную глупышку, с которой можно дерзко играть, между тем как героиня – иная: девушка, способная критически относиться к себе и другим, способная, ценя гений поэта, не поддаваться соблазну, не растаять при виде знаков внимания знаменитости, не согласиться с ролью пассивной жертвы.

С образом дерзкого "демона" соседствует в дневнике мужской герой совсем иного типа (и соответственно другой образ *Я*-героини на его фоне). Сразу после попытки романа *Непоследовательность* в записи от 13 августа начинается новое литературное предприятие. На даче тетушки Сухаревой Анета встречает молодого казака Алексея Петровича Чечурина, и он становится на некоторое время главным героем дневника. Рассказ о нем, как и ”роман” о Пушкине, строится по литературным моделям, недаром разные части повествования имеют названия и эпиграфы в основном из произведений Пушкина и поэмы И. Козлова *Чернец*. История дружбы-влюбленности между Алексеем и Анетой рассказана в дневнике с помощью сюжетных парадигм и стилистических шаблонов романтической поэмы (повести), ”скрещенных” с сентиментальными образцами, знакомыми нам по дневнику Анны Керн. Главные черты романтического казака – благородство и простодушие. Это ”чистый”, ”милый” ”сын природы” со всеми вытекающими последствиями. Героиня в рамках сюжета выполняет роль ”спасительницы”, которая пользуется его безусловной доверенностью, предостерегает от неверных шагов. *Я*-героиня показана как бы глазами простодушного героя, который сквозь внешнюю мишуру проникает в ее душу. В поле его взгляда автор дневника получает право сконструировать собственный идеальный образ. Его словами (в главе ”Первые впечатления”) она характеризует себя (*Я*-героиню) следующим образом: ”... вы стали со мной говорить и так пылко, искренно, так чувствительно, так умно, что я подумал: ”Так молода, а как разумна: какая доверенность, какая искренность...” (91). Во всех сценах, где рассказывается об истории с казаком внутри ”романной” ситуации, объективируя себя и создавая своеобразное алиби с помощью точки зрения ”простодушного сына природы”, Анета получает возможность говорить о себе позитивно, давать себе высокую самооценку, любоваться собой.

Преодолевая контроль цензурирующего *Ты*, которое навязывает ей конвенциональную роль ”девушки на ярмарке невест”, автор дневника пытается говорить о себе по-другому. Но, вероятно, ей трудно, нарушая патриархатные табу, говорить о себе прямо, и она прибегает к приему объективации *Я*, превращая *Я* в *Она* в *Я*-персонаж, пользуясь литературными клише или чужим словом или вообще передоверяя самохарактеристики другому персонажу (как в случае с казаком). Такое самоостранение, во-первых, создает ”эпическую дистанцию”, с которой возможны более смелые самооценки (в том числе позитивные), а игра в литературность позволяет ”прикрыться” чужим словом, снимая обвинения в нескромности (так как внутренний патриархатный цензор табуирует прямые нарушения "девичьей скромности").

Исходя из вышесказанного, ясно, что темы, связанные с жизнью тела или сексуальностью, полностью табурированы социумом и языком как неприличные и невозможные. Тело возникает в дневнике через мотив болезни или одежды. Прямое выражение телесных желаний не разрешено социокультурными конвенциями (может, у дворянской девушки для этого нет языка, а, если есть, то это не письменный язык). И это еще раз показывает, что степень свободы автора дневника очень относительная, что авторское *Я* дневника, это – локус, место столкновения дискурсов, которые предлагает ей/ему время.

Однако в дневнике есть места, где можем видеть неструктурированный женский субъект, который "неопредмечен" через чужой дискурс. Это такие записи, где, пользуясь термином Юлии Кристевой, можем увидеть, как через трещины и разрывы символического порядка прорывается "семиотическое", довербальное. Как известно, по Кристевой, "говорящий субъект", "субъект в процессе" – двойственный и расщепленный, что проявляется в том, что он одновременно зависим от существующих практик дискурса (символического уровня) и в то же время оказывает сопротивление им. Последнее, согласно Кристевой, обнаруживает себя в поэтическом языке, который есть вид семиотической практики гетерогенности, множественности, вырывающейся на поверхность структурированной упорядоченности символического уровня через такие явления, как повторы, аритикулирующие особенности интонации или ритма, не имеющие референции, глоссосалию – то есть через семиотические операции, эффекты, которые разрушают синтаксис, семантику, языковый порядок.[18].

На мой взгляд, некоторые записи дневника Олениной могут быть интерпретированы как такие "прорывы" фенотекста в генотекст, если применить еще одну пару кристевских терминов[19]. Например, иногда в тексте дневника появляются ритмические повторы (обратим внимание и на знаки препинания – многоточия и скопления восклицательных и вопросительных знаков). "<Я > восхитила его и Гурко своею любезностью. Ого ого ого." (105); "Граф приехал поздно, но тоже пел и оставался долго, очень долго... В. тоже пел и остался допоздна... Вот и все, вот и все, вот и все!"(121); "не ищи, не найдешь; но кто же, кто же жил без надежды !!! (131).Особенно интересна одна из июньских записей 1829 года :

> Тра ла ла ла, тра ла ла ла, тра ла ла ла, я презираю **всех и вся**. Ах, Боже мой, как весело на даче! Что за время, что за покой. Хоть весь день пой. Бог мой, какой... ты что... ах, не скажу... я **пережила** все, и теперь в сердечной или с сердечной пустоты пою, шалю, свищю, и все на **ю** с одним исключением – только **люблю** нет, я к сему слову прилагаю отрицательную частичку **не,** и выходит все прекрасно. **Не люблю.** Прекрасно, прекрасно... Чу, едет кто-то, не к нам ли? Нет, к нам некому быть, любимцы и любители все разъехались по местам, по морям, по буграм, по долам, по горам, по лесам, по садам, ай люли, люли, ай лелешеньки мои... смотрю и ничего не вижу, слушаю и ничего не слышу..." (123).

Для приведенной записи характерны музыкальные повторы, внутренние рифмы, песенный ритм, "бессмысленная" фиксация того, что происходит вовне и внутри себя, здесь нет никаких усилий придать этому потоку вид непротиворечивого сообщения, имеющего какую-то цель и смысл, ассонансы (перелив открытых "а", "о" и "влажных" "ю".[20]

В этой фразе "информация" – в музыкальном звучании, в ритме, понимаемом по Кристевой как "параметры желающего тела, то есть чувственные, эмоциональные, инстинктивные, несемантизированные доминанты речи, предшествующие всякому смыслу"[21]. Но надо заметить, что подобные "прорывы" в дневнике Олениной встречаются не часто.

Таким образом, можно сделать вывод, что и в дневнике Олениной, как и в журнале Керн, образ *Я* (как и образ *Ты*) не является цельным и осознанным. Но именно непоследовательность, нецельность, противоречивость *Я* и *Ты* женского дневника, отношения солидарности/вражды между ними, балансирование на грани открытости/закрытости, секретности/публичности, – все это превращает процесс писания дневника не в само*описани*е, а в само*писание*, сотворение себя, попытку создания собственной идентичности, в процесс, у которого нет результата, но который, пока он длится, позволяет женщине – *быть.*

Ссылки

[1] Felicity A Nussbaum, "Toward Conceptualizing Diary", in James Olney (ed.), *Studies in Autobiography* (Oxford University Press, 1988), p. 128.
[2] В. Н. Шикин, "Дневник", в *Литературный энциклопедический словарь* (М.: Советская энциклопедия, 1987), с. 98.
[3]М. М. Бахтин, *Эстетика словесного творчества* (М.: Искусство, 1979), с. 16.
[4] Domna C. Stanton, "Autogynography: Is the Subject Different?, in Domna C. Stanton (ed.*), The Female Autograph: Theory and Practice of Autobiography from the Tenth to the Twentieth Century*. (The University of Chicago Press, 1987), p. 13. См. также: Sidonie Smith, *A Poetics of Women's Autobiography: Marginality and the fictions of Self-Representation* (Indiana University Press, 1987), pp. 49–50.
[5] Рукопись, хранящаяся в Рукописном отделе Пушкинского Дома, впервые была издана в 1929 году под названием *Журнал отдохновения*. В данной статье текст цитируется по изданию: А. П. Керн, *Дневник для отдохновения*, в А. П. Керн (Маркова-Виноградская), *Воспоминания. Дневники. Переписка* (М.: Правда, 1989), сс. 129–246 с указанием страницы цитаты в тексте.
[6] Текст дневника был издан тиражом 200 экземпляров в 1936 году в Париже внучкой А. Олениной (в замужестве Адорно) О. Н. Оом. В данной статье текст цитируется по изданию: А. А. Оленина, *Дневник. Воспоминания* (Спб: Гуманитарное агентство "Академический проект", 1999) с указанием страницы цитаты в тексте. Редакторы и составители этой книги (Л. Г. Агамалян, В. М. Файбисович, Н. А. Казакова) исправили, сверившись с рукописью А. Олениной, ошибки, неточности и искажения предшествующего издания. Текст *Дневника* публикуется ими с сохранением основных особенностей орфографии и пунктуации оригинала.
[7] В России начала XIX века были очень популярны *Кларисса* Ричардсона, *Новая Элоиза* Руссо, Ст*радания молодого Вертера* Гете, романы Лоренса Стерна, Жермены де Сталь. См.: Н. Д. Кочеткова, *Литература русского сентиментализма* (Спб.: Наука, 1994), сс. 156–186.
[8] Готовые формулы для выражения чувств давал не только чужой текст, но и французкий язык сам по себе. "Степень автоматизации французского языка, языка зрелой культуры, выработавшей всеобъемлющий кодекс поведения, была очень велика. Французское языковое поведение давало набор клише, готовых к механическому воспроизведению" (И. А. Паперно, "О двуязычной переписке пушкинской эпохи", в: *Труды по русской и славянской филологии*, XXIV. Литературоведение, вып. 358 (Тарту, 1975), сс.148–156, см. также: Ю.М. Лотман, "Русская литература на французском языке", в Ю. М.Лотман, *Избранные статьи в 3-х тт.*, т. 2 (Таллинн: Александра, 1992), сс. 350–368.
[9] Е.Ф. Фрич, *Начало пути Л. Н. Толстого и документальная автобиографическая проза конца XVIII – первой половины XIX века* (Автореф. дис... канд. фил. наук. М., 1976), с. 8.

[10] См.: Luce Irigaray, *Das Geschlecht, das nicht eins ist* (Berlin: Merve Verlag, 1979), p. 140.
[11] Irigaray, *Das Geschlecht, das nicht eins ist*, p. 140.
[12] Аборт или любые иные попытки избавится от плода в русской церковной традиции считались безусловно тяжким грехом и наказывались длительной эпитимьей (см. Н. Л. Пушкарева, Ч*астная жизнь русской женщины: невеста, любовница, жена (X - начало XIX в),* (М.: Ладомир, 1997), с. 115). Не только церковь, но и врачи и общественное мнение в XIX веке рассматривали желание женщины прервать наступившую беременность как безусловно аморальное (см.: И. С. Кон, *Сексуальная культура в России: Клубничка на березке* (М.: О.Г.И., 1997), сс. 53–54). Конечно, и в сознании самой Анны Керн происходит сильная борьба "чувства" и "долга", и с утверждениями (самоубеждениями), что ее желание совсем не грешно, на страницах дневника соседствует покаянная молитва: "Боже, прости мне сей невольный ропот, ты, видящий все тайники души моей, прости мне еще раз за всякую мысль, всякое слово, вырвавшееся у меня от непереносимой муки..."(177).
[13] Suzanne L.Bunkers, "Midwestern Diaries and Juornals: What Women Were (Not) Saying in the Late 1800s",. in James Olney (ed.), *Studies in Autobiography* (Oxford University Press, 1988), p. 199.
[14] Заметим, что в женской прозе первой половины XIX века именно тетушка выполняла роль суррогатной матери героини, была персонажем, который обучал свою протеже социокультурным нормам и патриархатным стереотипам и осуществлял функцию контроля. См. об этом: Ирина Савкина, *Провинциалки русской литературы (женская проза 30-40-х годов XIX века)* (Verlag F. K. Göpfert, 1998), сс. 197–199.
[15] Stuart Sherman, *Telling Time: Clocks, Diaries and English Diurnal Form, 1660–1785* (The University of Chicago Press, 1996), p. 254.
[16] М. М. Бахтин, *Эстетика словесного творчества*, с. 31.
[17] См.: Susan Stanford Friedman, "Women's Autobiographical Selves: Theory and Practice", in Shari Benstock (ed.),*The Private Self: Theory and Practice of Women's Autobiographical Writings.* (Routleage, 1988), p. 40.
[18] Julia Kristeva, *Die Revolution der poetischen Sprache*, (Frankfurt am Main: Suhrkamp Verlag, 1978), pp. 35–42.
[19] Julia Kristeva, *Die Revolution der poetischen Sprache,* pp. 94–97.
[20] "Я без ума от тройственных созвучий и влажных рифм – как например на *ю* " (М. Ю. Лермонтов "Сказка для детей").
[21] Ирина Жеребкина; Сергей Жеребкин, *Метафизика как жанр* (Киев: ЦГО НАН Украины, 1996), с. 82.

"Чужая дому и звездам":

Female Stranger in the Diaries of Elena Andreevna Shtakenshneider

Arja Rosenholm

As with numerable other diaries and memoirs by Russian women, so have the diaries and the memoirs of Elena Shtakenshneider (1836–1897) been ignored as documents of scholarly interest. Elena Shtakenshneider is mentioned as an "eye-witness"[1], at the most, a reference of the Russian "woman question" of the 1860s, and her diaries are recommended in a utilitarian function to illuminate the life of the Petersburg male literati, as suggested in I. N. Rozanov's introduction to the *Дневник и записки* (1854–1886) when they were published for the first time in 1934[2]. It is without any doubt that the diaries and memoirs by Elena Shtakenshneider do richly chronicle the literary and social life of St. Petersburg in mid 19th century Russia[3]. Besides that I would suggest that her diary and memoirs give us a particularly sensitive focus on the rise of a new feminine consciousness of the "shestidesjatnitsa", those "new" women who came from privileged circumstances and found in intellectual activities a source for their new autonomy[4]. What fascinates me in these diaries is the intimate focus of a privileged woman who gives her life a cause by writing of it. Writing itself causes the subject-in-process[5] marked by the extreme pain of the dialogue between suffering and self-assurance. The story mediated by the diaries is split; it serves several "causes" of public and hidden selves, not just one Grand Cause hidden behind the autobiographical text.[6] It is this very dialogue led by the discordant diary-Selves constantly wandering in-and-between different stories and perspectives which shows the narrator both as alienated from the prevailing ideologies of femininity, and simultaneously, strongly influenced by patriarchal standards of female self-denial.

What is especially striking in the diaries is the boundary identity of the narrator. Although ambiguity is a common metaphor of self-interpretation in Russian women's literature of the 19th century[7], it is Elena Andreevna Shtakenshneider's diary which, in a highly dramatic way, is built on the rhetoric of the Otherness. Multiple experiences of isolation, aloofness, humiliation and rejection go hand in hand with the ennobling cultivation of an intellectual woman as a stranger. The feeling of extraordinariness prevails:

> Тоска, тоска! Теперь я вижу, как я мало похожа на других; мне ровни все нет. Все мои душевные силы направлены куда-то, где товарищей мне нет. Я стою вне жизни; только в отвлеченностях схожусь я с людьми, но с какими? – не с ровнями мне, не с товарищами. И остаюсь я вечно чужая и дому и звездам.(88–89)

The self-reflections, made in the diary over several years, follow the extreme "logic of exile"[8], characterizing, according to Kristeva, the very figure of instability she calls the "stranger" or the "foreigner". The self-representation of the diary-self embodies the "stranger" in an exemplary way, also revealing the anxieties of the contemporaries as *their* "image of the other", as their "hidden face of [*their*] identity"[9]. The figure of the foreigner bears the mark of "a crossed threshold"[10]. Something has definitely been exceeded, the insistent presence of a lining imprints the wanderings of the narrator, her being on the threshold, on the lines, in-and-between any solid structures: "Я нахожу еще в переходном состоянии" (139), states the narrator of her social, cultural and psychological locus. Shtakenshneider stands on several boundaries; in-and-between cultures and languages, East and West, individual and collective, Russian and German; she is affected by the Western European Enlightenment considering the citizen-individual as unitary and ideal, being simultaneously disillusioned about the liberalization of Russia against the totalitarian absolutism, she is brought up by two different cultural ideals; by the ideal of self-neglect embodied by the Russian hagiographic lives of saints, as her childhood reading, on the one hand, and the demanding individualism of German literature represented to her by Heinrich Heine, on the other hand. The end and the beginning are simultaneously present, the past continues to live in the presence, and the individual experiences are transformed into cultural signs: in one pocket Shtakenshneider carries poems of the idealistic F.N. Glinka, those of radical P.L. Lavrov in the other.

Her narrative is strongly marked by a double subjectivity[11] caught in the cross fire between two stories, between two rhetorical postures – paternal and maternal – on whose border the semi-public script is written. This corresponds to the role of Elena Andreevna as a mediator which she plays in the family circle being the messenger between "mama" and "papa" during their many conflicts. Her role in the family play is well reported:

> Я не спала всю ночь. Утром мама послала меня к папа, который не завтракал и не обедал с нами. Весь день я проходила от мама к нему и обратно, сверху вниз, и, наконец, он простил, они помирились. (156–157)

The female diary-self is devoted to boundaries, it leads an existence at the crossroads to different othernesses: As the eldest daughter of a court architect and an Academy professor, Elena Andreevna Shtakenshneider belongs to the social and cultural establishment, she is acquainted with the famous artists of her time and the literary elite coming together in the literary salon established by her mother, Maria Feodorovna in the years 1854–1862 in the imposing palace of the family. She is sophisticated, exceptional, hypersensitive, culturally privileged, yet speaks, simultaneously, from the margins. This is so, since Shtakenshneider is crippled from birth, hunchbacked, and walks with crutches. Mikulich, another Russian woman writer, depicts her after visiting the salon: "Елена Андреевна, пожилая, болезненная девушка, на костылях и с больными ногами, умная, добрая и приветливая."[12] Due to her invalidism the diary –"I" disqualifies herself into an outsider, an observer from beyond, a dropout, a wanderer on the borderline.

The rhetoric of Otherness – no place, no time, only the nagging instability of an existence – is overwhelming:

> Мне кажется, чувствуется даже, что я не стою на твердой почве, а нахожусь в воздушном пространстве, и над головой ничего, и ничего под ногами и кругом. (141)

The metaphors of swaying over some abyss of someone who has lost the soil under her feet, are recurrently pointing to the instability of the wanderer who has lost the ground of identity. It is as if one be receptive to conflicts only after the body has lost footing, as if a certain imbalance were necessary for conflicts to be heard[13]. The narrator writes that "[…] ощущаю что–то похожее на голод и жажду. […] жизнь мне обещает мало радости, горя много […]" (59). The language of starvation[14] – hunger and thirst (also 132, 168, 344) – shows the narrator as a woman who hungers and thirsts for a fuller life than her society can ever offer to any "privileged" woman. The anguish felt is "the problem that has no name"[15], not even by herself to discover. It is as Epstein Nord says of 19th century Western women of ambition and achievement, that

> […] the resolution of struggle and satisfactory discovery of sexual and spiritual identity remained painfully elusive and, therefore, virtually impossible to describe[16].

In accordance with Heilbrun who calls us to take seriously the "privileged" women's nameless anguish, I would suggest that the very complaints and reflections made by this privileged woman, Elena Shtakenshneider, are "at the very heart of women's oppression", including "sexual abuse and the miseries of a hunger that is not physical" but "that can be felt by women of all races and classes"[17]. The painful ambiguity is caused by when the consciousness of the difference arises, since "the foreigner lives within us"[18]. So is also the diary-self made conscious of her handicap: of never being able to be a "normal" woman: "я не невеста" (103), "я не выйду замуж" (188), "я не кандидатка в жены" (278), "я не выйду замуж" (288), as is the difference repeatedly established. Not only does she feel herself different compared to bodily healthy, but the invalidism makes her receptive to conflicts of being a different kind of a *woman*. The limp makes her difference audible, but not only as a cripple.

The experience of the "unfitting" boundary identity is fixated by a scene which shows the Otherness bound to gender identity. The narrator is on a quest with the "normal" femininity which, as she feels, she cannot adapt any more, quite analogously to her denial of the masquerade:

> Эти два вечера мы провели в *маскараде*, […]. Уже одно то, что принуждена я была туда ехать, было противно. Маме пришло вдруг в голову показать мне маскарад. Меня эта идея повергла в ужас. Мне, хромоногой, надевать домино и маску, т. е. скрываться, когда

> при первом шаге походка выдаст меня. 'Будешь, – говорит, – сидеть и по крайней мере составишь себе понятие, что такое маскарад'. Но к чему мне это понятие? [...] А вдруг какой–нибудь знакомый меня увидит и подумает, что я сама захотела туда. Но с мама не бороться. (154)

The very power of the masquerade-scene lies in its implication of a taboo: the reader is pointed to the fact that the narrator knows why she feels hostile towards the masks, though, what the real reason is, is left unutterable. It can, however, be deconstructed from the bindings between the definition prohibition of a taboo and the metaphors of masquerade pointing to Otherness and femininity[19]. On the one hand the narrator is at odds with "normal" femininity, being no "bride", no "wife", nor a "mother", on the other hand the focus from which she sees her limited possibilities as a woman to enunciate her desire assents just to those of others' wishes, she is the Other but yet not as "me":

> Все знакомые девицы меня чуждаются, и неудивительно: кому я интересна? Я не могу ни в чем, что их занимает, принимать участие; не могу ни танцоватъ, ни наряжаться, ни кокетничатъ [...]. (53)

> Конечно, жизнь моя, ради моего убожества, примет иной оборот, чем у других девушек, я не выйду замуж. Так что же? И здоровые не все выходят. И будто уж это такое несчастье? (188)

> Ну, да, я из несчастных, я калека. Не могу ходить, бегать, танцевать, как другие. Моя жизнь пойдет не торным путем, не с другими, а в стороне, и как не намечена. Я не выйду замуж, не буду любима, не буду иметь детей, свою семью, свой дом. Я брак в жизни. (288)

For sure, the narrator-I offends different kinds of taboos, since Shtakenshneider does not fit into the dualistic world of the binary models with only two alternatives acceptable: right or false, political and aesthetic mainstream or its radical nihilist challenging, we or the others. The main taboo, however, concerns the relationship which the masquerade scene brings about, that between Otherness and her gender identity. The relationship between masquerade and femininity, as it is discussed by Joan Riviere in her article "Womanliness as a Masquerade"[20], is grounded on the hypothesis that there is no "true" femininity, that masquerade is a representation of femininity, but its travesty, too; a twofold issue inscribed also within Irigaray's understanding of female mimicry[21]. Shtakenshneider's denial of the masquerade is in accordance to her analogous attitude to the "normal" femininity, as it was prescribed to Russian gentry women in the 19th century. Shtakenshneider denies the normative "roles" prescribed to women, she is filled with an ambition to enter the male domain, presented as that of literary activities. Exceptional, as she thinks she is, she identifies with a male world; the female "I" slides into a male-identified posture:

> Я так привыкла к обществу мужчин и к их спорам, что мне просто лень говорить с дамами, [...]. (130)

Simultaneously, however, she is not free from being looked-at as a female object of the scopic economy which offers men an active gaze to be (self)reflected by the practice of the mirroring female masquerade. "[...] на меня все [...] смотрят" (91), knows the woman. She is, however, evaluated not only by others, but she by herself disqualifies herself by the standards of "normal femininity" which she cannot fit into. No mask or role of normal femininity will cover what is always present to everybody, her crippled body that reduces her, as she feels, into an unattractive "disfigure". This is how she wants to learn to look at herself, to learn not to feel like a "normal" woman but to discipline her desire and to become modest, silent and acceptable as an unattractive intellectual woman.

However, the desire, strong as it is, is only partially to become stifled, what makes the disciplinary training into a life-long project. The diary is a witness of fighting needs shifted into scopic struggle between two "gazes"; the "spiritual" and the "bodily" eye (умственное – телесное око, 80, 123). The narrator fears someone would say to her that a woman sexually not attractive is not allowed to have any desire at all, whether intellectual or sexual. This, having desire and trying to suppress it, is her very private quest, which she does not bring up in publicity, acting there in a quite defensive way. When the cultural establishment makes Julia Zhadovskaya, a contemporary woman writer, into an object of ridicule, as a woman and a cripple but yet writing of love, Shtakenshneider keeps silent:

> Была у Глинок Юлия Жадовская. Над ней смеются за то, что она, убогая, немолодая, незрачная, – пишет про любовь; над ее убожеством даже смеются. Я не решилась (...) сказать Василью Курочкину, что он это напрасно делает, чтобы не нашли меня слишком заинтересованной в деле подобного рода. (195)

While in privacy desiring influencing public opinion as a competent literary specialist, which she knows she has all the expertise, she is also aware of the nonfemale character of her challenge in public. A conflict, also pointed out by the masquerade concept of Riviere, comes up when a woman with ambition is to challenge the symbolical authorship of the paternal father-figures, whose favour she would, yet, "woo"[22] after having conscious feelings of competition. There is, in the diary, this covered pleasure of an intellectual woman to be signified as such by getting reassurance by an equal; an intellectual man (340). The diary notes twice how the woman enjoys being in public the object of an extraordinary man, as was Lavrov to her:

> Мне нравится, когда в гостиной, (...) он начнет искать своими близорукими глазами меня, и все уже знают, кого он ищет, и, смеясь, подводят его ко мне. Он садится тогда возле меня, и тут тотчас же и образуется центр [...]. (181)

And later:

> Мы сходились на нейтральном поле вопросов нашей тогдашней общественной жизни или научных вопросов. Но моему личному сознанию было любо, когда он, войдя в гостиную, искал меня своими близорукими глазами, и другие, догадываясь, кого он ищет, улыбаясь, направляли его ко мне. (367)

The position of a "neutral" confidante who in a womanly conforming manner only sits and waits to be spoken to is the mask of the female Stranger to avert society's judgement. Because of her visible bodily handicap Shtakenshneider cannot play with the heterosexual rules and the acceptable feminine roles, neither is she to play the innocent dilettante. Shtakenshneider's strategy is not the narcissistic mimicry cultivated by the very expert of Russian feminine masquerade, the poetesse Evdokiya Rostopchina, who openly and joyfully proclaims to "love the masquerade": "Я только женщина, гордиться тем готова, Я бал люблю!.. отдайте балы мне!"[23] When Rostopchina makes herself into an object of desire by an ostensible consent to the negative reputation, given to her by Belinskii, Dobrolyobov and Chernyshevskii, as an idle and frivolous "poetess of the ball"[24], Shtakenshneider chooses another strategy; that of masochistic pleasure in over-identification with her a-femininity and a-sexuality. The normal femininity is likened to the "attributes of her bodily torture"[25], she says. Shtakenshneider's strategy is that of her "martyrology" (416), which she, however, utilizes as her liberation, too: it is her conscious – and thus "playful" – denial of the "normal" masquerade which allows her to enter the male literary and philosophical circle. It is the anti-masquerade which becomes her mask. While insisting on not being a bride, wife, or mother she seeks comfort in her otherness which, indeed, becomes a contradictory place of exile from and engagement with intellectual male establishment. In her anti-femaleness and assumed unattractiveness she does not challenge the male gaze, but, sooner, she becomes a safe, i.e. harmless companion without any sexual appeal of a potential Woman to be conquered by a man as the very mirror of his male self-reflection. Through her stressing on the anti-masquerade the exceptional woman is no more a threat to a man and, in accordance with the duality of feminine "roles" prevailing, the bodiless woman can now be accepted as a man's confidante without being a "wife candidate" (278), the role which was both given to and enjoyed by Shtakenshneider especially in the relationship with Lavrov. The diarist is the "wallflower", the outsider beyond the masquerade who, yet, knows to use the marginal locus as her shelter from where to observe, to see and hear things unattainable to those "normal" women who are engaged within established heterosexual hierarchies and rivalries:

> Но шплиттергексе, кажется, поглядела иное, [...], т.е. именно оттого, что губы не открываются и не дают воли действовать языку, она и имела досуг поглядеть многое. (273–274)

This, the bodily marginality combined with fine talent to transform the subtle observations into sensitively drawn cultural scenes, makes the diary enjoyable reading. Shtakenshneider acts from the exile, simultaneously under the shelter of bodily integrity – from an ambiguous place shared by other Russian women, too, like Maria Zhukova or Julia Zhadovskaya, other bodily handicapped women writers.

Shtakenshneider avoids becoming lost in the masquerade of normal femininity while refusing to play the heterosexual roles of a bride, wife or mother. She sees herself too much as lacking the "normal" standards. To win back some of the lost desire she identifies with that of men and suppresses her "own" instead[26]:

> [...] я сделалась восторженной поклонницей Лаврова. Стала смотреть на вещи его глазами, повторять его слова, любить, что он любил, ненавидеть, что он ненавидел [...]. (362)

She sees her role as the one who gives, enables a mirroring dialogue for her discussant, she is the silent listener, takes care of and inspires men, enjoying the public attention of men directed to her as their confidante. In this role she does play with the mask of "unattractiveness", of an innocent getting pleasure from her secret ambition:

> Лавров [...] сблизился со мною. Я не думаю, чтобы он смотрел на меня, как на прозелитку: я по многим причинам для нее не годилась, да и тон наших бесед был иной. [...] А со мной, я думаю, напротив того, Лавров, если и были у него прозелиты, отдыхал от них. У каждого, даже самого ничтожного, человека, бывает же какой–нибудь талант. Есть, я знаю, такой и у меня, это талант слушать и, сказала бы, понимать, да боюсь, не будет ли слишком, скажу: схватывать смысл на лету и вовремя бросить слово, которое действует на собеседника, как масло на огонь, давая ему уверенность, что его слушают и понимают. При этом я никогда не перебиваю, не делаю охлаждающих вопросов или попыток самой завладеть речью. Вот что, вероятно, нравилось во мне Лаврову. Я многих даже невольно обманывала таким образом, т.е. меня считают поэтому гораздо умнее и более знающей, чем я на самом деле. Другие находят, что я люблю льстить, и это, пожалуй, правда. (366–367)

Simultaneously, however, a feeling of never being able to fulfil the own creative power gives the diary its sad undertone. The key metaphor of the female self – manifesting the disillusionment towards one's desire and creative power – is a "bird with broken wings": "[...] чаще чувствую себя птицей с подрезанными крыльями". (93)[27] The female narrator herself is involved in the surgery operation. The narrator is the agent and the victim of her own creative power. The conflict between the two "I's", the public and the private selves – both needed for the dialogue working on the identity – is recognized: "[...] я в жизни и в дневнике не одна и та же"[28] , she acknowledges, since it is "impossible to say in public what she tells to the diary". Meanwhile the balancing act of the "inner struggle" (141) is built on keeping the hidden desire apart from the willing self: The "stranger" should become indifferent to all the insults and rejections, she should rise above any pain, should not complain, but be dauntless, brave, a good daughter. Any suffering should be kept under control and repressed. The loss of love shall not reveal any public wound, but be silenced, the pain "murdered": "Я свою [тоску] заморю". (91, also 346) The key scene treating the loss of her great love (Osipov) shows the sublimation of the private pain exercised as a rationalization of the loss into a moral virtue

> [...] знала, что чувство цельное отдать одному человеку нельзя; и забылась, и отдала было. Не приняли – беру его назад и разменяю, чтобы хватило на всех, на весь мир. А разве одним чувством только живут? А голова? Я еще ничего не знаю; я хочу все знать, и голова будет знать. Но кто научит? Нет у меня учителя, нет никого. Ведь Осипов этим учителем и был. Ну, поищу другого. Вот только бы одолеть себя, одолеть болезнь. (91)

The challenge to "overcome" one's "wound" ("на дне души только ранка болить" 117, "победить себя" 169) silences the complaint; proud and stubborn she holds on to what she lacks by fanatically denying it: the love of an ordinary woman. The denial reveals her very anguish: to remain out of love (недостаток любви, 188), forgotten and abandoned (345).

The writer employs the private diary-dialogue in order to survive the painful difference, the insults and rejections, and to delegate the male protagonists to represent her in public. The hidden desire for an empowered life story rests on assurances to another; public, puritan and disciplined "I" that the diarist has successfully escaped the narcissistic desire for love. The intoxication goes to the extent that the public self reaffirms her subordination to all transcendental fathers, not only her beloved "papa"[29], but all the men in her life, her brother Andrei, dyadushka, Osipov, her youth love, Polonskii, Lavrov and Dostoevskii. Men represent the culturally valued positions as teachers, revolutionaries, apostles, prophets, as god-like (47, 184, 210, 284, 364, 366), as implied in her attitude to Lavrov:

> Я вовсе не желаю быть ему [i.e. Lavrov, A.R.] ровней, а, напротив того, желаю на него смотреть снизу вверх, и близко вглядываться в него даже вовсе не желаю. (180–181)

However, as Féral suggests, a woman "cannot assume the identification with the Father except by denying her difference as a woman, except by repressing the maternal within her"[30]. This is what indeed happens: While showing strong empathy for her father the daughter feels herself misunderstood by her mother, and assumes in return an attitude towards her which is almost patronizing: "Правду говорит мама, что я душой старше нее [...]". (130)

The self of Shtakenshneider’s diary is not any spontaneous or “true” presence, nor do we have any teleological development into an authentic self-consciousness[31]. Rather is the diary writing exercised in the function of a life-long self-education and self-disciplining: writing as a strategy for self-protection, for avoidance of more “wounds”. The rhythm of writing is the rhythm of self-disciplining and its subversion: the language is a defence against the unconscious, pre-symbolic logic, although not at all a successful defence network, punctuated as it is by messages from the unconscious semiotic desire. When the inner and outer reality collide, faith in the powers of persuasion through language turns into astonishment: “Я видела сегодня свой портрет, фотографию, которую делали для папа; не думала я, что у меня такое наивно–робкое лицо” (131). The female narrator tries to intoxicate the desire of the hidden self, hurt and humiliated in her yearning for ordinary love; that this shameful female vanity would be left behind by the invalid spinster to lead a docile life. The rational I is her own censor:

> Но будет об этом! (89)
> Но будет об этом. (92)
> Ну и конец. Ставлю крест на все. (96)
> Ведь поставила же я крест на все. (99)
> Все одно в голове! Попробую о другом. (92)

The narrator gives herself orders to write inside the defensive network. The self-censoring is, however, potentially damaging, since the female narrator’s desire finds articulation in the very terms of its repression. Even when Shtakenshneider experiences her own dramas, she frequently fails to report them directly[32]. Of the central psychosexual drama in her life she says almost nothing, she is silent about the romantic predicaments, only hinting at the pain and unhappiness of losing the Great Love, although Osipov’s name will come up even years after their separation. Not only does the “I” avoid self-revelation and personal narrative, she also deprecates her creative “wings” – her musical talent and the sculptural activities – which she reports as failures (152, 153, 206). She places herself into the role of a “child”[33], a pupil, recurrently looking at herself through the eyes of others. This certainly corresponds to the most pervasive characteristics of female self-representation defined in relation to significant others[34], and implies what Spacks has called the female “suppression of narrative about the self"[35] . The significant others are men acting as substitutes for the narration of the female self. Her own story is told through the lives led by others, by men.

This way of creating one's female life as a non-story around the public and heroic life of men[36] goes parallel with the pattern of the "*двойная жизнь*"[37], the female double consciousness, which was strongly developed in the texts by Russian women writers of the last century. The female narrator's story is told from "the place of the Other"[38], that is, it comes from the "place of absence", spoken by "no one" as "not One", as Irigaray argues, woman's discourse as "pluralized"[39], as imitative and disruptive. The narrator speaks from several different positions, not from any One centre. She feels herself as a unique "exception" in a male world which fascinates her much more than the "closed" world of her mother and the sisters. Only rarely does she touch on domestic life, but tries, instead, to fulfil the cultural expectations imposed on her by the literary "fathers", as was Shcherbina, who "[…] постоянно уговаривает меня писать дневник и вносить в него все, что я вижу и слышу" (103), as the narrator states.

> Щербина опять говорил мне вчера: 'Пишите свой дневник как можно подробнее, знаете, все мелочи записывайте. Не пишите о том, что и без вас будет известно из газет, но то записывайте, чего не могут все знать; подробности, которые будут интересны через несколько лет'. Я рада слушаться Щербину, но уменье–то, уменье выбирать! (107)

The literary ideal is far away from her female domestic life, being:

> Один старичок, сенатор Жихарев, знакомый и товарищ по Московскому архиву дедушки, [который] пишет в "Отечественных Записках" свои воспоминания под заглавием "Дневник Чиновника". Вот бы мне так уметь! (108)

Despite the many male idols, "apostles" and patrons in abundance, woman's own voice in the male establishment is muted, or masqueraded: in the area of language the woman remains a silent Polyglot[40] . The semipublic strategy, which Shtakenshneider adapts as a diarist, is present through her other literary activities, too: Proudly and in a self-conscious manner the narrator proclaims: "Когда Полонский сделается цензором, немецкие книги цензуровать буду я". (322) She delivers Ya. P. Polonskii, who was the official censor, her expertise of the Western, especially German literature, her name and her actual contribution, however, remain in silence, without any established name. Rozanov comments:

> По словам сына поэта, А. Я. Полонского, означенная должность [как “иностранный цензор”] мало утруждала поэта: почти все иностранные книги не только немецкие просматривала Елена Андреевна и Яков Петрович в большинстве случаев только санкционировал ее мнение[41] .

In the same manner, as she feels that as a diarist, as she frequently complains, she would fail to follow her ideal diarist-*starichok* to depict “details” and pure “facts”[42], in the same manner her voice remains mute in the presence of men:

> [...] перед ним [Lavrov, A.R.] я как можно тщательно скрываю свое горе, – радостей у меня нет, – свои сомнения и недоумения, иначе.... Что иначе? (340)

Only as an elderly woman looking back at her life, has she the courage to confess:

> [...] вечно занятая чужими делами, я никогда не находила времени говорить о своих делах. Когда я была еще молода, я все себя спрашивала: когда же наступит мой черед говорить, выгружать свою душу? Каждый раз, когда я раскрывала рот, при первом слове тот, с кем я говорила, вспоминал, что вот что с ним было, если у него точно так же, – и приходиалась слушать, а не говорить самой. Так мало–по–малу я говорить о себе разучивалась, [...] я умела слушать и не беспокоила их [людей, A.R.] своими делами. (345)

The radical confession above demonstrates the logic of the female double consciousness. The “effaced” voice (мой задавленный голос, 64) of self-reflections of this kind will disrupt the continuity of the “pure facts” aimed at by the calm observer. The actual story of a female “stranger” to be told by the diary becomes a puzzle put together from different pieces of numerous meditations and self-reflections which go roaming through the text-continuity. Telling of incoherence, of Otherness, these self-reflections are caused by an outbreak of the effaced voice which will never totally submit to the version of the public Self as denying “normal” love and passion. On the one hand, she states: “Я не выйду замуж, не буду любима, не буду иметь детей, свою семью, свой дом” (288), on the other hand, the other selves, those unrealizable in her own life, live in other women’s lives, as does that "Self" identifiable as a "young mother": "Вон тоже 'я', только зовут его не Лена Штакеншнейдер, а Лиза Шульц, молодая мать". (288–289) In its very silence and incompleteness the suppressed story begins to dry out the assurances of the story the narrator thinks she tells; of "details" and pure "facts" about the male establishment. The self-reflections, as a "coming out" from behind the repressive silence, lead to a mythological expansion of the Self – the outpouring of her personal identity with its pain and fear providing the subject with a strong self-assurance. These are the dramatic passages in the diary, "the paradox of continuity in discontinuity"[43], where the narrator speaks directly about her womanhood and reveals the degree of her self-consciousness about her position as an exceptional woman, as a stranger.

Shtakenshneider does not go into a public contract but cherishes her exceptionality by means of her private diary. In an unsentimental tone she withdraws her desire to act *in* discourse as a public subject: in order to avoid the shame of becoming an object of laughter, as was Julia Zhadovskaya taking the risk, when writing of love in public, as a woman and a cripple (195). Shtakenshneider's choice to retain privacy shows the doubleness of her happiness, or is it rather the double bind of the female stranger? For, as Kristeva writes,

> [...] curiously, beyond unease, such a doubling imposes upon the other, the observer, the feeling that there is a special, somewhat insolent happiness in the foreigner. Happiness seems to prevail, *in spite of everything*, because something has definitely been exceeded: it is the happiness of tearing away, of racing, the space of a promised infinite. Such happiness is, however, constrained, apprehensively discreet, in spite of its piercing intrusion, since the foreigner keeps feeling threatened by his [or her, A.R.] former territory, caught up in the memory of a happiness or a disaster – both always excessive[44].

This kind of happiness, caused by the experience of an existential transformation as a price for her autonomy, is inherent in her self-definition as the sceptical but unique Cassandra: "Опять Кассандра видит что-то" (160, 159, 179). On the one hand there is a strong voice of resignation which shows the writer, as being quite hopeless towards the option which would combine both happiness and female Otherness:

> Не ошибается ли Белинский... В самом ли деле так отвратительна и так неуместна, уродлива (лучшего слова не нахожу) женщина-писательница... Есть исключения, я, например [...] но женщина

> эта исключение, – она не имеет прав, не имеет голоса, у ней только отнято и взамен не дано ничего.(311)

On the other hand, in order to survive in these desolate circumstances, she has the strong will to develop positive self-experience and inherent self-value which would not only depend on this perishing world. She creates for herself a shield of inaccessibility and indifference to protect herself, she cultivates her difference and ennobles her status as a stranger: "Я живу слишком богатой умственно жизнью. Вижу, слышу, даже понимаю – слишком много". (170, see also 132, 312, 342). This dual signification is inscribed into the Otherness of the mythical Cassandra-figure bound with a "double life" of

> [...] гордость и горечь: гордость, что я ни в ком не нуждаюсь, и горечь, это меня забывают. Эти два чувства заставили меня совершенно скрывать свою личность и отдавать от себя все. (345)

Shtakenshneider as Cassandra, a daughter and a priestess: she identifies herself with the mythological daughter of the Troian King Priamos, a female figure engaged with social and political questions, a female stranger in the androcentric world, and a foreigner, running the high status of a priestess, an oracle with the gift of prophesy. She sees the future, since not involved in the power conflict of the colliding parties. Simultaneously she is not understood, not heard by her nearest, nor by her enemies[45] . Shtakenshneider is the seer with a prophesy unheard by others:

> Мне все кажется, чувствуется даже, что я не стою на твердой почве, а нахожусь в воздушном пространстве, и над головой ничего, и ничего под ногами и кругом. Я испытываю то же ощущение, которое испытывается, когда находишься на краю бездны и смотришь в нее с высоты. Мне кажется, весь мир находиться на краю бездны и должен погибнуть; что наступили последние времена, о которых сказано в Евангелии, и я удивляюсь, как этого никто не замечает. И в то время то, что этого никто не замечает, поддерживает мой ужас, потому если бы заметили и поверили, то образумились бы, и пророчество бы не исполнилось.(141)

Without any sentimental self pity Cassandra knows she has no place among ordinary women. Neither can she have a status as an "apostle" reserved for men, as she knows. What then could be the female ideal to be identified with for a Russian woman who is supposed to be not a beauty, neither a mother, but is rather a woman who wants to nourish her society with spiritual gifts? This is the self-quest of which the diary tells us; of her inner transformation: "Я все ищу идеальную женщину [...]" (111). Shtakensheider is attempted to find a female ideal which she hopes to discover occasionally in different types of women, so in the extrovert salonniere, Shelgunova (111), or in the "young mother", Liza Schulz (288–289). As the above Belinskii-quotation shows, she is meanwhile quite confused, almost despairing to arrive at any adequate positive identity presented her by patriarchal images, and, as the gender question being too aggravated with taboos to be challenged on a conscious level, she makes use of those mythical associations which seem to nourish her needs and sympathies[46].The mythical woman Shtakensheider identifies with is not any of the beauty objects submitted under the verdict of Paris, neither is it a Gorgoean monstrum, nor the anasthesized "Sleeping Beauty", the "new woman" of the 1860s[47] to be awakened by the Apollonian Genius. On the contrary, it is a woman who wants to be a female priestess herself. The mythical associations as a self-conscious Cassandra liberate her imaginative potential to be creative among the patriarchal "apostles", although, yet, among that society of male spiritual leaders she is to carry the reputation of a woman whose wisdom is turned into a gloomy prophecy of future prospects.

However, she is not only a tragic figure, as Christa Wolf's Cassandra was not a woman without hope[48]. It is rather the way in which she learns to cope with her physical and intellectual Otherness, special pain which makes her strong and liberates her from the naivite of the "norm". Although it would be easy to feel sorrow for the destiny of this exceptional woman, so sophisticated, and so placeless in the established Russian male history, we shall not ignore the strength of the Cassandra-figure by which Shtakenshneider herself refuses to be pitied. She creates a figure to mediate between her uniqueness and the world, to bring consolation into the painful isolation from normal femininity and the paternal establishment. Cassandra is for Shtakenshneider a figure which is provided with the most important values she identifies with; the cultural and moral superiority, as the highest. This is obvious by her sympathy for a young radical woman of the 1860s, Masha Mihaelis, who was arrested shortly after showing her sympathy for Chernyshevskii, already on his way to exile (334, 339):

> Это не нигилистка, это московская барышня, т.е. в ней больше сознания. Она вышла из общей колеи не во имя идей, потому, что в ней ей было неудобно; пошлости, мерзости ее натура не хотела

> переносить. Смелости у нее хватило, на то она и барышня. [...] Почувстовав себя выше среды, ей было нипочем бросить родовой быт свой и семью. (335)

Due to her invalidism Shtakenshneider identifies her life as a "martyrology" (416,105) which provides her with a higher sensibility for moral issues than allotted to ordinary people and who are healthy in body:

> Сейчас принесла мама и положила мне на стол мои бриллианты, серьги, брошку, браслеты– все атрибуты моей пытки. Сегодня бал у Бруни. Она их принесла с таким видом, точно знает, что обрадует меня; точно слезы, которые навертываются на мои глаза, – слезы радости. Она смотрит на меня и улыбается. Слепая она, что ли, или хочет не видеть? (117)

The profane pain is transcended into a mythological self-assurance and self-survival. The identification as Cassandra acts in the function of transcendence, to help to interprete the solitude as uniqueness "larger than life" and so, with calm indifference to observe ordinary women's roles which the diary-Self cannot play. Shtakenshneider cannot identify with any of the binary womens' roles prevailing in the middle of the century: neither is she the *kiseinaya baryshnya*, as the glamorous aristocratic salonniére or an innocent *institutka,* nor is she any pure type of an "emancipated woman" as a *nigilistka*. She is a both-and, a creature split by different cultures and languages as her uneasy home: "Я своей длинной косой только принадлежу к аристократкам, впрочем: *every inch a nihilist!*" (325)[49]. She is a wanderer on the borders; in the sexlessness of a "maiden" (маленькая девочка, 93) and an "old woman" (старуха, 93), as the repentant Mary Magdalene (345–6), or as the "Splitterhexe" (273) she is beyond any sexually determined femaleness. Cassandra is the figure who, due to her position at the border – from her very "highness" (167) – can see the false "roles" of ordinary women, as they are disqualified by the unordinary woman as "nonauthentic" (несамостоятельное), as "masks" set up on women by men.

> Ах, сестры, мои сестры! Как бы хотела я открыть вам всю душу, сказать вам правду, – и нельзя. И найти вас не могу, и не дадут нам, да и духу нет, в себя веру потеряла. (318)

Cassandra prophesies her gloomy prediction.

Consequently, Cassandra rejects both normal femininity and the masquerade, as we already pointed out (141, 154). Equally false in their meanings, femininity and masquerade are both denied by the limping Cassandra. Instead, in a discussion about George Sand, who was for the Russian liberals the true representation of an "emancipated" woman, Shtakenshneider seems to point to some utopian moments of her term of femininity not prescriptive as male-oriented political or cultural model and located beyond the masks. George Sand she sees as "half-male":

> Она полу–мужчина. [...] разве вполне развитая женщина должна походить на мужчину? (167): Я не верю, что для женщины нет иного развития, как на этот образец. [...] А мне вдруг показалось, что мужчины из самомнения и самообожания выдумали это развитие, и не могут себе представить иного и самостоятельного. (167–168)

This utopian place of an "authentic" feminine is given to Cassandra. She is brought up from the mythological past into historical time, from beyond, and outside the dominant ideology of gender as an egalitarian but implicitly a male-centred project[50].

Cassandra is a radical non-conformist. The exceptional woman will not only mirror the "new man", the *бурсак* (284), as the writer snobbishly calls Chernyshevskii. Sooner, and this, indeed, is important: she finds an other voice, an autonomous place for her to get along with her individual emancipation development. The main focus is on, how the diary-self learns to get along with the conflict of not being an ordinary woman who is haunted by ordinary desires. Over-identification with suffering is part of her "martyrology" and the necessary lot of the hyper-sensitive Other. This is a rhetorical and psychological tradition which seems to be more common for Russian women than playing with the irony of narcissism, successfully adapted by her Western women contemporaries[51]. Provided with an armour of indifference the Russian Cassandra[52] detaches herself from ordinary women, as she does from her own suffering. The experience of a "Stranger" gives her – unlike those ordinary women with routine and rest – the lofty sense of having a biography[53] , however ambiguous between the lacking "self-confidence" (327, 340, 345, 346) and mythological self-expansion. With this identification as the self-steering Cassandra with a gloomy prediction we have a life script which in a realistic manner anticipates the fact that a woman does not have any "public" story to tell under the historical circumstances, and which is simultaneously provided with that fundamental yearning, to be found in the journals of her sister-soul, Maria Bashkirceva[54], of being called to a higher mission and fame.

Notes

[1] Richard Stites, *The Women's Liberation Movement in Russia.* (Princeton, 1978), pp. 29, 33, 70, 76; see also В.В. Стасов, *Надежда Васильевна Стасова: Воспоминания и очерки.* (СПб. 1899). This has also been the fate of Vodovozova's memoirs which are often quoted as documents, being not, however, of any interest to literary research.
[2] И.Н. Розанов, 'Елена Андреевна Штакеншнейдер и ее дневник'. In Елена Андреевна Штакеншнейдер, *Дневник и записки* (1854–1886). Ред., статья и ком. И.Н. Розанов. (Akademia 1934), 7–27. The quotations are from this edition. The editor points out that "[...] мы принуждены были делать большие пропуски и сокращения: в дневнике ее много повторений, много деталей, понятных и интересных только для ее домашних, общих рассуждений и случайных мыслей и оценок, мало для нее характерных и только разбивающих впечатление." p. 27.
[3] See also Barbara A. Engel, 'Shtakenshneider, Elena Andreevna', in Marina Ledkovsky, Charlotte Rosenthal, Mary Zirin (eds.), *Dictionary of Russian Women Writers.* (Greenwood, 1993), pp. 593–594.
[4] See Bianka Pietrow-Ennker, *Russland's "neue Menschen".* (Campus, 1999), pp. 257–312.
[5] I refer here to the instability of language and the fundamentally split character of the subject as a speaking/writing being who, according to Kristeva emerges through the process of signification; the "semiotic" chaos inherent in the pre-"symbolic" meaning goes beyond the authorial intention which is not to read as the only meaning of the sociosymbolic texture. Julia Kristeva, *Die Revolution der poetischen Sprache.* (Suhrkamp, 1987); Julia Kristeva, 'The System and the Speaking Subject', in Toril Moi (ed.), *The Kristeva Reader.* (Basil Blackwell, 1990), pp. 24–33.
[6] See Beth Holmgren, 'For the Good of the Cause: Russian Women's Autobiography in the Twentieth Century', in Toby W. Clyman, Diane Greene (eds.), *Women Writers in Russian Literature.* (Greenwood, 1994), p. 144.
[7] Mary Zirin, 'Butterflies with broken Wings? – Early Autobiographical Depictions of Girlhood in Russia', in Marianne Liljeström, Eila Mäntysaari, Arja Rosenholm (eds.), *Gender Restructuring in Russian Studies.* Slavica Tamperensia II, Tampere 1993, pp. 255–266; Ирина Савкина, *Провинциалки русской литературы.* (Женская проза 30–40-х годов XIX века). (Verlag F.K. Göpfert, 1998); Arja Rosenholm, *Gendering Awakening.* Femininity and the Russian Woman Question of the 1860s. (Kikimora, 1999).
[8] Julia Kristeva. *Strangers to Ourselves.* Tr. L.S. Roudiez. (Harvester Wheatsheaf, 1991), p. 6.
[9] Kristeva, *Strangers to Ourselves*, p. 1.
[10] Kristeva, *Strangers to Ourselves*, p. 4.
[11] See also Sidonie Smith, *A Poetics of Women's Autobiography.* (Indiana University Press, 1987), pp. 17ff.
[12] В. Микулич, 'Встреча с знаменитостью'. In *Женское дело*, vol. 2, (1899), pp. 5–29, here p. 7.

[13] This is how Kristeva sees the sensitivity of a stranger. Kristeva, *Strangers to Ourselves*, p. 17.
[14] See also the issue of starvation in the quotation of Florence Nightingale in Elaine Showalter, *The Female Malady: Women, Madness, and English Culture, 1830–1980.* (New York 1985), pp. 128, 144.
[15] Carolyn, G. Heilbrun, 'Non-Autobiographies of "Privileged" Women: England and America', in Bella Brodzki and Celeste Schenk (eds.), *Life/Lines. Theorizing Women's Autobiography.* (Cornell University Press, 1988), p. 64. She refers to Betty Friedan.
[16] D. Epstein Nord, *The Apprenticeship of Beatrice Webb.* (Amherst 1985), p. 65. Also Heilbrun, 'Non-Autobiographies of "Privileged" Women: England and America', pp. 62–76.
[17] Heilbrun, 'Non-Autobiographies of "Privileged" Women: England and America', p. 63.
[18] Kristeva, '*Strangers to Ourselves*', p. 1.
[19] Kristeva, '*Strangers to Ourselves*', p. 8.
[20] Joan Riviere, 'Womanliness as a Masquerade', in Victor Burgin, James Donald and Cora Kaplan (eds.), *Formations of Fantasy.* (Routledge, 1989), pp. 35–44.
[21] Luce Irigaray, *Speculum. Spiegel des anderen Geschlechts*, (Suhrkamp, 1980), p. 139.
[22] Riviere, 'Womanliness as a Masquerade', p. 37.
[23] See her poem "Зачем я люблю маскарады?" Е.П. Ростопчина, *Талисман.* (Московский рабочий, 1987), pp. 131–133.
[24] Н.А. Добролюбов, 'У пристани'. in *Собрание сочинений в 9-ти томах.* Т. II, (СПб. 1962), pp. 70–87, here pp. 74, 76, 77, 80, 82 and Н.Г. Чернышевский, 'Стихотворения графини Ростопчиной', in *Полное собрание сочинений в 10 томах.* (СПб. 1906), II, pp. 309–310.
[25] "Сейчас принесла мама и положила мне на стол мои бриллианты, серьги, брошку, браслеты – все атрибуты моей пытки". Штакеншнейдер, *Дневник и записки*, p.117.
[26] Irigaray, *Speculum. Spiegel des anderen Geschlechts*, pp. 139, 78. Irigaray comes to contradictory conclusions interpreting the masquerade: on the one hand women would lose themselves in the masquerade while playing femininity. In order to win back some of their lost desire women would identify with the male desire and deny their "own" desire. On the other hand mimicry can be understood as voluntary adoption of the role of woman, to relocate her oppression through a new discourse without reducing themselves in it, they would stay elsewhere. See also Liliane Weissberg (ed.), *Weiblichkeit als Maskerade.* (Fischer Taschenbuch, 1994).
[27] See also Zirin, 'Butterflies with Broken Wings? –early Autobiographical depictions of Girlhood in Russia', pp. 255–266.
[28] Штакеншнейдер, *Дневник и записки*, p. 262.
[29] Unlike the mother the narrator gives her "papa" softening attributes calling him "добрый папочка", "бедный папочка". On "papa" see Штакеншнейдер, *Дневник и записки*, pp. 58, 93, 97, 103, 112, 127, 142, 144, 153. There is a kind of rivalry inscribed in the relationship with the mother, see pp. 117, 130, 168, 343.

[30] J. Féral, 'Antigone or the Irony of the Tribe', In *Diacritics* 8, (Fall 1978), pp. 2–14, here p. 4.
[31] As proposed by Rozanov in Штакеншнейдер, *Дневник и записки*, p. 10.
[32] "Но я не все вношу в дневник, что слышу и вижу, и что случается. Так, я не передала, что в январе еще виделась раз с Осиповым, [...]". Штакеншнейдер, *Дневник и записки*, p. 153.
[33] Her development she depicts as that of a "child" between the "nanny" and the "teacher" represented by two men, Benediktov and Lavrov. Штакеншнейдер, *Дневник и записки*, p, 363.
[34] Nancy K. Miller, 'Representing Others: Gender and the Subjects of Autobiography'. *Differences: A Journal of Feminist Cultural Studies.* Vol. 6, no 1 (1994), pp. 1–27, here p. 2.
[35] Patricia Meyer Spacks, 'Female Rhetorics', in Shari Benstock (ed.), *The Private Self.* Theory and Practice of Women's Autobiographical Writings. (The University of North Carolina Press, 1988), pp. 177–191, here p. 181.
[36] The literary memoirs written by her are devoted to P.L. Lavrov and F.M.Dostoevskii.
[37] Каролина Павлова, 'Двойная жизнь', in В. Брюсов (ред.), Каролина Павлова, *Собрание сочинений в двух томах.*. (Москва, 1915), т. II, pp. 3–152.
[38] Jane Gallop, 'Snatches of Conversation', in Sally McConnell-Ginet, Ruth Borker, Nelly Furman, (eds.*), Women and Language in Literature and Society.* (Praeger, 1980), pp. 274–283, here p. 274.
[39]Nancy Furman, 'Textual Feminism', in McConnell-Ginet, Borker, Furman (eds.), *Women and Language in Literature and Society,* pp. 45–54, also Susan Lanser, 'Toward a Feminist Narratology', in R.R. Warhol and D. Price Herndl, (eds.) *Feminisms. An Anthology of Literary Theory and Criticism.* (New Brunswick, 1991), pp. 611–629.
[40] Kristeva, *Strangers to Ourselves*, pp. 15–16.
[41] Розанов in Штакеншнейдер, *Дневник и записки*, p.530, комм. 322.
[42] "Хочу записывать факты, а все свожу на какие-то размышления и вопросы". Штакеншнейдер, *Дневник и записки*, p. 130, also pp. 107, 157, 175.
[43] F.R. Hart, 'Notes for an Anatomy of Modern Autobiographer', in *New Literary History* Vol. 1 (1970), pp. 485–511, here p. 500: "[...] effective access to a recollected self or its 'versions' begins in a discontinuity of identity or being which permits past selves to be seen as distinct realities."
[44] Kristeva, *Strangers to Ourselves* , p. 4.
[45] E.g. Robert von Ranke-Graves, *Griechische Mythologie*. 2. Bd. (rowohlts, 1960), pp. 379, 658ff.
[46] See Irma Korte, *Nainen ja myyttinen nainen.* (Yliopisto, 1988), p. 118.
[47] See *Рассвет*, no. 1 (1859), also Rosenholm, *Gendering Awakening*, pp. 1–35.
[48] Christa Wolf, *Voraussetzungen einer Erzählung: Kassandra.* (Luchterhand, 1984), pp. 86, 88, 96.
[49] She points to the duality prevailing in the women's movement, which she also joined, whereby the ideological positions were marked by those preferring the liberal "aristocratic" way, and by those manifesting their radical "nihilism" by cutting their hair.

[50] Rosenholm, *Gendering Awakening*, pp. 83–126, 127–208.
[51] Such as Emily Dickinson or Jane Austen.
[52] A figure of self-identification also for other women writers. See Арья Розенхольм, 'Рассказчица–писательница в противоречиях или взгляд Кассандры', in Михаил Файнштейн (ред.*), Русские писательницы и литературный процесс в конце XVIII–первой трети XX вв*. (Verlag Frank Göpfert 1995), pp. 91–114, here pp. 92, 112.
[53] Kristeva, *Strangers to Ourselves*, p. 7.
[54] Marie Bashkirtseff, *Le Journal*. (Mazarine 1980, orig. 1887).

В поисках собственного образа:

Людмила Вилькина в своем дневнике и переписке (1890-е – 1900-е гг.)

Елена Тырышкина

Л. Вилькина не создала автобиографии[1], не оставила мемуаров, дневник она вела в течение ряда лет (с ранней юности до 28 лет, правда – нерегулярно) и затем к нему не возращалась. Она написала много писем, и в самом этом факте нет ничего необычного, так как эпистолярная культура в то время была очень развита, особенно в среде писателей и художников. Более того, дневники и письма читались вслух, но не непосредственным адресатам, а всем тем, кто хотел послушать. Все, кто доверял свои мысли и чувства бумаге, вполне отдавали себе отчет в том, что их жизненные реалии и факты тут же становились фактами эстетическими. М. Кузмин читал свой дневник Вяч. Иванову, В. Нувелю, К. Сомову, а сама Л. Вилькина своим друзьям – весьма откровенные письма В. Розанова, обращенные к ней[2]; в своих письмах Д. Мережковскому и К. Сомову[3] она просит, чтобы они не читались посторонними, ибо ей хорошо были известны нравы в символистской среде. Однако дневник Л. Вилькиной не был предназначен для чтения вслух третьему лицу (лицам). Какова же была функция ее дневника и эпистолярных материалов?

Л. Вилькина вела дневник активно в1890-е гг.,[4] в период исканий смысла своего существования. Дневник был формой исповеди и самоанализа в то время, когда она искала устойчивых семейных отношений и не могла обрести их, а также, когда пыталась найти для себя дело жизни – действительность как таковая не давала ощущения своей значимости. В дневнике встречаются наброски стихотворений и рассказов (т. е. отчасти он является записной книжкой писательницы), но – нечасто. Почти нет выборочной фиксации самых интересных моментов своей жизни, чтобы использовать их в литературной работе. Л. Вилькина фиксирует чужие мнения о том, что ее особенно волнует – о роли женщины, о любви.

1890-е годы были для Л. Вилькиной не слишком счастливым временем сомнений и разочарований в браке и в собственных творческих возможностях (традиционные женские роли ее не устраивали, детей она не могла иметь). Она искала свое место – на сцене, в науках (учеба за границей), в качестве дамы-благотворительцы, театрального критика, переводчицы, поэтессы.[5]

Сложность позиции Л. Вилькиной как личности состояла в том, что она, постоянно окруженная выдающимися писателями и художниками (К. Бальмонт, В. Брюсов, К. Случевский, Д. Мережковский, В. Розанов, К. Сомов и др.), чувствовала свою меньшую одаренность. Она была хорошей переводчицей с французского – ее переводы пьес М. Метерлинка (совместно с Н. Минским) переиздаются до сих пор, но тогда эта деятельность невысоко ценилась. Семейная жизнь не была счастливой, хотя с мужем она не рассталась, их все же связывали общие (отчасти – литературные) интересы. Приходилось ревновать не только к временным увлечениям мужа – Н. Минского, которого она также считала талантливее себя, но и к своей тетке, известной переводчице и литературному критику, Зинаиде Венгеровой, которая всю жизнь любила Минского, – и с чисто женской точки зрения, и как к сильной женщине-личности, сумевшей устроить свою судьбу и завоевавшей признание.[6]

Обратимся к дневнику Л. Вилькиной, выбирая наиболее типичные фрагменты:

> 26 сентября
>
> Начинаю снова дневник – по необходимости. Столько за день намолчу, что мне начинает казаться что я не живу, а вспоминаю о – пустой – жизни. Дни проходят так, как будто бы если бы они не

проходили, не было бы иначе. Я никого не вижу, ни с кем не говорю, а с <нрзб.> почти знаками. Например: завтракать подавать? – да, хочешь чаю? ... Холодно. – Ужасная погода... Какая разница между мной уже умершей и мною еще живущей, но так? <...>

26 ноябрь 90

Снова пишу тебе, всепонимающий и несуществующий друг. Теперь о истории с НК. Не знаю зачем все это сама устраиваю: выхваливаю, заведомо восхищаюсь, когда совсем не восхищена. И зачем мне влюбить Н. М. <...> Но скажи мне, почему я хочу этого. Быть может, я хочу, чтобы Н. М. упал в моих глазах. Быть может, хочу таким образом извинить свое будущее и хочу это будущее развратным. Не знаю. Но чувствую, что с большим презрением, спокойствием слежу за этой историей. Сегодня пошел к ней, говоря, что идет в последний раз, что боится влюбиться, что не в его годы и т. д. Вот уже 1 час ночи, а его все нет. Мне нисколько не неприятно. <...>

О любви (разговор)

Бальмонт. Надо самому возвыситься и с вершины всех любить – красивых и уродов. Мер. – Акт совокупления <нрзб. – являет?> в себе несомненно нечто свиное. Надо его избегнуть. Это придет. Люди должны перевоплотиться. Плоть когда-нибудь будет иная. Люди будут вроде ангелов – и мужчина, и женщина, ни мужчина, ни женщина. Пола не будет. Бакст – Женщина – фабрика детей. Она должна рожать. Я говорю одно и думаю другое. <...>

15/2 Апрель (Понедельник)

Выехала из Петербурга прошлый вторник – 27 марта. Приехала в Женеву в четверг. Отъезжая от Петерб. страшно трусила. Вот вред жизни вдвоем – делаешься ребенком. Здесь наняла себе комнату и уже была на одной лекции – Gonrd' a l'hestoire de la philosophie – о Декарте. В первый раз я была истинно счастлива от лекции. Не потому, что читал он слишком хорошо, <лист оторван по лев. краю> потому что я целый час, наверное, не должна была думать <дефект. лист – о себе?> и о том, что надо, наконец, действовать – часы проходят <...>

Конспект Дж. Льюиса "История философии в жизнеописаниях" <18 страниц текста> <...>

Вчера и тритьеводни принимала морфий. В первый раз – разочаровалась. Ничего не чувствовала и не могла заснуть. Вчера приняла два порошка сразу и было чудно приятно. Как будто я умерла, и меня положили в холодный и каменный склеп. И что не склеп, а длинная и сводчатая зала из серого камня и я в ней, а тела не чувствую, тела нет и постепенно сознание пропадает, а в черном воздухе – серебряные цветы и ветки. Только действие морфия скоро прошло. Я снова почувствовала себя, тело болело, был жар и головная боль. Получила еще 6 порошков, но решила более не трогать и оставить на тот случай, когда надо будет взять все сразу и заснуть надолго. <...>

<1898>

Д. Мы с ним живем слишком близко от земли. Жизнь, как силок, нас беспощадно опутывает. Н. М. целые дни только и думает, что о процентах и жидах. Что это? Неужели вина моя. Меня тяготит это бесконечно. Хочу перенести мысль на что-нибудь иное, а он опять, опять. Неужели я убила в нем поэта. <...>

День

Полов. чувство не имеет ничего общего с чувством любви. Это только человеческая хитроумная выдумка для извинения полового чувства. Мечтая и любя Г., Н. М. <зачерк.> меня. Если бы я теперь была девушка, я никогда бы не <зачеркн. – отдалась?>. Я начинаю понимать красоту невинности. Мы <зачеркн.– ласкали друг друга?> через две минуты после смертельной ненависти и искреннего негодования. Любовь прекрасна, фактический брак – уродство. Говоря Г. о любви, он не переставал со мной. Где же тут любовь. Да наконец причем любовь и – Извинение уродства и все. <...>

Д. Вчера получила от Н. М. телеграмму, что он приехал ради статьи в П. и уезжает, и просит чаще писать, что без меня скучает. Между тем я уверена, что если он встретил в это время женщину, то за ней ухаживал. А в П. просидит все время у З. В., быть может свидится с Г. и – – Подумать и представить себе как мне здесь тошно, – куда! <...>

Урусов: Нравственность, как башня в Пизе – создана быть падающей. <...>

Красота жизни в нескольких отдельных личностях. Они – планеты среди млечного пути жизни. И на них нельзя уже смотреть как на "женщину" или "мужчину". Это существа без пола и лет; это "их светлости" и они только в жизни и интересны. <...>

19 января 1901 г.

Вот что произошло: я, как я, – умерла, а живу для Н. М. Должна от него терпеть всё. Всё, включая в это всё, все унижения. Иду на это. Я неживая, но в образе человека. Личных радостей быть не может. Всё для Н. М. и с его точки зрения. Я когда-то истая декадентка, я самолюбка, я торжественно убиваю свое "я". Вот так было вчера. У меня были две дороги – жить одной, для себя и чтобы и другие были для меня, и я была бы не около Н. М. – Но мне стало жаль и я увидела, что он из-за меня болен. Тогда я спросила себя: что лучше – чтобы Н. М. умер или я? И что-то во мне, ясно решило, что лучше, чтобы умерла я, а он бы жил и как можно радостнее и как писатель, и как человек. Тогда я к нему возвратилась, чтобы уже жить для него. <...>

Я не совсем права. Ведь живет же во мне это глупое желание поклонения. И зачем мне книга чужих стихов. Неужели я себя настолько еще не вижу, что требую поклонения других. И стоит ли для этого хоть пальцем пошевельнуть. <...>

Мне грустно, меня мучают мои годы, моя неплодотворная жизнь. Могло ли быть иначе? Как выразить реально тот огонь, который сжигает меня? Как найти себя?"[7]

Как можно заключить из этих материалов, рассуждения рефлексивного характера доминируют над событийными описаниями. Для Л. Вилькиной очевидно, что реальность записанного слова противостоит не-реальности рутинного бытия. Она находится в плену литературных (романтических и символистских) идеалов, когда пишет об отношениях мужчины и женщины и примеряет искусственные модели к жизни. Она ищет ответов на те вопросы, которые касаются прежде всего ее женского "я". В этом смысле показательны ее признания о несовместимости любви и брака (точнее, телесной страсти) – прямо-таки в духе *Крейцеровой сонаты* Л. Толстого (и не без влияния концепции "влюбленности" З.Гиппиус).[8] Л.Вилькина сравнивает чужие мнения о роли женщины и значении любви, чтобы сделать неутешительные выводы о невозможности достигнуть идеала в земном браке. Ее текстовый образ в дневнике – это мучительные поиски собственного "я" путем обращения к перебиранию чужих мнений о себе и мире.

Там, где речь идет об ее интимных отношениях с мужем (записи конца 1890-х гг.), она еще настолько стыдлива и связана общественными табу, что зачеркивает все глаголы, означающие близость, либо ставит прочерк на месте табуированного слова (здесь нужно заметить, что постоянная сверка своей жизни с высоким – литературным идеалом, приводит к цензурированию текста: возможность прочитывания дневника третьим лицом не исключена совершенно, и перед ним, неведомым критиком, она должна ”прилично выглядеть”). Со временем Л. Вилькина будет куда смелее в облечении своих чувств и поступков в слова – дневник заканчивается записями 1901 г., а в ее письмах середины и конца 1900-х гг. будут встречаться уже весьма ”нескромные” пассажи. Страдания по поводу невозможности соответствовать идеалу, где на первом месте фигурирует ”красота невинности”, наконец, оставят ее, и Вилькина начнет вполне сознательно жить в двух пространствах:реальной действительности и действительности игровой, эстетической, моделируемой. Если в первой – можно было быть вполне откровенной и рассуждать и о реалиях быта, и о подробностях своих романов весьма натуралистическим языком, то во второй – вольности, если и допускались, то облича-лись в поэтически-романтическую форму. Вот фрагмент из ее письма к мужу второй половины 1900-х гг. (опущены наиболее откровенные подробности романа с голландцем, о которых она сообщает Н. Минскому):

> Получила наконец редакционные деньги. На дом. 748 fr. 35c. – Сегодня нельзя внести в банк – кладу под замок, под скатерть – Завтра внесу. Мой любименький, как я чувствую себя глупо без тебя. И зачем это. Даю честное слово, что это последний раз в моей жизни. Еще Себастьян – понимаю, но все другое – Ужасно глупо. Вчера не было от тебя письма и я здорово мучилась. Сегодня пришло. – Не хочу голландца второй раз, мой миленький. Посылаю тебе одно из его писем и портрет. Но не хочу. Поехала вчера нарочно в Версаль и оттуда написала, что еще не вернулась. <...>[9]

В конце-концов – в начале 1900-х гг. образ жизни Л. Вилькиной определился: стилем существования становится то, что называется ”жизнетворчеством”, во многом – компенсаторного характера. Это был богемный стиль жизни, где большое место занимает следование канонам искусства, моделирование поведения по образцам. Собственный салон (”легальная” возможность дилетантизма), театры, рестораны, литературные вечера. И везде – следование чужому.

После 1901 г. она не пишет дневника, но переписка ее весьма обильна: это способ формирования собственного эстетического образа, возможность манипулирования своими адресатами и транспонирования этих выстроенных отношений – в реальность первичную. Знаковая сотворенная реальность станет более значимой, нежели данная. Л. Вилькина использует для себя роль *femme fatale* и *femme enfente* в одном лице, а также – "новой" женщины, стремящейся к особым "платоническим отношениям" ("рождение в красоте" в концепции Вяч. Иванова)[10] . Эта стратегия во многом объясняется самозащитой – после неудачных попыток устроить счастливую семейную жизнь и состояться в искусстве. Она самоутверждается посредством низведения другого на уровень объекта для манипуляций. Правда, эта стратегия только иногда давала желанные плоды (Д. Мережковский, В. Розанов) – В. Брюсов и К. Сомов довольно быстро уклоняются от предложенных "алгоритмов" поведения, когда речь идет о принципиальных вещах, хотя "поиграть в любовь" они готовы.

Мужчины всегда выступали по отношению к Вилькиной в качестве верховного авторитета – она же пыталась их подчинить с помощью своей внешности и игры в такие "особые" отношения, которым нет места в низкой реальности. Письмо становится для Л. Вилькиной конструктом автобиографии – она копирует собственные письма к наиболее важным для нее адресатам в особую тетрадь и хранит ее. Вот несколько ее писем к В. Брюсову:

Бс -у

Вот видите – я не пишу Вам, не зову Вас. Я знаю, что теперь приехала "другая". А Вы, хоть и язычник, а двум поклоняться страшитесь. Да и надо было бы бороться, а я считаю борьбу уродливой – борются низшие организмы. Но мое "женское" сердце противоречит человеческому во мне рассудку и мне отрадно было бы знать, что Вы иногда думаете обо мне. Придумайте, как бы de temps en temps давать мне об этом знать. <...> Так : помните обо мне.

Л.

О нашем "сближении" никому. Да?

Б-ю-у 26 ноября 902

Сегодня я недовольна. Было много, что не должно было быть. И именно для Вас не должно быть. Какое детское утешение говорить, что любите. Но я знаю, что любите, потому, что хочу, чтобы любили. И именно "изменно" любите. Вот теперь Вы видите мои глаза, Вы видите недобрые глаза. Завтра я Вас не увижу, но я хочу слышать Вас и завтра. Пришлите стихи. Я хочу твою душу, невольник.

Elle

Бр-у

<...> Ну, а еще я глубоко уверена в том, что может <зачеркн.> человек пройти мимо меня не заметив – как проходят мимо лучших картин – не замечая их, но если уж кто-нибудь остановил свой взор и почувствовал мою душу, тот ”уйти” не уйдет, тот не изменит: – ”от меня дороги нет назад.” А я ведь не борюсь. Вам легче думать, что Вы отходите от меня. Пусть так. Вот Вы в сегодняшнем письме пишите о посылаемых мне конфетах. О да. Я жду их с болезненным нетерпением. Я найду в коробке не только конфеты, а символ Вашей мне ”принадлежности”. Духовного, прекрасного, ”экстазного”. <...>

Elle

Бр-у

Какой Вы милый, какой Вы милый! Ваши удивительные конфеты – я и Н. М. – едим целые дни и шлем за них большое спасибо. А мне еще отраднее и бесконечно отраден ваш другой подарок – кольцо. Как хорошо, что вы себя смело отдаете всего, в жизни обыкновенно так мало смелого, законченного – хотя бы на миг. У меня лично, за время вашего отъезда – много случилось печального. А я так не люблю печальное! <...> Но не буду говорить подробно об этом.

Жизнью пользуйся живущий,
Мертвый в гробе мирно спи.

Отчего Вы мне не присылаете ”новых” стихотворений? Я жду, я верю, что они есть. Я хочу их. И пишите – же Валерий.

Ваша Elle

Бр-у

Валерий, друг мой, наконец, вот и Ваши стихи. Мне их так надо было, так недостало. А прощания не боюсь – ведь не в силах Вы уйти без моего согласия. Но принимаю прощание, как переход к радостному приветствию. Ваше отклонение к работе меня не пугает. Я ”тоже” отреклась от людей – никого, кроме книг и тетрадей, и стен, и свода своей комнаты не вижу. Но Вы часто бываете у меня, я говорю с Вами не о том, о чем мы с Вами говорили уже, но о новом, еще более ”настоящем” и обоюдно близком. Я написала Вам несколько сонетов, но по ”робости” писательской не посылаю. Взяты они в ”Н. В.” Через недели две может быть напечатают.

Elle

> Я думаю о вас нежном и ласковом. Я вижу, что цветы наполняют мою комнату. Ваши и только Ваши. Что если бы?
>
> <без обращ., даты, подписи>
>
> Если это искренне, серьезно и действительно, если Вы, наконец, поняли себя, и разглядели и верно оценили и свои силы, и свои желания, я с радостью принимаю Ваше решение, которое дает лучший, вернейший, чистейший исход. Лучше тропинка через бездну, чем дорога, бесконечно текущая по краю пропасти. Я верю в то, что между нами может быть настоящая дружба, такая, какой не знает большинство людей, и тщетно ищет меньшинство. Ваша страсть была обыденной страстью, несмотря на всю силу и глубину Вашей любви, и это я не раз пытал <так в тексте> Вам показать."[11]

"Театральный" характер этих писем очевиден: даже подпись – в третьем лице (Elle – фр. "она") свидетельствует о сконструированном образе. "Она" пишет об их "любви" в возвышенных тонах и о себе – как об особе тонкой и творческой. "Она" откровенно пытается уловить тон и стилистику брюсовских рассуждений о стихах и чувствах, "подделываясь" под своего адресата, – иногда попадая впросак, так как В. Брюсов был готов играть лишь до определенного предела, – пока речь не шла о его свободе распоряжаться собой. В ответ на письмо Л. Вилькиной, где она замечает: "... как хорошо, что Вы себя смело отдаете всего...", он опровергает эти слова, отказываясь от подобного "суггестирования":

> 1902 декабрь
>
> Нет, Вы неправы, Людмила, Все-таки я не отдал себя всего. <...> В своих стихах я часто говорю от лица раба, от лица невольника, о котором Вы помянули в одном письме. Но сам я этой сладости – быть рабом – так и не испытал до сегодня. Упрямо, пошло, грубо я всегда оставался свободным, – даже когда сам покорно подставлял шею под ярмо. <...> Быть безвольным, быть покорным, быть рабом, отдать свою душу до конца – это сожгло бы меня безмерным счастием, крайним, предельным. Целовать следы на песке ("не ноги, следы твоих ног", как говорит Ваш Рафалович) – значило бы для меня изведать сладострастие несказанное, о котором я только мечтаю безнадежно. Я не целовал следов ничьей ноги никогда, ни даже в дни "первой" любви. Принадлежать кому-либо другому – вот завет, которого я не умел исполнить, тайна, которой я не достиг."[12]

Л. Вилькина, будучи писательницей-эпигоном декаданса, следовала такой модели авторепрезентации, где привычная патриархатная модель фемининности (жена и мать) была заменена моделью "лайф-артиста" в женском варианте (креативность вместо репродуктивности). Основные женские роли декаданса, перекочевавшие в быт из литературы (Ш. Бодлер, С. Малларме, О. Уайльд) – это роли агрессивной, притягательной и пугающей Красоты. По отношению к сложившимся стереотипам женского поведения в обществе эта стратегия носила явно провокативный характер. Женщина становилась в позицию самодовлеющего субъекта, превращающего себя в эстетический объект. Законы природы и общества подменялись законами своевольной игры. Стремление сделать себя и свою жизнь "текучим" произведением искусства означало стремление к постоянному трансцендированию, погоню за "инобытием".

Самым типичным примером в этом отношении может служить З. Гиппиус. Вилькину считали ее подражательницей, "двойником" – и небезосновательно. Однако, если Гиппиус действительно удалось найти особый тип поведения творческой женщины, сочетавшей в себе несочетаемое (Мадонна и Дьяволица, прекрасный андрогин), создавшей вокруг себя напряженную атмосферу особых чувств, то Вилькиной пришлось примерять уже чужие маски и играть чужие роли. Л. Вилькина стремится идентифицироваться с демонической женщиной-соблазнительницей, которой присущи отчасти детские черты (классический пример – Саломея[13]), типичной героиней декаданса; или же с прогрессивной "новой женщиной", исповедующей особые "платонические" формы любви[14]. Характер идентификации носит, как правило, эстетический характер. Сама ориентация на литературную героиню (причем, не на конкретное лицо, а на некий тип, набор функций), либо на несуществующую "идеальную" модель "женщины будущего" выводит Вилькину за рамки этического пространства, обрекая на существование в границах эстетического, лишая перспективы внутреннего роста. Принципы подобной идентификации во многом схожи с театральной.[15]

В этой ситуации Вилькина совмещает позиции персонажа и "внутреннего" зрителя одновременно (при том, что "внешний зритель" ей жизненно необходим). К тому же, здесь в одном (ее) лице сочетаются исполнитель и персонаж. В идеале внешний зритель должен – хотя бы на время – поддастся иллюзии правдоподобия, переживая общение с персонажем как с реальным человеком. Такая стратегия, с одной стороны, нацелена на переживание ситуации как реальности, а не вымысла – это касается прежде всего "внешнего зрителя", который должен принимать все происходящее за чистую монету, хотя бы некоторое время. С другой стороны, исполнительница в роли персонажа и "внутреннего зрителя" одновременно, имеет возможность испытать удовольствие от самой возможности свободного перехода от вымысла к невыдуманной /немоделированной реальности (удовольствие от "сдвигания рамки") и возможности проживания в чужом образе. Однако "внешний зритель" в контексте декаданса/символизма (будучи к тому же литератором или художником) был посвящен в правила подобной игры и непосредственности был чужд – точнее, он также наслаждался двойственностью – свободой перехода от эстетической реальности к вне-эстетической: В. Брюсов определил характер своих отношений с Л. Вилькиной одной краткой фразой: "Играли в любовь."[16] Д. Мережковский также довольно быстро перестал питать иллюзии относительно заданной искусственности манеры обращения с ним[17].

Быть актером и зрителем одновременно – значит обречь себя на призрачность как вымысла, так и реальности. То, что предлагала литературная мода, на самом деле оказалось фикцией и ловушкой, – следование клишированным образцам поведения не способствовало раскрытию и развитию личности, не лишенной способностей. Конструирование реальности (не без помощи эпистолярной стратегии особого рода) привело лишь к конструированию фантомного "я", где одна маска сменяется другой.

Ссылки

[1] Сведения о биографии и творчестве Л. Вилькиной см. : *Русские писатели, 1800–1917,* т. 1 (М., 1989), сс. 442–443; M. Ledkovsky, Ch. Rosenthal, M. Zirin (eds.), *Russian Women Writers* (London, 1994), pp. 711–713.
[2] Н. А. Богомолов, *Михаил Кузмин: статьи и материалы* (М.: Новое литературное обозрение, 1995), сс. 223–225; ”Распоясанные письма В. Розанова”, вступление, публ. и прим. М. Павловой: *Литературное обозрение*, N. 11 (1991), сс. 67–71.
[3] ”Письма Д. С. Мережковского к Л. Н. Вилькиной”, публ. В. Н. Быстрова, в *Ежегодник Рукописного Отдела Пушкинского Дома на 1991 г.* (СПб., 1994), сс. 209–251; Письма Л. Вилькиной к К. Сомову хранятся в Отделе рукописей Государственного Русского Музея (Ф. 133. Ед. хр. 216), часть этих писем опубликована мною в сб. *Женский вопрос в контексте национальной культуры. Из истории женского движения в России.* вып. 3, ч. 1 (Спб, 1999), сс. 107–117.
[4] В 1890 г. Л. Вилькиной было 17 лет (годы жизни – 1873–1920). В начале 1890-х гг. она становится гражданской женой Н. Минского (официально брак был зарегистирован в 1905 г.).
[5] О разнообразной деятельности в различных обществах и кружках, попытках учебы за границей и о корреспондентских опытах Л. Н. Вилькиной можно судить по ряду следующих архивных материалах, хранящихся в РО ИРЛИ РАН (Ф. 39. Ед. хр. 809. Л. 8, 10, 11, 12,13, 14,15):

Член. билет русс. женского взаимно-благотворительного общества в С-П-ге
1896/97 No 683
Людмила Ник. Вилькина-Юрьева;

Universite de Geneve
N 4973 Carte d’Autiteur, semestre d’ete 1901
M-elle Wilkine, Ludmila
cours Litterature franc. Prof. Bourier;

Первый Дамский Худ. кружок
среда
1903–1904 Л-ла Ник. Минская-Вилькина;

Новый театр
сезонный билет 1903–1904
Дубликат Г. Вилькиной-Минской
на свободное место

Дирекция Нового тетра
быв. Кононова – Мойка, 61;

Рус. театр. общ-во, Билет действ. члена Л-лы Ник-ы Вилькиной-Минской на 1904 г. N.642;

Удостоверение кор-та журнала "Театральная Россия" Л. Н. Вилькина
СПб. янв. 2 1905 г.
редакция Театр. Россия:
"Театр. газета"
и "Музыкальный мир";

Билет для входа в лит-худ. общ-во 1907 г.
Вилькина на 1 месяц с 1 февр. по 1 марта.

[6] Об отношении З. Венгеровой к Н. Минскому см.: "Письма Зинаиды Афанасьевны Венгеровой к Софье Григорьевне Балаховской-Пети", publicationes, commentaries et notes de Rosina Neginsky, in *Revue des etudes slaves*, t. 67, fasc. 2/3 (1995), p. 474.

[7] Л. Н. Вилькина. *Дневник.* РО ИРЛИ РАН. Ф. 39. Ед. хр. 779. 1885. Сент. 19 – 1901. Янв. 19. Л. 9, 10, 11, 34–54, 62, 63, 69, 73, 99, 100, 106, 110. Многие записи не датированы. Сокращения: Д. – день, Н. М. – Николай Максимович Минский, НК – неустановленное лицо, Мер. – Д. С.Мережковский, Г. – вероятно, З. Н.Гиппиус, П. – Петербург, З. В. – Зинаида Венгерова. Урусов – вероятно, князь А. И. Урусов (1843–1900), см. о нем: Е. А. Андреева-Бальмонт, *Воспоминания* (М.: изд-во имени Сабашниковых, 1996), сс. 248–87. В угловых скобках даны предположительные написания зачеркнутых или неразборчиво написанных слов. Орфография и пунктуация приведены к современной норме, но с сохранением наиболее типичных особенностей авторского письма (на основе того же принципа публикуются и эпистолярные материалы).

[8] Olga Matich, "Zinaida Gippius: Theory and Praxis of Love" in Ronald Vroon, John E. Malmstad (eds.), *Readings in Rissian Modernism. To Honor Vladimir Fedorovich Markov* (Moscow: Nauka, Oriental Literature Publishers, 1993), pp. 237–250.

[9] Л. Н. Вилькина. *Письма ее к Н. М. Минскому. 1899 г. февр. – 1910 г. июль 20.* РО ИРЛИ РАН. Ф. 39. Ед. хр. 185. Л. 5. Письмо не датировано, но содержание его позволяет говорить о предположительной датировке – конец 1900-х гг. "Себастьян" – испанский город Сан-Себастьян, где Л. Вилькина часто отдыхала и лечилась во второй половине 1900-х гг.

[10] Вяч. Иванов, "О любви дерзающей", в Вяч. Иванов, *Родное и вселенское* (М.: Республика, 1994), сс. 87–90; Н. Бердяев, "Метафизика пола и любви", в *Перевал*, N. 5, сс. 7–17; N. 6, сс. 24–36 (1907).

[11] Л. Н. Вилькина. *Тетрадь с копиями писем ее (17) к Брюсову, Бальмонту, Случевскому, А-у и неизвестн. лицам 1902 ноябрь 26–29.* РО ИРЛИ РАН. Ф. 39. Ед. хр. 791. Л. 2, 5, 8, 9, 11–12,14. Оригиналы писем Л. Н. Вилькиной к В. Я. Брюсову хранятся в РО РГБ (Ф. 386. Карт. 80. Ед. хр. 13,14,15). Письма приводятся, как правило, без дат. Сокращения – Бр-у, Б-ю-у – Брюсову; "Н. В." – еженедельный журнал "Новое время". "Другая" – А. А. Шестеркина. О взаимоотношениях В. Я. Брюсова и А. А. Шестеркиной см.: "Письма к А. А. Шестеркиной. 1900 – 1913", предисл. и публ. В. Г. Дмитриев. в *Литературное наследство, Валерий Брюсов*, т. 85 (М.: Наука, 1976), сс. 622–656; "Жизнью

пользуйся живущий, Мертвый в гробе мирно спи" – цитата (перепутан порядок строк) из баллады Ф. Шиллера "Торжество победителей" в переводе В. Жуковского.

[12] 12 В. Я. Брюсов, *Письма его к Л. Н. Вилькиной. 1902–1907 г. янв. 18*. РО ИРЛИ РАН. Ф. 39. Ед. хр. 833. Л. 16–17. Из этих писем была опубликована меньшая часть (8 из 47, те, где нет упоминаний о близких отношениях В. Брюсова с Л. Вилькиной): В. Я. Брюсов. "Письма к Л. Н. Вилькиной", публ. С. С. Гречишкина и А. В. Лаврова, в *Ежегодник Рукописного Отдела Пушкинского дома на 1973 г.* (Л.: Наука, 1976), сс. 126–135. "Рафалович" – С. Л. Рафалович (1875–1943) – поэт.

[13] О функционировании сюжета Саломеи-Иродиады и его особенной популярности в литературе рубежа 19-20 вв. см.: Елена Тырышкина, "Сюжет Саломеи-Иродиады в литературной традиции XIX – начала XX века", в *Literatura rosyjska. Nowe zjawiska. Reinterpretacje* (Katowice, 1995), сс. 82–98.

[14] На практике эти отношения означали "тройственные" союзы – у Л. Вилькиной был свой опыт такого рода: некоторое время З. Венгерова жила вместе с ней и Н. Минским в одной квартире на Английской набережной, 62. Другой опыт касался сложного романа (?) Л. Вилькиной с К. Сомовым, который был гомосексуалистом.

[15] Патрис Пави, *Словарь театра* (М.: Прогресс, 1991), с. 157.

[16] В. Я. Брюсов, "Переписка с С. А. Поляковым", в *Литературное наследство, Валерий Брюсов и его корреспонденты*, т. 98, кн. 2 (М.: Наука, 1994), с. 65.

[17] *Письма Д.С. Мережковского к Л. Н. Вилькиной*, сс. 210–217

A War in Her Own Translation:
Elena Rzhevskaya's *Distant Rumble*

Irina Novikova

The idea of war seems difficult to seize without the ideas referring to the absence of war, thus making war present as a standard.

Marina Warner

When I found out that the author of a story was a woman, I did not read it. It is most ridiculous when a woman looks into the life of a man and tries to depict it. However, a woman-author has all advantages when she refers to a woman's sphere.

Lev Tolstoi

The historical, political and cultural developments of the 20th century marked significant changes in accessible positions, roles and statuses for women and proposed no less controversial scripts of their inclusions, engagements and commitments in the range between the home and the stars. Karolina Pavlova could not have dreamt of Literaturnii Institut, could not have thought of a career as a military interpreter at war, could not have been frustrated with the silence of a woman author in the conditions of political censorship.

After the sweeping warfares of World War I, the Russian Revolutions of 1917 and the Civil War of 1918–1922 Roman Jakobson wrote about what he defined as "the context of the female warrior masquerade" in Soviet Russia:

> For many women their only liberation from the confines of domestic responsibilities was experienced during wartime. They exercised skills, traveled with security, socialized freely, found comradeship and acceptance; the male world became accessible in an exciting way. The military gave them an identity and, under the guise of patriotism, an understandable motive for rejecting hearth and home. Many never readjusted after this experience but found their awareness of their superior status snatched away from them after the war ended.[1]

Pre-war Soviet gender ideology indoctrinated a new woman's image as a self-sacrificial militant and active fighter for a common larger cause. It infiltrated both women's access to the labor market and the performance scripts of their traditional roles in the family. Soviet women were exposed to the ideology of emancipation in the conditions of enforcement economy and war regime. The war became the only trope of desire for women to genuflect, and the military economy of oneness dramatically transformed women's relation to sexual difference.

Autobiographical practices create fictitious unities of a historical subject thus becoming elaborate analogies between the individual *bios* and the nation as a collective social form in its historical development. Military memoirs privilege war as an organizing collective experience for the politically and historically legitimate temporality of the nation, for textual spacing of the imperial idea of linear time. In re/producing mythologies of the masculine transcendental subject, historical imagination of modernity appropriated the subgenre of military memoirs as a powerful textual tool forwarding the dichotomy of peace/war in pedagogy for the nation, its borders and territories.

The Soviet woman as a subject-at-war has been little investigated through autobiographical domains. Svetlana Aleksievich is, perhaps, the only widely known writer whose books *War Does Not Have A Woman's Face* and *Zinky Boys* were against the mainstream memory works that either celebrated or mourned women's sacrifice at war. She interviewed women who participated in the World War II. The women belonged to the generations of mothers whose sons and daughters treated the Afghanistan military adventure through the lenses of war mythology. Before Aleksievich very few writers tried to destabilize representations of women at war as inflected and mediated by structured violence and power, and the importance of such off-stream memory works is still not recognised. Christa Wolf formulates the problem in *The Patterns of Childhood*:

> An unused memory gets lost, ceases to exist, dissolves into nothing - an alarming thought. Consequently, the faculty to preserve, to remember, must be developed. Haunting questions persist – what is crime? Who is the perpetrator and who is the victim? If the mother is the transmitter of cultural values in a culture that pretends it has no recent history, then what is the daughter's place in that continuum? To frame these questions in such a way, to break silence, is to say the least, to exceed acceptable cultural boundaries.[2]

My tribute, thus, is to Elena Rzhevskaya whose engagement with making sense of and integrating her life and wartime memory in *A Distant Rumble* was also an attempt to interpret and think of the extent of profoundly changed gender relations for Soviet women at the crossroads of Soviet emancipation ideology and militarization of women's consciousness, "as an equal among equals". Her novella scraped off the patina of Soviet public accounts about women at war that functioned as ideological instruments for muting women's alternative performances of memory.

A student of Literaturnii Institut, Rzhevskaya went to the front as a translator. Her second "birth" took place near Rzhev, where bloody battles took place in 1943 ("...I was killed near Rzhev"). The name of the city became Rzhevskaya's nom-de-plume. She finished the war in Berlin. At the very end of the Second World War a young military interpreter Elena Rzhevskaya was affiliated into the secret group of Soviet intelligence officers charged with finding Hitler's body, dead or alive, in Berlin. It is now known that counter-intelligence agents took the bodies of Hitler and Braun. Each night the remains were buried, often in the woods, and then dug up when it was time to move on with the army. Finally, the bodies were buried in Magdeburg, and remained there for 25 years under a yard purchased by a waste-disposal firm. On Stalin's order, the findings and evidence were kept in secret files. The witnesses were obliged to keep silence. As Elena Rzhevskaya was one of them, she ventured to start writing about Hitler's end only after the death of Stalin. The full version of *A Distant Rumble* (*Dalekii Gul*) was published only in 1989. With the definition of *A Distant Rumble* as *povest'*,

Rzhevskaya posed a question about fact and fiction, reality and textuality, life and autobiographical representation of a woman's memory narrative. Disappearance (not death), exhumation and autopsy employed for identifying the bodies, are central metaphors of *A Distant Rumble* as a memory narrative about the Operation Myth.

Rzhevskaya recounted her own experiences as a wartime woman, a disappearance behind its multiple "operation myths" in constituting the Soviet historical time. She examined the effects of the Second World War on women and remembered her experiences at the end of the war in the context of postwar mobilizations of women's lives fractured and destroyed by war. At the same time, Rzhevskaya confronted rigid canons of Soviet war memory narratives in the established ideological tradition. The very act of remembering women's experience at war, not along established genre and ideological boundaries, but breaking through them, brought a powerful dissenting voice into the still life of Soviet woman's iconography in the Soviet discourses of war. The memoir plot of the journey to freedom is at the same time a different, muted story of the Soviet woman who is given an "identity" by the military, from a sniper to a military interpreter. What Rzhevskaya discovered for herself would remain veiled until she started publishing the first notes. The unveiling is a prerogative of a man-victor; the veiling, thus, becomes a trope of a military woman's postwar invisibility – in her experiences, memories, discoveries. For many years this final plot of World War II belonged to the range of unknown, or the least known, excluded "episodes", veiled in mysteries beyond the official historiography of war and its end and, inevitably, in Rzhevskaya's personal life story.

Rzhevskaya does not create the self-portrayal of an exemplary heroine, a female warrior at the moment of historical victory. Rzhevskaya's job as a military interpreter is marginal to the laws of war as she has to provide a contact between the two hostile realities. It is Rzhevskaya's role as a translator in the given spectrum of women's roles at the front that conditions her relational function in subverting the Self/Other dichotomy in its extreme political manifestation of the war. Out of this marginality, subversive to the laws of war and by using the montage technique, Rzhevskaya transforms several interweaving plots. She assembles the narrative intrigues of detective (search), encounter, discovery and origin as plots rewritten from a military woman-interpreter's "incidental" point of view.

In translation theory, translation is actualized only when the meanings of language/Other are possible to translate into the meanings of a target language. In case of untranslatability, compensatory strategies are employed to "negotiate" the meaning into another language. Translation and un/translatability (or in/visibility in terms of her story) are appropriated by the professional translator/interpreter Rzehvskaya for framing her experience as a woman at war into the memory narrative. Moreover, the "translation" of the past experiences is contested by Rzhevskaya in terms of the definition of what constitutes a "life" in autobiography. This latter question of *bios*, the accumulated historical events that comprise the "biography" of the writer, is problematic from "the perspectives of both women's autobiography and the critique of a metaphysics of the subject"[3]. In the Soviet metaphysics of the subject, the referential mobility of an autobiographical writing in which "repetition of the facts of a life can never merely mirror them but always transforms them"[4] was threatening to the flawlessly determinist historiography produced for the transcendental goal. An autobiographical project as interpretation of individual past and "translation" of a subject-in-process into the text would have challenged

> carefully determined and recycled plots, characters, and metaphors that would legitimize state power and rationalize the irrational atrocity of the state's actions[5].

The Soviet tradition of war memoirs, the least flexible genre subtype, was lavishly represented by the famous heroes and the military from high echelons of political-ideological power. In their memories the repetition of the script "from the defeat to victory", based on the selective narration of large-scale facts, contributes to the panoramic effect of the historical course/cause, with the authorship and personal story "derived from the politically sacred"[6]. The genre status of a public legend such as a military memoir has to be justified by the representativity of an author's personal experience at war. As Liz Stanley argues:"The past, like the present, is the result of competing negotiated versions of what happened, why it happened, with what consequence"[7]. The negotiated version of a representative memory narrative about war formalizes the status of an author's representativity for this collective experience through the script of inclusions. Exclusions, on the contrary, – historically invalid or simply unimportant details, fragments, episodes – are sifted away when an unchallengable war/

peace record is elaborated. The textual interpretations of a self as an individual representative of the collective historical experience are at the same time the evidence of his/her witnessing the representative collective *bios*, or "the accumulated historical events". Consequently, the historical meaning assigned to a series of representative collective experiences functions as the context that invests a self with an individual coherence, comprises the "biography" of the writer and authenticates a remembered self-image in *graphe.*

Exceeding acceptable cultural boundaries means perpertrating the privileged textual strategies of a military memoir by impairing the time-space structuring of the canon with a different "translation" of an individual lived experience. As Shlomith Rimmon-Kennan points out, the model of reality is found in chronology and causality as well as through the contiguity of space[8]. Through chronology and causality, the narrative linearity of a memoir text would also relate about a narrator's consciousness exposed to or inscribed in the effects of history. The narrative linearity of *Distant Rumble* is "contaminated" with untypical digressions, either episodes-flashbacks-questions, or private elements of notes or letters. The text is organized around a specific tension between the unselective immediacy of notes, confessional comments, questions, personal letters, incidental episodes, private moments of the war and the selective contextualization of the end-of-the-war events.

The self-reflexivity of the narrator is accentuated through questioning which is a challenging rhetorical tool subversive to the production of a textual, historical and imperial cohesion in the military memory narrative. Questioning is combined with breaking the linear cohesion as the narrative digresses from linearity due to the textual tension between description and narration. Descriptive flashback episodes transform the linear narrative time effectively and undo its political prescriptions dichotomized into the war–peace opposition. The effects of chronology in the plot synthesis of the events are minimized by montage and fragmentation of the text. Descriptive parts conspicuously revert the perspective from the central plot of the search for the enemy and monumental historical time to the margins – to spaces for women at war – to their destroyed territories and bodies, empty and burned-down houses, brothels, prisons and concentration camps. At the same time, the montage deprivileges "great history" by confronting it with its own incidentalities, side effects, episodes and fragments such as Rzhevskaya's "incidental" episode at the end of the World War II.

A military woman's fragmentary notes at the war front borrow from the genre of a diary that Suzanne Juhasz described as classical verbal articulation of dailiness. The perspective of the diarist is not distance, but immersion. Fragmentary notes on slips of paper, scribbled lines carefully preserved since the war symbolise the years of unwritten diaries and the erasure of private memories. Diaries were banned at the front during the war, but Rzhevskaya as well as others still wrote down their impressions and thoughts: "In general, how easily, willingly, on the run, episodes were just scribbled down (I wish writing diaries had not been banned!). How difficult it was to begin and to write down at least something with intention, on purpose"[9]. A scribbled incident, an "ornamental" detail, provokes the loss of panoramic distance and transgresses the boundaries of the genre. "Details threaten orders based on dominance; they get too close: we become immersed", – argues Rebecca Hogan[10]. They threaten the rules of the genre in *Distant Rumble* that "translates" the origins of power in the post-war worldviews as structured by virtue of the binary opposition of war/peace only.

The tempting "detective" plot – the search for the dead body of the one who "sired" the war – is based on the gen(e)ric assumption that only the author of the detective story knows the real end and where the criminal can be found. On the other hand, the intrigue of the search encapsulated in the plot of liberation/journey has been traditionally rendered in the motif of the hero's death. The search and the burial of a(n) (unknown) hero symbolizes the nation's rebirth. Paradoxically, the death of Hitler, the other "author" in the Berlin bunker, its performance *a la death of a hero* in *tragedie classique*, becomes only a possible but silenced (unknown) "episode" in the politically-informed "rebirth" of historical coherence and historiographic continuity derived from Stalin's desire, from the victorious author's ambitions. The construction of historical, political – and individual – time belongs to Stalin's desire. His will and craving for authorship of the future imperial order actually revert the paradigmatic relationship between the context and the text. The context is replete with the literary, the aesthetic, the canon-producing "unsaid", that would make the cultural status of texts into a senseless attempt to write a story-difference of a self. The tragic parody sired by the author of postwar narrative – the hidden body/ memory/self – turns into an obligation for the "heroine" to share an equal part in the war narrative, to find the body of the anti-hero and to participate in her own muted war story behind the heroic public accounts about "unknown heroes".

By silencing Hitler's "death of author", Stalin asserted the power of his authorship in politics and making of history. Reality, thus, is his art, and since life is turned into an aesthetically organized process, what is left to art except for its "realistic" representations? Stalin appropriated the author function to narrativize the myth of rebirth and origins: "When the wooden Arch of Victory with Stalin's portrait in its center was being hastily constructed, the dead were patiently waiting to be buried".[11] At the same time, the mystification of the enemy's death became a disclosure into a long-term suspense plot. Otherwise, Hitler's suicidal death in his "own bed", under his own name, would undermine the totality of victory and its author. A ritualistic moment of the suicidal enemy's burial would complete the act of victory but would create no space to impregnate clean pages of future with potential battle plots in its name.

A silenced episode literally excludes the body of the enemy and, paradoxically, those who searched for it. The anonymity, thus, extends far beyond the experiences of a woman as a military interpreter in the counter-intelligence group. The anonymity extends to millions of "unknown" episodes and bodies for Stalin's authorial desire to birth the post-war world order of dominance and as such it is equally important to the political narrativization of the war's end and to Rzhevskaya's personal experience. The authorship function is to ensure the virtue of mystification by which the origin of the postwar peace order is conceived. Exclusion of detail in a particular marginal experience for producing the negotiated version of the origin is as central to mystification of history as it is essential to the genre as a form of multiple textual "subversions and the capitulations of woman's writing in a patriarchal culture that "fictionalizes her"[12]. Mystification is sustained by excluding experiences and dismantling the negotiated version of the post-war origin. In *Distant Rumble* Stalin's plot of mystification as his mark of the paternal origin is re-constituted in Rzhevskaya's quest for mystifications of the "maternal origin" in women's public accounts about war negotiated into the mainstream memory production. Rzhevskaya's "translation" of the figures of "woman" from the past is organized around the trope of a journey, typical of Russian travellers' writings with the autobiographical-philosophical quest "Is there any truth in that distant kingdom for me?" Within the trope, she creates a different story of women's experiences, memories and selfhood as a challenge to her disappearance into unrepresentable/ untranslatable otherness in the Soviet iconography of the feminine.

The act of victory as the act of discovery arrogates to victors the power of origins. The portrayal of Stalin crowning the arch of victory in Berlin is a mirror-substitute that guarantees his legitimate and definite patrimony and secures his name for the mythology of origin. Textual investments, such as military memoirs in the Name of the Father, would become substitutes for a forbidden story and tongueless identity. The re-birth of the new world out of death – authorship, "real" and "fictional", erase the portrayal of a self. However, textual subversions shift the original "detective" plot of searches to the secondary – episodic – plane of narration, and this deliberate backgrounding of a search-intrigue contributes to Rzsevshkaya's rewriting a discovery plot. Rzhevskaya's memory-map of the end of the war embodies the contradictions of liberation as legitimate political liberation/conquest of the territory. The intertext of typological historical, cultural and literary parallels contributes to the powerful defamiliarization of the overwhelming context of the unsaid. The deviation from a Tolstoyan War-and-Peace plot, the temporal stretch of war-And-peace (spring – summer 1945), moves the reading to the boundaries of the genre as negotiable spaces for the interpreter's "translation" of silences, episodes, exclusions by telling a story of her own. "And" is a marginal time that, paradoxically again, is her "translation" of the past as a discovery of stories about other women and women of Europe as Other.

Rzhevskaya opens the memory narrative with crossing the border and entering the territory of Poland for the first time as a military officer. Her memory retrieves and "translates" flashbacks of Other territory – European blank spaces embodied in faces and figures of women. The first episode as an initiation rite is a meticuluously described meeting with an old Polish woman. Pani Maria becomes the symbol of the *ewig Weibliche* in Rzhevskaya's first gaze into the unknown and different story of women:"I was a servant of war, so the war took care of me. But there was no concern whatsoever as to pani

Maria, a private person. Live if you can survive."[13] On the other hand, in Luce Irigaray's argument, it is femininity that can be converted from a form of subordination into an affirmation[14]. For pani Maria, her femininity is a protest performed against masquerades of female militancy. Pani Maria's explicitly romantic performance of femininity is what the narrator – always an imperfect form of heroic masculinity – would long for as an unreachable form of affirmation and protest beyond prescribed phantoms of sex "equality".

After performing the role of the Soviet heroic womanhood that is threatening to the masculine subject of the enemy at war, the narrator tries to mimic pani Maria's femininity and, in a way, to revive her own memories of femininity in a romantic dress. However, the narrator does not recognize herself as a masquerade mask in the mirror reflection. The young woman's transformation during the war, initiated in her "rebirth" during the battle near Rzhev in 1941, is completed, and the image is assimilated so that the question is how is it possible to return into the roles ascribed in peace. What would have been "natural" before the war – the mirror reflection of her body in a feminine dress – is now perceived as alien. In this split a woman becomes dangerous as soon as she is aware that the performance of both codes at war (militancy) and in peace (femininity) is always disempowered by the hegemony of the male imaginary. The mirror also metaphorizes her silence as a woman-author who represses memory, thus, participating in the production of history in which the mystery of re-burial is hidden behind the clarity of the birth of the new order, thus, coveting death in the rituals of the return to the past, including autobiographical discourses.

Further in her discovery journey, Rzhevskaya describes a shapeless female body in a soldier blanket, an unnamed and abandoned body beyond different cultural signifiers of the feminine. The body becomes the embodiment of women's muted story, not an autobiographical "I", but a silenced slash "/" in warfare genealogies:

> Sidewalks are empty. Only at the corner there was a crowd of weird, short creatures, clad in dark soldier blankets. We drove closer to the downtown area, and again the same strange figures. You can catch a glimpse of a face in a blanket – female, dark, sharp, and a glance, empty and blind.[15]

At the moment of And, between war and peace, a woman is just a biological "no-body" – / – an anonymous and sexless 'slash' between the two cultural signifiers, the two orders of the opposition of war/peace. However, a de-signified body cannot be tolerated by patriarchal positionings of the feminine, and it has to be re-signified in compliance with post-war gender ideologies. Moreover, an anonymous female body in a soldier blanket mimics – as in the mirror – the narrator herself, one of many in a military outfit unable to recognize herself (her Self) in the mirror.

The end (And) of the war is more of a question to the narrator's own origin in the past of ambiguous and controversial lacks. Is a new Soviet woman different from this re-signified dead of war as she has always been taught? A mirror is a significant repetitive image, a mute de-familiarizing reflection of a woman passing-by and her stories, faces, images and shadows. The mirror becomes a metaphor for her own Otherness, her muted story in the postwar textualizations and representations of the Soviet militant feminine. What does Rzhevskaya see in the multiple mirror reflections that make her think about her self-image as the reflection of somebody's will? Why does her first encounter with difference and femininity of the Other woman become the first page of her war memoir story? What is this hidden alterity in her memory which survives beyond the genre of a representative her/oic story?

On the other hand, the slash as the symbol of collective anonymity is re-inscribed as the space of transcending the limits of the binary givens of cultural ideology that gender a woman's body and consciousness. Paradoxically, as a translator, Rzhevskaya is always in the territory of a slash "/". The position challenges the fixity of her belonging as it lets her "translate" her own experience outside the power of collective imaginary and transcend it into the alterity of the experiences of women on the roads of Europe. The experiences are acts of discovery and at the same time a part of her "re-birthing" ritual. Women on all sides of the war – pani Marias, victims of concentration camps and brothels, a Soviet military interpreter – are objectified even more, in mutual alterity. It was fixing them in constructing borders between "West" and "East", to the level of "zero" at the end of the war as they are "re-born" into the re-dichotomized world order. The "slash" becomes a trope of invisibility and namelessness of a Self dichotomized in Self/Other, war/peace, etc. The Self/Other dichotomy goes not only along the front line and the coming post-war East-West divide across which Rzhevskaya encountered anonymous, lost women of Europe. The Self/Other divide reveals itself not only in the war/peace historiography authorized by trans-Atlantic fraternal signature to secure and stabilise the post-war narrative of origin and genesis of the world order. The Self/Other divide in the birthing of the post-war order annuls her agency into "oneness" by Soviet politics of gender substitution.

The final episode of *A Distant Rumble* describes the narrator's walk with Tanya, a Soviet woman who has to replace the interpreter in post-war Berlin. The episode as a different end of that war – for women – is paralleled to the "incidental" and just mentioned context of the peace-builders' meeting in Potsdam whose decisions would authorize the post-war development. The memory-re-enactment of a leisurely stroll around Potsdam represents two Soviet women who re-center their functional obligations in socialist warfare patriarchy. The autobiographical narrator/translator is a figure of margin, threshold and as such she is dangerous. From the position of the system, she is herself "in danger and emanates danger to others"[16]. The role of the militant female, with so many questions and doubts about the freedom of liberators, has to be stopped. Tanya who dreams of a family and children in Germany is a needed replacement, a returned social persona of a post-war woman. A woman is relegated to a space within a particular history to function as a double agent in its political domestications built on "a concept of natural time as *familial*"[17]. As Anne McClintock points out, "the family offered an individual trope for figuring *historical time*"[18]. In *Distant Rumble*, there is an explicit doubling of the family as an individual trope. On the one hand, the army is a f(am)ilial image of true masculinity in historical time that has to incorporate into its operational mythologies the tragic masquerade of female militancy, truly filial to the "mother-figure" of war. On the other hand, the family as an individual trope of historical time centers around the mother-figure. Soviet motherhood was scripted in biological-political terms. A woman's naturally-given reproductive functions were considered central to reproducing the "nature" of the order into the future.

Both heroines fulfill the given gender roles. Both, with traumas of the past war as well as dreams and fantasies about the future peace, are strangely divided in the transient present by mutually silenced war stories. This mutual distancing de-fuses potential subversions of their own in "unnecessary details" of Soviet women's experiences at war. Elena and Tanya shift active positions in the transition between war and peace that will never seriously threaten gendered power relations. The appearance of Tanya, a substitute, a replacement, with her desire to start a family, offers both desire and family as metaphors and fetishes for a single genesis narrative in which a politics of such role substitution unveils an art of double appropriation – territorial and gender. This appropriation process expels a woman from her military outfit and mimickry of oneness. The situation is suggestive of Kristeva's argument,

> ... the expelled abject haunts the subject as its inner constitutive boundary; that which is repudiated forms the self's internal limit. The abject is something rejected from which one does not part[19].

A military woman-translator as a border figure should, thus, become a socially appointed agent of abjection in writing about the war as an "abject zone"[20].

A colander is the first thing that Tanya buys in Germany. However, a colander in Tanya's hands turns into a metaphor of disruption, of sifting the "essence" from "unnecessary details", remembering to be a wife and mother and forgetting to be a soldier. The re-constituted Soviet feminine subject has to expunge "incidental" impurities as the historical order cannot be threatened with disruption[21]. A colander functions as a fetish instrumentalised by those in power of sifting, cleaning, purifying, mythologizing the Soviet mother-discourse and its post-Soviet multiplications.

When a national order re-articulates its gender relations more in terms of the post-war rebirth of the new global order, a woman of the nation has to be appropriated into radically changed positionalities in the reconstructed gender system. In the authorized globalized narrative of origins the trope of the mother's labors and creative powers receives a tragic resonance as it relegates us to the gendered cultural narrative of war/peace as death of hero/rebirth of the nation. In the mystifications of the "death of the hero"/paternal origin, the maternal is mystified in the rebirth of the nation as well. How the body returns to the state of difference is the fantasy for women with no access to significations of the return. Thus, the reproductive metaphor appropriated in the war/

peace dichotomization of history is essential to producing the stable and fixed identity of the Soviet woman as the autobiographical subject.

The war becomes literally the monstrous womb of the narrator's rebirth and renaming. Elena Rzhevskaya survived where only few survived. She was "bathed in blood" in the battles near Rzhev. Her *nom-de-plume* as the act of self-renaming in the womb of the war articulates Rzhevskaya's symbolical re-birth as a child of the collective dead body of the dead in opposition to the dead author of their lives, her own life included. The episodes with the mirror are interesting to read through Lacan's notion of the mirror stage when a child comes into consciousness through the self-reflective operation. The mirror-stage of the child (or the "child" of the war in this case) is connected with the acquisition of language, and the resistance to its acquisition arises from seeing Other, reading Other, seeing herself as Other. The young military woman is always "displaced" and she is always "a divided, a pluralized subject which occupies multiple and mobile sites"[22], thus, a resisting writer and reader is always in the process of dissolving and deconstructing the woman's "stable identity".

The narrator returns to Moscow by plane, and the flight soars her up into the sky, as the finale of her re-birthing out of the war "womb". Her substitute Tanya remains on the earth and she will possibly become a sanitized mother-figure in the process of abjection. Her self-sacrificial sacraments of maternity will serve the phantoms of women's historical agency produced in the politically hygienic memory narratives by women "authors". Rzhevskaya feels that she herself, with her experience at the front, is becoming a fetish, a doll, a substitute for a woman author who would silence traumas into the single authoritative narrative of the war. What constitutes a woman's "life" in the metaphysics of the Soviet "subject" is a critical question-mark behind numerous questions in the text. The delegated agency of woman at war constructed as female militancy and necessity of the war is disavowed as the political re-territorialization has to be assured in the post-war narratives of the new European order and its origin. The female militant who is a phallic substitute suggests "an unbidden fear of emasculation"[23] and threatens with defying the sacred borders of phallic power. Can a militant female become the history's organizing figure, with the right to female authorship? This would mean transgressing the dominant tropes of military and heroic masculinity to ritualize the policing of boundaries – in territory, history and gender.

A doll as the only trophy from the war on the plane testifies to her rebirth into the fetish that marks her expulsion in the process of abjection:

> It was empty on the plane – no cargo. Only a cardboard box with my doll travelled on its floor. I could not even think about this in the fear of heights [...] lying helplessly on the bench [...][24].

Her militant agency of a phallic substitute becomes the object that is "something rejected from which one does not part". Disawoval includes the veil of maternal iconography thus putting her into a silenced position in the Soviet narrative of war as historical change and its political effects. Domesticity here functions as a relation of complex possession – territorial appropriations and domestic frameworks. Domesticity functions as a conversion project for transforming a space and political and social relations to power. Domestication of liberated territories as domination in the future colonized lands of the Soviet globalization script also functioned for historical time to be collected, assembled and mapped in post-war historiography. Thus, a woman undergoes a double displacement in which family and a disciplined woman-mother has to offer a genesis narrative for Soviet history and to translate it to her children in the roles of the mother and the first teacher at school.

The generic collective identity of a soldier at war (Soviet soldier), which is questioned by Rzhevskaya, intervened in her memories so radically that a full text was published only in 1989. She undid a Soviet myth of "writing the body of coherent victorious history" and touched upon the issue of how a perpetuated warfare supplied this "history" with symbols and representations through women's/mothers' "colanders" of memories. Moreover, Rzhevskaya's memory narrative articulates how femininity and motherhood were constructed and instrumentalised in the Soviet historiographic dichotomy of war/peace. For her, it was also a question of a "new Soviet" woman's autobiographical self-representation in the culture of ideological censorship. Rzhevskaya managed to "translate" political re-colonization of women's possible emancipatory agency into the most rigid form of autobiographical practices. This form was subversively re-written to expose its stabilizing function in the instrumentalizing politics of memory narratives against a woman by alienating her from inhabiting her own memories of "history proper" in the production of personal and collective legends.

Notes

[1] Edward J. Brown, *Major Soviet Writers. Essays in Criticism.* (Oxford University Press, 1973), p.13.
[2] Bella Brodzki, and Celeste Schenck, (eds.), *Life/Lines: Theorizing Women's Autobiography.* (Cornell University Press, 1988), p.254.
[3] Julia Watson, 'Towards an Anti-Metaphysics of Autobiography', in Robert Folkenflik (ed.), *The Culture of Autobiography. Constructions of Self-representation.* (Stanford University Press, 1993), p.63.
[4] Paul John, Eakin, 'The Referential Aesthetic of Autobiography', *Studies in the Literary Imagination*, Vol. XXIII, No2, Fall 1990, p.143.
[5] Beth Holmgren, *On Lidiia Chukovskaia and Nadezhda Mandelstam*, (Indiana University Press, 1993), p.7.
[6] Holmgren, *On Lidiia Chukovskaia and Nadezhda Mandelstam,* p.7.
[7] Liz Stanley, *The Auto/biographical I.* The Theory and Practice of Feminist auto/biography. (Manchester University Press, 1992), p.9.
[8] Shlomith Rimmon-Kenan, *Narrative Fiction: Contemporary Poetics.* (Methuen, 1983), pp.123-124.
[9] Elena Rzhevskaya, 'Dalekii Gul', in *Druzhba Narodov*, No 7, (1988), p.45.
[10] From: Shirley Neuman (ed.), *Autobiography and Questions of Gender.* (University of Alberta, Indiana, Frank Cass and Co, LTD, 1993), p.99.
[11] Rzhevskaya, 'Dalekii Gul', p. 5.
[12] Sidonie Smith, *A Poetics of Women's Autobiography: Marginality and the Fictions of Self-representation* (Indiana University Press, 1987) p.18.
[13] Rzhevskaya, 'Dalekii Gul', p. 7.
[14] Luce Irigaray, *This Sex Which Is Not One.* Trans. by Catherine Porter (Cornell University Press, 1985), p.76.
[15] Rzhevskaya, 'Dalekii Gul', p. 30.
[16] Mary Douglas, *Purity and Danger* (Routledge and Kegan Paul, 1966), p.78.
[17] Anne McClintock, *Imperial Leather. Race, Gender and Sexuality in the Colonial Contest.* (Routledge, 1996), p.45.
[18] McClintock, *Imperial Leather,* p.71.
[19] Julia Kristeva, *Powers of Horror: An Essay on Abjection.* Trans. by Leon S. Roudiez (Columbia University Press, 1997), p. 4.
[20] Kristeva, *Powers of Horror,* p. 4.
[21] Kristeva, *Powers of Horror,* p. 9.
[22] Michelle Boulous Walker, *Philosophy and the Maternal Body.* Reading Silence. (Routledge, 1998), p 105.
[23] McClintock, *Imperial Leather*, p.72.
[24] Rzhevskaya, 'Dalekii Gul', p.69.

Voicing M/other in Russian Women's Autobiographies in the 1990s

Marja Rytkönen

This article has been inspired by theories concerning "other" women in psychoanalytical plots – mother and daughter – and the issue of representing others as a necessary constituent of autobiographical writing.[1] Theories of "female self" give a starting point for my interpreting the role of mother, or "other", in three contemporary Russian women's autobiographical texts. These theories seek to explain the mother-daughter relationship from a psychoanalytical point of view, emphasising that "maternal dominance in early childhood and the mother's closer identification with daughters than with sons"[2] makes "growing girls come to define and experience themselves as continuous with others".[3] As Miller shows, these theories have also inspired theoreticians of women's autobiography, notably, Mary G. Mason's seminal "The other voice" in 1980. The author constituted a model of female autobiography that represents the female self first and foremost through her relation to others. This theoretical assumption proliferated in subsequent writings on women's autobiographies.[4] Here, my aim is not to "prove" any of these theories right or wrong, but to consider them as a reference point for interpreting models of writing about the self in three contemporary autobiographies where a female "other" plays an important part.[5]

If we look at Russian memoirs concentrating on the period of the 1930s and 40s, the purges, the loss of parents and disintegration of family and home[6] are all elements of the story of "poteryannoe pokolenie"[7]. Descriptions concerning the relationship between mothers and daughters, children and parents, are restricted to glimpses of happy family-life before the tragedy when everyone was still unaware of the events to come. Thus, the story between parents and children is absent; it is a story that did not take place, because mothers and fathers were separated from their children, husbands from their wives, sisters from brothers, due to the state's intervention. Instead of the story between children and parents, we can read the story of the individual and the state, the symbolic mother/father.[8] One author, for instance, recalls the words of one investigator who accused her of abandoning her duties of daughter towards the state and Stalin.[9] However, in the 1990s there have also been published autobiographical texts in which the focus appears to be more on the individuals' and families' experiences than on the description of the relationship between the individual and state. The intersubjective element of autobiography can be attended to in these autobiographies.

I would like to look at the representation of "other" in three texts written by contemporary women. In one of the texts the author memorizes her life through her relationship with her mother. I will read this text as writing in order to recover and revise the relationship between mother and daughter, understanding one's own self and life in accordance with this relationship. In another text written by an author born after Stalin's death, the mother-daughter relationship is described as one of dependence, exploitation, and separation – in it the image of mother appears to be a counter figure, a "negative" model of a woman's life. The third text I will look at, does not deal with familial relationships but represents a female subject in search of coherence and identity, and in this process another female figure plays a significant part, helping and making the writing subject confront the past self, i.e. the self as other/the other in the self.

1. Recovering m/other

Elena Bonner in her memoirs, *Dochki – materi*, focuses on her girlhood years, the time before the purges of the 1930s, which coincided with her adolescence.[10] This focus and narrative viewpoint enable the writing subject to concentrate on and, in my view, to revise her relationship to her mother. The time and its events were taboo issues during the Soviet Union era, and could be articulated only with the period of glasnost' and perestroika.[11] Noteworthy in Bonner's narrative is that it is spoken through the young girl's "I/eye", but, with the voice of the adult "I", who recalls and reconstructs her childhood in order to recover (it for) herself. The mother plays an important role in the memory-work and in the writing process which start after her death. This loss triggers in the writing subject an urge to remember and write down her mother's life. It is writing against death, against forgetting, but it is also writing to recover her mother's life, "to tell [mother's] story from [her] place in it".[12] This process also brings up the questions of who her mother was, what was her life like, and who "I" is.

The memories begin with a dream where the narrator is able to express her deepest feelings towards her mother, which was not allowed when she was still alive:

> Я болела в маминой комнате, и это как-то приближало меня к ней, мне было уютно быть почти на ее месте. И впервые за это время мама мне приснилась. Она сидела за столом в красной вязаной кофточке поверх какой-то очень нарядной белой блузки, совсем такая, как в последнее время до болезни, а я сидела по другую сторону стола, и мы через стол держались за руки, вернее, я держала ее левую руку и целовала ее – никогда в жизни этого не было, мы просто не могли себе такое представить и позволить – ведь всю жизнь внешне отношения были такими, что это сделать было нельзя. (...) А в последнее время, последние месяцы мне часто хотелось как-то физически приласкать маму, но все стояло это "нельзя".(...) А во сне все было легко – и руку ее целовать, и плакать – все было можно. (...) С этого сна начались воспоминания. [13]

> I lay ill in Mama's room, and that brought me closer to her somehow. It was cozy being almost in her place. And for the first time since she died I dreamed about her. She was sitting at the table in her red sweater over a very dressy white blouse, just the way she had been right before

> her illness. I was across the table from her, and we were holding hands. Or rather, I was holding her left hand in mine and kissing her. This had never happened in my life; we simply would never had imagined or permitted ourselves such behavior – after all, our relationship had never made that possible. (...) And lately, in the last months I had often wanted to show some physical expression of my love for her, but that "Forbidden" sign was always there. (...) But in the dream it was so easy – to kiss her hand, to weep – it was all permissable. (...) The memories began with that dream.[14]

From this dream on, begin the remembering and writing of a letter to children and grandchildren, where the story of mother's family is told. Thus "family genealogy defines itself in female terms" and women are "survivors, ...who outlive men and enable other women's continued existence".[15] In the figure of mother both past and future are present, as the daughter grows up to be a mother herself.

The narrative technique enabling the voicing of revised perspectives is first of all focalization. The adult "I", the narrating subject, voices the experiences and thoughts of the small girl, experiencing subject. The adult "I" is herself a mother, and sees past experiences both in a different and in the same way as the small girl. This becomes apparent in the description of this younger self's experiences. In the course of the narrative, the narrating subject moves freely in time and place, but in representing the small girl's experiences the perspective is "restricted". Thus, the experiences remain unanalysed, the events are not explained from the viewpoint of the omniscient adult narrator so, her perspective is not imposed on the small girl's experience, but instead there is a striving for understanding. This is possible because the narrator is divided into the experiencing and the narrating subject who share the experience of the same events, but whose perspectives are different. This is connected with the role of the narrator as daughter and mother.[16]

The relationship between mothers and daughters in *Dochki – materi* is characterized as problematic because there is a considerable (un)identification involved: the mother "sees" herself in the daughter and vice versa. This makes it difficult to see oneself as "other", and see the "other" in oneself. The process of remembering childhood also leads the writing subject to ponder upon this dilemma. In *Dochki – materi* mothers have problems in communicating with their own daughters, but they are able to express their love towards granddaughters:

> У мамы было чувство вины перед бабушкой за свою судьбу, которая рикошетом прошлась по бабушке. У меня – перед мамой за мою судьбу и мое счастье. Дочки – матери! Дочки – матери! [17]

> Mother felt guilty in front of Grandmother because her fate ricocheted into her mother's life. I feel guilty toward my mother for my life and my happiness. Mothers and daughters! Mothers and daughters![18]

However, the narrator's consciousness has changed, she has grown to understand mother, understand herself, now that she has children of her own. The stories of the daughter's and the mother's development are told in the text simultaneously: it strives "...to bridge a personal, generational, and ideological division which has been present during her entire life. As the 'I' becomes ever more inclusive, it transforms itself into 'we'".[19]

The narrator's mother is a busy career woman rather than a warm, caring and loving mother, and, according to the narrator, her methods of raising children do not include much affection. However, the mother's absence in girlhood (physically and emotionally) and the "new" relationship with her in adulthood after her camp years, create a new way of seeing the whole relationship from this "past-present-future" -perspective, which is available for the writing subject. The writing subject creates "a meaning to her mother's death and a pattern to her life, to both of their lives" through the writing and remembering process.[20]

In her book Bonner articulates "the problematic attitude to mother in patriarchy", but, she also reaches for the mother – the narrative seeks to heal the scars of the "radical surgery" as Adrienne Rich calls the separation between mother and daughter[21] – the daughter's obligatory separation from mother in order to be independent. The reaching for mother as a daughter structures the model of writing, first and foremost, the model of focalization in this text. The retrospective focusing of the narrator on her childhood memories and experiences enables her to bring back those memories and revise them without losing her own voice, to describe her experiences as if through the small girl, but with the consciousness of the grown up woman. "Writing is the passage way..., the dwelling place of the other" in oneself as Cixous defines the process of writing. Woman also experiences the "other", "not-me" within her self and in the relationship to mother in particular.[22] Bonner's writing can be seen in this light of writing oneself, because the woman narrator articulates the "so-far" inarticulate, the relationship to mother, not by becoming, absorbing the m/other in herself, but seeing, experiencing, acknowledging the other in herself. Thus, it is not only the relationship to mother which is recovered, but also the formation, the growing up of a small girl. Through the process of writing, the narrator dwells on her memories and faces (by representing) these feelings and events of her life. Comparing Bonner's story to the other two texts I will concentrate on, hers is different, because it focuses on her personal development as a child and girl, emphasising the connection to mother, and in addition representing the narrator's development as woman, not suppressing corporeal experiences of femaleness.

2. Mother and other myths

In the autobiography of Mariya Arbatova, *Mne 40 let*[23] , the relationship between mother and daughter forms a different kind of story than in Bonner's text. The playwright and tv-personality Arbatova (Gavrilina) was born in 1957, and she belongs to the free hippie-generation of the 1970s. In her story the mother plays the part of a negative model for a woman's life. Arbatova's book can overtly be characterized as a Bildungsroman, describing how the naive, wild child Mariya becomes – after many trials and adventures – a feminist liberated from myths concerning masculinity and femininity. Arbatova's plays have been characterized as stories about superfluous women, who are apparently successful, who have families and careers, but in the end are nevertheless expelled from the male dominated world, and denied the fruit of their work.[24] This plot is partially repeated in her autobiography, where the narrator, despite her successful combination of work and family, her happy second marriage which is based on equality between two independent partners, and despite the fact that in the modern world women have proved themselves as competent as men, she is rejected from the male dominated society, simply because she is a woman.

The depiction of the mother's life in the chapter "Mama" and other descriptions of mothers, undermine the Soviet ideal of motherhood as the only rewarding, satisfying mission in a woman's life. The narrator describes her own mother as a "professional victim", whose biography's "idiotism" was the main reason for her becoming a feminist. Writing about her mother and criticizing her conduct seem to be a "liberating act" for the writing subject, because the expression of negative feelings towards her mother is allowed, but at the same time also the understanding of those negative feelings is possible. This expression of love/ hatred for mother is possible only after having herself become a mother, taking her mother's place.[25] The narrator seems to be able to understand her mother's life better than the latter herself:

> Я совершенно не понимала, зачем надо было обменивать собственный творческий потенциал на обручальное кольцо.
>
> I did not understand at all, why Mama's own creative powers had to be exchanged for an engagement ring.[26]

However, on the other hand, she sees mother's life as a consequence of the idealized Soviet image of woman's mission of being the "self-denying, good mother"[27]. According to the narrator her mother was disappointed in her own life, and therefore made everybody else's life miserable. In order to compensate for the loss of her own space and life the mother devours others' lives:

> Ей хотелось, чтоб мир близких начинался с неё и заканчивала ею, она не имела частного пространства и не подозревала, что частное пространство другого священно.
>
> She wanted others' world to begin and to end with her. She did not have any private life of her own, and she did not understand that the private space of others is sacred.[28]

In this autobiography the narrator has made the mother's story into an educational example: how a woman should act in order not to become like that. On the basis of the text, the narrator has herself been able to separate herself out from the "syndrome of generational replication".[29] Her career as a writer, success in raising children, and active love-life serve as a positive example for women in that being a mother is not an obstacle to self-realization, and something her mother had not realized. It is told how relaxed she takes care of her twin sons and simultaneously writes plays. This is due to her ability to write "fast" and "effectively". Contrary to her own mother, the narrator considers herself a good mother, because writing offered an escape from domestic duties.[30] Some mothers that come across the narrator's path are described as being too strict towards their children, because their own lives are miserable. These descriptions of "monster-mothers" are aimed at criticizing the onesidedness of motherhood as sole mission in women's lives in (Soviet) Russia, and representing her own image as "other", "different", not identical with these mothers.

The text's numerous accounts of the narrator's love and sex life, are aimed to serve as an example and education for Russian women and men who are trapped inside the conventional, patriarchal gender roles, as she herself was before her personal emancipation. The alleged purpose of this female "Decameron" was, that women would be able find points of identification and men learn what women really want, so that both could be liberated from myths about feminine and masculine conduct.[31] However, the narration about these experiences can also be interpreted as a need to share the experiences, a need for a listener/reader. Although the text is written primarily as a public account of life, and the narrator claims to set her life and experiences as an example for others, in my view, the writing subject's constructing of the "self" as altered is linked with the female others, and especially with the mother: "Думаю, что феминисткой меня прежде всего сделал идиотизм маминой биографии." ("I think, that I became feminist first and foremost because of the idiotism of Mother's biography").[32]

3. Self as "other"

Narrating about one's life by "way of alterity"[33] is a model used in the memoirs of Emma Gershtein[34] . The focus of the text is on the literary circles and their life in the 1930s: the Mandel'shtams, Anna Akhmatova, Lev Gumilev are among the main figures in this text. The most striking effect of this book according to the Russian media[35] has been the anti-canonical representation of, especially, Osip and Nadezhda Mandel'shtam: the author is said to have deconstructed the very myth of a classic poet and his wife, the dissidents' heroine, Nadezhda Mandel'shtam. In this text the lives of others intertwine in a most complex way with the author's life. The writing subject dwells on her "past", and her "self" by narrating about these other figures and their lives, predominantly about Nadezhda Mandel'shtam. It is true that Emma Gershtein writes about intimate sides of the Mandel'shtams' life, but on the other hand, it can be said, that in doing so the writing subject also touches upon intimate aspects of her own life. The writing subject confronts the "other", "past" self with the help of other female figures, most notably Nadezhda Mandel'shtam.

According to the narrator, her aim in writing these memoirs is twofold: she wants to describe what life was in the 1930s – since the later generations cannot imagine it – what "really" happened to Osip, Nadezhda and others. The narrator expresses on many occasions her aim to correct certain false accounts concerning the poet's life, and in particular, to correct Nadezhda Mandel'shtam's faulty accounts concerning several events in their life. But, on the other hand, Gershtein writes a story of her own life, her personal friendship with the Mandel'shtams, her love life, her status in the society of the 1930s. The interrelations and shifts between these two perspectives in the text create an ambiguity in the reader. On the one hand, there is the authoritative voice of the literary scholar, who represents her views together with recently discovered documents, which back up her claims. On the other hand the narrative includes passages of utter subjectivity, of personal involvement: it is as though the narrator actually re-lives, or at least re-stages in her mind some scenes of her life. In these passages, the point of view, or focalization, is the experiencing narrator's, who is a participant herself in the scene. For instance, when the narrator speaks about herself as a young woman aqcuainted with the Mandel'shtams, who, as the narrator says, represented for her an important alternative way of life she longed for at that time, especially a certain disquieting experience, the narrative perspective shifts from objective, external focalization, to subjective, internal focalization: the focus is on the narrator's consciousness and perception:

> Он (Osip Emil'evich, M.R.) говорит с обычным своим тревожным красноречием, но по его лицу пробегает скрытая улыбка, которую я скорее угадываю, чем вижу: он испытывает удовольствие, украдкой поглядывая на меня. И мне кажется, что Яхонтов это тоже понимает. Ведь спектакль разыгрывается специально для меня, для того, чтобы понаблюдать за мной, нанося мне раны. Я молчу. Это злит его.

> He is speaking with his usual troubled talkativeness, but over his face runs a secret smile, which I rather guess than see: he experiences

> pleasure in giving me stealthy glances. And I think, that Yakhontov also realizes this. You see, this performance is especially prepared for me in order to watch me, to cause me pain. I keep quiet. It irritates him.[36]

This passage illustrates the merging of the narrator with the "past self": with the help of the present tense, the detailed description of feelings connected with the situation the narrator lives the events once more in her mind. The consciousness of the narrator is merged into the consciousness of her "past" self, that is, the narrating and experiencing subjects seem to have merged. Anni Vilkko calles this kind of narrating the "presence of memory". The distance between now and then diminishes – the present tense figures the immediacy of the memory.[37] The memory is part of the subjectivity, it belongs to the present, as much as to the past. Although passages of this kind are aimed at being illustrations, or rather, evidences of other people's behaviour and character, they seem to reveal as much about the subject of writing.

Although the figures of both Osip and Nadya are represented as a cause of a certain ambivalent feeling for the subject of writing, these figures also serve as constituents of the coherence of the writing subject. By asking herself/the reader some rhetorical questions after having revealed some "scandalous" details about Osip's and Nadya's lives, the narrator explains her own conduct to herself. Overtly she merely describes the peculiarities of the others' lives, but these questions, nevertheless, involve the narrator:

> Свой союз с Осипом Эмильевичем Надя называла "физиологической удачей". В ту пору все ее рассуждения и шалости были пронизаны разговорами об эротике. Как я относилась к этому? Моральная и эстетическая сторона подобных сюжетов меня нисколько не беспокоила. Мы жили в эпохи сексуальной революции, были свободомыслящими, молодыми, то есть, с естественной и здоровой чувственностью, но уже выработанной манерой истинних снобов ничему не удивляться. (...)
>
> Сейчас я понимаю, что в моей голове была нелепая мешанина из искусственной теории и совсем не подходящей к ней моей собственной манеры поведения.
>
> Nadya called her union with OM a "physiological success". In that time all of her tricks were filled with erotica. How did I react to this? We lived in the age of a sexual revolution, we were free-thinking, young,

> that is, with natural and healthy sensuality, but we had developed already a blasé manner not to marvel at anything. (...) Now I understand, that in my head was a ridiculous jumble of artificial theory and my own manner of behaviour, absolutely incongruous.[38]

This narrative technique can be interpreted as the writing subject's confronting of the "other self", that is, her past self with the help of these other figures, especially Nadya Mandel'shtam. It is not insignificant that this other is female, because much of the otherness in the past self is connected with sexuality and relations with the other sex: in this light, nor are the passages insignificant with Osip Mandel'shtam, whose behaviour the writing subject sometimes describes as offensive, even aggressive.

By explaining the disquieting memories with the spirit of the times, with youth's wildness, the writing subject strives to create the coherence of the "I". The past, however, is filled with memories and experiences that cause ambiguity in the narrator, and many such experiences are connected with the figure of Nadya and Osip. For the narrator, writing about the past is a way of confronting the other in herself. Especially Nadezhda and Osip seem to serve as "counter-selves" of the past, experiencing self. It can be stated, that the narrator's "grounding of identity through relation to the chosen other ... enable[s] [her] to write openly about [herself]"[39]. The passages of others' lives and life with others are of special importance for the constituting of the subject in writing.

As Nancy K. Miller suggests, it can be said that for autobiographical writing in general, and for writing memoirs in particular, the relationship to others is one of the constituting principles, for female, as well as for male autobiographers.[40] In Gershtein's text this argument is valid in many ways: the reader is the ultimate "other" in autobiographical writing as the rhetorics of the text constantly refer to the reader's position; Nadya Mandel'shtam's figure lurks everywhere in the text. The author/narrator lets the reader understand that her presence is motivated by the fact that she was connected with the most important experiences in Gershtein's life, and that she had contributed a great deal to the picture of many other persons and events of that time. However, if we look at the matter from a meta-narrative and psycho-narrative level, this significant female other seems to be one of the constituents in the creation of female subjectivity in the text: sexuality, relationship between the sexes, friendship between women are connected with depictions of this significant female figure. This conclusion can be drawn if attention is given to the gender of the narrator/author. It can be concluded that the narrative includes important experiences for the writing subject herself that she, however, feels are not identical with herself. But in this writing, the "other" in oneself becomes apparent[41]. Writing through the experiences of another woman helps the writing subject to confront these experiences, which seem very fresh and alive, even after so many years. In this text the writing subject confronts/represents the repressed "other woman" in herself.

Notes

[1] Nancy K. Miller, 'Representing Others: Gender and the Subjects of Autobiography', in Yvonne Hyrynen (ed.), *Voicing Gender.* (University of Tampere, 1996), p. 111.
[2] Marianne Hirsch, *The Mother/Daughter Plot. Narrative, Psychoanalysis, Feminism.* (Indiana University Press, 1989), p. 20.
[3] Nancy Chodorow, *The Reproduction of Mothering.* (California University Press, 1978), quoted in Miller, 'Representing Others', pp. 107–108.
[4] Miller, 'Representing Others', pp. 106–107.
[5] Miller, 'Representing Others', p. 117.
[6] For example one author writes how she lost her father, mother and sister during the 30s and 40s, and how the son she gave birth to in prison was taken away from her – and that this was a common feature of women's lives in a prison camp.
[7] Vera Pirozhkova's memoirs *Poteryannoe pokolenie* depicts the author's childhood and youth during the 30s and 40s in the Soviet Union.
[8] Adele Barker, 'Women without men in the writings of contemporary Soviet women writers', in Daniel Rancour-Laferriere (ed.), *Russian Literature and Psychoanalysis.* (Benjamins, 1989), p. 433.
[9] Tamara Petkevich, *Zhizn' – sapozhok neparnyi.* (Astra-Lyuks, 1993), p. 450.
[10] Elena Bonner, *Dochki – materi.* (Chekhov Publishing Corporation, 1991/1994).
[11] Accounts of this time and its events were printed as samizdat and tamizdat publications. See, for instance, Laura Engelstein's review, which deals with emigrant memoirs in Stalin's time, published in the 1980s in the USA. Laura Engelstein, 'In a Female Voice', *Slavic Review*, vol. 44, no. 1 (1985).
[12] Miller, 'Representing Others', p. 130.
[13] Bonner, *Dochki – materi*, p. 14.
[14] Elena Bonner, *Mothers and Daughters*, transl. by Antonina W. Bouis (Alfred A. Knopf, 1992), p. 11.
[15] Helena Goscilo, *Dehexing Sex. Russian Womanhood During and After Glasnost* (The University of Michigan Press, 1996), p.37.
[16] Hirsch, *Mother/Daughter Plot*, p. 159.
[17] Bonner, *Dochki – materi*, p. 302.
[18] Bonner, *Mothers and Daughters*, p. 333.
[19] Hirsch, *Mother/Daughter Plot*, p. 159.
[20] Kathleen Woodward, 'Simone de Beauvoir. Aging and Its Discontents', in Shari Benstock (ed.), *The Private Self: Theory and Practice of Women's Autobiographical Writings.* (Routledge, 1988), p. 102.
[21] Adrienne Rich, *Of Woman Born: Motherhood as Experience and Institution.* (Nortong, 1976/1986), p.236.
[22] Hélène Cixous, Catherine Clement, *The Newly Born Woman.* (Manchester University Press, 1975/1987), pp. 85–86, 90.
[23] Mariya Arbatova, *Mne 40 let.* (Zakharov-Ast, 1999).

[24] Marina Ledkovsky, Charlotte Rosenthal, Mary Zirin (eds.), *Dictionary of Russian Women Writers*. (Greenwood Press, 1994), p. 36.
[25] Julia Kristeva, *The Kristeva Reader*, Toril Moi (ed.), (Basil Blackwell, 1986), p. 184.
[26] Arbatova, *Mne 40 let*, p. 32.
[27] See for example Tat'yana Okulova's eulogy of self-sacrificing, altruistic motherhood, and the role of woman-mother as the preserver of Russia's sacred traditions. Tat'yana Okulova, 'Nam dobrye zheny i doprye materi nuzhny...' *Nash sovremennik*, no. 3 (1990), pp. 183–184.
[28] Arbatova, *Mne 40 let*, p. 32. In this aspect the depiction of mother-daughter relationship is similar to Lyudmila Petrushevskaya's depiction in "Время ночь", where mothers' and daughters' lives intertwine with each other repeatedly.
[29] Helena Goscilo, 'Mother as Mothra: Totalising Narrative and Nurture in Petrushevskaia, in Sona Stephan Hoisington (ed.), *A Plot of her Own. The Female Protagonist in Russian Literature*. (Northwestern University Press, 1995), p. 113.
[30] Arbatova, *Mne 40 let*, p. 175.
[31] Arbatova, *Mne 40 let*, pp. 122–123.
[32] Arbatova, *Mne 40 let*, p. 32.
[33] Mary G. Mason, 'The Other Voice: Autobiographies of Woman Writers', in James Olney (ed.), *Autobiography: Essays Theoretical and Critical*. (Princeton University Press, 1980), p. 231.
[34] Emma Gershtein, *Memuary*. (Inapress, 1998).
[35] *Moskovskie novosti*, 'Besposhchadnaya Emma', no. 40 (1998), p. 22.
[36] Gershtein, *Memuary*, p. 425.
[37] Anni Vilkko, *Omaelämäkerta kohtaamispaikkana. Naisen elämän kerronta ja luenta*. (Tammer-Paino, 1997), pp. 167–169.
[38] Gershtein, *Memuary*, p. 424.
[39] Mason, 'The Other Voice', p. 210.
[40] Miller, 'Representing Others', p. 109.
[41] Instead of "other", Hélène Cixous writes that homosexuality is repressed in the "I", but that it becomes apparent symbolically in traits of character, behaviour, manners, gestures, and more specifically – in writing. Hélène Cixous, 'Sorties', *niin&näin*, no. 2 (1995), p. 20.

Part III
Scenarios

Sexual Scripts in Women's Biographies and the Construction of Sexual Pleasure

Anna Temkina

This article is devoted to the analysis of scripts about women's sexual behaviour reconstructed on the basis of biographical interviews with 18 middle-class women of two generations in Russian society. Data were collected in the realm of a Finnish-Russian project in 1996–1997. The article concentrates on the following questions: 1) the script approach as a methodology of social constructionist research of sexuality; 2) ideal types of sexual scripts represented in women's sexual biographies; 3) the script of sexual pleasure as a means of constructing sexuality, and the process of "doing gender" in the sexual script.

Methodological approach

In this article the concept of "script" is applied to the analysis of the construction of sexuality in women's sexual biographies. The social constructionist approach is based on the following assumptions: First, the way we study the world is determined by certain concepts, categories and methods, and second, the meaning of the concepts and categories we use are varied across cultures and time.

The social constructionist approach has been applied to research on sexuality since the 1970s.[1] Sexuality is understood as a cultural construct (a set of learned behavioural patterns), and the theory of scripts has been applied to the research on sexuality in Western sociology and psychology[2]. Scripts are considered as trajectories of the sexual life course. According to Laumann, Gagnon, Michael and Michael[3] the scripting theory is applied to explanations of how sexual scripts specify with whom people have sex, when and where they should have sex, what they should do sexually, and why they should perform certain sexual activities. Socio-cultural processes play a fundamental role in determining what is perceived to be "sexual" and how sexuality is constructed and interpreted. Patterns of sexual conduct are assumed to be culturally determined. Individual scripts (as presented by informers) are studied as cases of implementation of cultural instructions.

The sexual script approach is a version of social constructionism within the framework of research on sexuality. Cultural scenarios are interpreted as instructions for sexual and other conducts embedded in cultural narratives. This approach is mainly applied to the analysis of sexual practices in a certain order, i.e. in different generations and different strata[4]. Less attention has been paid to those meanings of sexual behaviour which could be said to influence the construction of the script.[5]

I assume that cultural meanings of sexual behaviour (appropriate for a milieu, generation, age, status, and gender) frame the individual stories about sexual life. Those meanings might change during life courses, meanings of sexual behaviour need justifications and explanations. A person categorises sexual experience by means of available cultural instruments. Biographical data give possibilities to analyse the categories through which sexuality is constructed in personal narratives. By this is meant analysis of both the categories in which a person describes sexual experience, and analysis of the instruments which are used for this categorisation, i.e. procedures of comparison, opposition, and moral approval. I use Silverman's method of Membership categorisation (an adaptation of Sack's method) for text analysis.[6]

In this article my aim is first to explore ideal types of scripts. Second, I analyse the work of categorisation in narratives where sex is constructed as "pleasure". Third, I consider gender construction as an instrument for interpretation of sexuality. Different sexual scripts both express and construct gender culture, which is presented by respondents in the narratives as appropriate gender behaviour, gender norms, and gender expectations.

The empirical data consists of biographical interviews with 18 middle-class women, of whom five belong to the age group 27–34 years, seven are between 39 and 48 years old, and six between 57 and 63 years. The interviews include the following issues: childhood, adolescence, sexual debut, marriage, and divorce, parallel relationships, relationships with steady partners. The interviews involved also questions about sex talk with a partner, love and jealousy, adolescent sexual experiences, violent sex, contraception, childbirth, abortion, and sexually transmitted diseases.

Sexual scripts in women's biographies

Based on the interviews with Russian middle-class women I distinguish the following ideal types of sexual scripts: the *pronatal* script, where sexual life is described as reproductive/ family life; the *romantic* script, where sexual life is described as an expression of emotions and feelings (above all love); the *hedonist* script, where sexual life is described as an orientation towards sexual pleasure; the *communicative* script, where sexual life is described as a way of informal (or intellectual, or friendly) communication; the *market* script, where sexual life is described as oriented toward material benefits; and the *achievement* script: sexual life is described as the means of self-realisation. Depending on stages of a person's life cycle or specific sexual relationships in one life-story several scripts can be found. The ideal types of scripts differ in accordance with the meaning ascribed to sex concerning the following issues:

– What does the story tell about on a general level?
– How is the loss of virginity (and/or sexual debut) described?
– How are preferences in sexual relations described?
– Who is the partner and how is he described?
– What kind of sexual relationships are the most common?
– What does sexual pleasure and satisfaction depend on?
– How are sexual practices described?
– What categories are used in the sexual vocabulary?

Pronatal script

"Sexual life was defective, but I got used to it" (63 years)

The story concerns relationships between mainly married couples and it has the following traits: The first sub-sexual experience is formed by a lack of sex education and romantic love. The husband is the first sexual partner and sexual life takes place within the marriage. Sexual life is synonymous with marriage and reproduction, which forms the story into a narrative about pregnancies, childbirth and abortions. It is difficult for the narrator to discuss sexuality and sexual satisfaction. As a rule sexual practices are not described, and when it is done these practices are described as monotonous, routine and unsatisfactory.

Romantic script

"Sex is the consequence of feelings and the instrument of love. You have sex if you are attached to a person" (46 years)

The script describes sex as love, as an attribute of "love", as "amorousness". The narrative is constructed as a series of romantic and emotional stories, where sex is a by-product of feelings and does not concern questions of technique. Love is the basic category of the sex vocabulary through which a reflexive project[7] of the self is organised. The narrative tells about steady relationships with a lover, but sexual practices are described with some constraints and difficulties.

Communicative script

"Sexuality exists since it exists in language. We are getting closer to each other not in order to have an orgasm, but in order to talk and communicate. We have sex to talk" (32 years)

In this script sex is described through the category of "communication". Sex is interpreted as an instrument to show respect and friendship and to express commonal interest[8] which also forms the main reason for having sexual relationships (within or outside marriage), and which is also rooted in joint work or milieu. Sexual relationships are described as a series of marital, extramarital or parallel relations, both steady and casual, and sexual pleasure and satisfaction are seen as objects of negotiation. Sexual practices are widely described, but mostly as a response to the questions of the interviewer. "Understanding", "common interests", "language", "personal relationship" are the main categories of the sexual vocabulary.

Hedonistic script

"I decide not to confuse sex and love... I can have sex with a person for whom I have no feelings. Sex is the greatest pleasure given to human beings by nature" (31 years)

The script describes sex as an autonomous sphere of life, it is distinguished from love, marriage, and reproduction, and understood as a natural drive and expression of personality. Detailed descriptions of sexual technique are given in the story. Sexual feelings are described as inborn, and virginity is considered something that one should lose as soon as possible, even with a casual partner. The main reason for having sexual relationships is "to give pleasure and to take pleasure", they are compatible with the satisfaction of hunger or appetite. A sexual relationship is a "game" or an "art", and a subject for discussion. Sexual relationships can also include lesbian sex and group sex. The main categories in the sexual vocabulary are those which directly describe sexual practices.

Market script

"I pay with sex for material benefit" (34 years)

Sex is described in this script as a means of receiving material benefits: sex is "work" to be done and therefore men should pay for it. The stories tell about selling sex, about prostitution. The main reason for having sex is to receive material support, money and/or expensive presents, and a partner is looked upon as a "sponsor" or "client". Relationships can be both casual and steady. Sexual pleasure is usually absent, but sexual practices are described in detail, and contraception is a subject for discussion. The story tells about sex in the terms of "using", "consumption", and "resources".

Achievement script

"Sex improves my self-evaluation, it proves my value... I am important, I am needed" (34 years), "It proves that I am pleased" (39 years)

This story is about self-evaluation and self-realisation: the motive for sexual debut, sexual relationships and marriage is to give proof of self-esteem, and relationships are both casual and steady. Sex tells about "recognition", "calls for (her) sexuality and femininity", and thus it is not important to receive sexual satisfaction, which can be faked. Sex is considered the means to "status achievement", to female competence demonstrated by male desire.

These frames do not embrace all the possibilities of interpretation of sexual conduct. Other interpretations can also be found in the texts, for example, sex as an "esoteric practice" and sex in relation to orthodox beliefs, but they are rarely presented as integral narratives. Another important theme is "violence", but it could be looked upon as organising the whole life. In an individual biography there is seldom an ideal type of script, and the frames change during the life course. Different frames of interpretations create frames of references, in comparison and in opposition to which the moral approval of sexual behaviour is constructed.[9] Next I will reconstruct frames of references and categorisation in order to explore how sexual pleasure is constructed in the biographies.

Sex as a pleasure

I will now analyse sexual biographies, which include narratives of the autonomous sphere of sexual pleasure. There is not one biography organised as a project of implementation of sexual behaviour as "pure" pleasure. This kind of sex is always described in comparison with other meanings of sexual conduct. My task is to uncover the frames of reference for description of sex as pleasure. These frames include sex education and sex initiation, sexual relationships, preceding attitudes of informants and their partners. An implicit and explicit comparison and opposition of different sexual meanings in different relationships create a system of classification (distinction). Differentiation of sexual meanings and its "cultural classification" is implemented through conscious reflection. The informant's own version of reality is constructed through it.

How is sexual pleasure constructed into an autonomous sphere of life and how is the distinction carried out? Most stories present the combination of sex, love and marriage (steady relationships) as an ideal composition of sexual relationships. This combination serves as the main frame of reference, presuming moral justification of the autonomous sphere of sex. In what follows, I will consequently define the systems of reference, the classifications of sexual meanings and its moral approval and the re-interpretation of gender as part of such moral approval. Three cases will be analysed in detail. I would like to note that a lack of sexual satisfaction and sexual pleasure are mentioned in relationships during the life span in several biographies of the same generation (27–48 years) and in the majority of biographies of the oldest generation (57–63 years). These biographies are about marriages, love and relationships. Generally sexual pleasure is a problematic aspect in women's biographies.

Case 1. "Sexuality as a learning process". M, 46 years old

"In the course of my life I have had more and more casual sexual encounters".

Both during her marriage and after M had parallel, steady and casual, relationships. In the interview she characterises her orientation as striving for sexual pleasure in multiple relationships. I will now look at how this script is constructed.

M provides two interpretative variants of sex as pleasure: first, it is a component of "true love", of "passion", or of a "mad love affair". This means harmony and liberation in unique personal relationships. Second, it means technical, "simple, good, easy" sex, where it is enough "to desire each other" and to love each other's bodies. The second variant is being separated, on the one hand, from "true love", love feelings, common interests, and intimacy. "Such a love does not happen more than 2–3 times in life". Marriage, on the other hand, is considered a "complicated system of financial, material, moral, kinship relationships, which also includes problems of housing, ageing, health". These distinctions are made through categorisation of different attitudes in different relationships with partners, through their comparison and opposition. The informant refers to sex education in the parental family as an important context. She connects sex problems in marriage with lack of sex education. She often mentions the lack of sex education and describes her behaviour as a way to overcome this problem.

M reproduces recollections of her youth in a double sense. On the one hand, she understood sex as something "indecent", "non-understandable" and "dangerous". "I had strange views in my youth. When I was 19, I was thinking about pregnancy after petting". She explains this as the consequence of upbringing: "nobody told me anything", and underlines the lack of knowledge and understanding. On the other hand, she characterises the atmosphere in the parental family as one of love and intimacy. This formed the basis for her idea that wife and husband are sexually happy. Thus she also expected herself to have a happy sexual life in marriage and oriented herself towards not having sex before marriage. The main categories – contradictory to the interpretation of sex later in her life – are "lack of knowledge" and "orientation toward having sex in marriage". Her biography is constructed as a process of improving her own sexual experience and as a process of separating sex from marriage.

The second frame of reference is her marriage in her twenties. The marriage script represents traditional variants of sexuality (pronatal script). M gives the following descriptions. Her first sexual contact was with her husband. She characterises the husband as being an "honest, good person" and "intelligent" whom she respected, but lacking in love and sexual attraction. She was not happy in her sexual life with her husband. She explains this by their attitudes towards sex, by their lack of experience and knowledge. Her husband is characterised as a non-experienced person "without culture of sexual communication", he treated sex as "satisfaction of needs like hunger, thirst". "I felt that sex was indecent, he that it was harmful". She describes the marriage as lacking in love and sexual satisfaction. A person "whom she respects" is distinguished from a person "whom she loves and/or sexually desires". The difference between sex-communication-love-marriage is formulated referring to marital experience.

Another contradiction in her story is based on gender relations in marriage. She describes her husband's feelings as those of a "typical male", which are oriented towards conquering women, of making a wife belong to him and treating her as property. Throughout her life she wants to overcome these gendered attitudes. She refuses women's position as property and orients herself towards an egalitarian choice, and even towards the task of teaching a "sexually inexperienced man". The opposition between "belonging to a man" and "free choice" is formulated.

The next frame of reference is an extramarital relationship with her first lover, which lasted for several years after she had been married for five years, and for whom she had a "strong passion". She compares this relationship with her marriage in three ways. First, this relationship is evaluated as love, as "passion", based on common interests. Secondly, there was a powerful sexual attraction, desire and strong jealousy. Thirdly, there was no such personal relationship ("such as respect") as with her husband. This relationship is described as a process of learning sex: "due to him I understood what sex was". Therefore love, passion and sex are separated from friendly personal relationships and marriage. This relationship is not only compared with the previous one (marriage), but also with the last one. In the former case she describes herself as passive, as a pupil, in the latter as active and free in choice, and also as a teacher for her partners.

M describes her life in her thirties (after the divorce) as "strange" or "different", with both casual and permanent relationships. This period, characterised as sexually satisfactory, is opposed to the previous one. She uses the previous categories in interpreting her relationships with two steady lovers. With the first lover the relationship lasted eight years, consisting of rare dates considered as "holiday occasions". The context of this relationship is constituted by the status of the partner, who was married without intentions to divorce, and her own status, a single mother living with her son. The relationship developed from love to a habit in the contextual condition of limited choice. Later on, when her son was older, casual relations began to occur.

The relationship with her second lover lasted nearly three years, and she describes it as "strong love with passion". She pictures it as "harmony", "sexual perfection" with "mutual sexual abilities and skills". Her "sense of inferiority was overcome" and her relation to the body changed. At that time "I did not need any other partners". Her narrative about this partner is very short and there is no explanation for why the relationship ended. This was the only relationship she did not feel like giving any details on. "I know what I did for him, but I don't want to speak about it". A unity of love and sexual satisfaction is the basic frame of reference for this relationship. In other cases the lack of love is approved on the basis of an assertion of the possibility of separation of sex from love.

The connection between the different periods is also explicitly mentioned. Casual relationships began when "I recovered from being sick after my divorce" and after being desperate for a love affair. "I was physically sick, and one of my friends, a psychotherapist, told me that I should immediately have sexual contacts... And I did...This happened after I turned 40".

Thus, contemporary relationships are described in reference to a previously constructed system of categories. Firstly, they are separated from love (they differ from relationships with lovers she felt love for). Secondly, they are separated from the "complicated system of marriage" (they differ from her own marriage and from "generic" marriage). Thirdly, they are not based on common interests, views and intimacy (they differ from her own marriage and such relationships with lovers, which were based on common interests). Fourthly, they presuppose experience, abilities, skills, highly developed technique of sexual practices (they differ from her marriage and are similar to relationships with her last lover). Female sexual satisfaction derives from practice and becomes a "mechanical experience".

She teaches men who lack such skills (the situation is different from the one in which she was taught). These men are evaluated as "helpless in sexual life", their attitudes towards sex are "terrible" (they are similar to her husband's and her own when she was young). A man as a teacher (first lover) turns into a partner in training (last lover) and then into a pupil. This man "has no idea about his abilities", and "hesitates to speak about sex". He has "complexes and fears", "feels shy about the body", his "sensuality is not developed", he could not "enjoy and get pleasure from sex", and he cannot "give pleasure to a woman". These men are "shy and vulnerable".

What kind of woman can teach sex? The informant compares her abilities with her own early experiences and with other women's. She does not want to "own" the man, she feels no jealousy and considers herself sexually superior, she knows her own body well, she expresses respect for wives and mistresses, she has no financial problems (she is currently working in business), she has experiences that younger women usually do not have. She makes her own sexual choices and she "teaches all her partners". Sexual relationships can, however, lead to "strong feeling and love": "[i]t is desirable to have love and sex. But this is not what happens every time".

These features are distinct from her early life. Sexual relationships oriented towards autonomous sexual pleasure are connected to experience, knowledge (learning), status, and age. Her own and her partner's attitudes depend on the parameters which are formulated as the opposition to earlier attitudes, to lack of experience and knowledge. These features distinguish the informant from other women, making her superior. She compares herself to *others*. She was *other* when she was young, her parents are *others,* and so are also young inexperienced and sexually undeveloped women. In constructing such *otherness* she implements those types of behaviour, which she considers to be male. She argues for differences in female and male attitudes towards sex. "Men realise themselves in sex; for women this is not necessary, for her it is enough to be desired". "There is no necessity for women to have multiple partners, but men need them". Implicitly she follows the patterns of behaviour she considers to be male. Her identity is constructed through internalising male norms. The informant distinguishes herself from her own youth, and from other women by using patterns of male behaviour in order to justify sexual pleasure as an autonomous sphere of life. Sexuality is thus explicitly described as a cultural construction.

Case 2. "Sexuality as natural drive". S, 31 years old

"Sex is the greatest pleasure given to a person by nature"

S is divorced and now has numerous sexual contacts. Also during her marriage she had both parallel steady and casual relationships. For her sex as pleasure means the opposite of sex which is described as "shame-duty in marriage" and which is "secondary and not important". She separates sex as pleasure from love relationships and from paid sex.

She makes these distinctions through comparison and opposition of attitudes in different relationships with reference to certain contexts, and she mentions the following types of relations: marriage, love, passion, paid sex, sex as joy, lesbian sex, group sex.

The first important context which the informant addresses is sex education in the parental family and adolescent sexual feelings and experiences. She considers her sexuality inborn: "I knew everything throughout my life, I was born with sexual feelings". She contrasts her "natural sexuality" with parental upbringing. According to parental attitudes she was supposed to lose her virginity only with her (future) husband in order to have "a normal family". These attitudes are evaluated as "sex is shame-duty in marriage". In her adolescent opinion a "normal family" presupposes virginity and then sexual experiences. In this way she formulates a contradiction, which serves as a pivot for further interpretation of sexuality. Sexuality as an natural expression (interpreted as existent from birth) is opposed to its cultural limitation. This interpretation then helps to separate sexuality from marriage.

The second reference system is the first experience of sexual intercourse. She had two partners: one, whom she was going to marry, and another to whom she had a strong sexual desire without any intention of establishing a firm relationship. Thus, sexual desire is separated from marriage. The sexual debut happened with the latter partner, who became her lover. "I fell in love with a terrible passion". Sexual relationships are characterised as sexual pleasure. In the story she continues her interpretation of sexuality: "I wasn't taught by anybody. I knew everything by myself. Probably a woman has a genetic sexual instinct. I don't understand how it is possible to teach a woman to make love ".

Her fiancé became the second partner. The sexual debut happened with another person because of the fiancé's lack of sexual experience. "If I had known this in advance I could have helped my fiancé". She stresses her natural sexual ability and the partner's lack of sexual experience. When she compares her first two partners (in response to the interviewer's question), two dimensions are singled out. The first one is the characteristic of personal relations. "It was interesting and lively with my fiancé". The second dimension is a sexual one. "He [fiancé] was more loving and sensitive in sex... he paid much more attention to me than to himself". The personal relationship is being separated from the sexual one. The following categories for partners are constructed: "a person with whom it is interesting" and "a person with whom sexual relationships are satisfactory".

The next frame of reference is her marriage. Her husband as well as her former fiancé were virgins, and this "was the tragedy of our life". "He was sexually inexperienced". But where do male skills come from if they are supposed to be "given by nature"? She does not speak about this. Two assumptions could be made out of her system of categories. First, she differs from her partners by having sexual abilities "naturally". This is her characteristic trait as well as of all women. Second, her interpretation of sexuality implicitly includes the necessity of learning it (as this was done referring to her youth) though it is explicitly denied ("I don't understand how it is possible to teach a woman to make love").

The personal relationships with the husband are described generally as getting worse ("he suppressed me morally and physically") while they sexually were getting better ("maybe he became more experienced or our bodies got used to each other"). Sexual satisfaction was also the obstacle for divorce, which nevertheless happened after five years of marriage. The informant, using marriage as the system of reference, separates, firstly, personal relationships from sexual ones, and secondly, natural expression of sexuality from social experience. The second distinction is made through a detachment of her own expression of sexuality from those of her partners .

"A promiscuous sex life began after the divorce". She describes herself as "morally suppressed by living with her husband" and "after the divorce I was surprised by men who expressed sexual interest in me". The referent during this period is her female friend who had "a stormy sex life", and who decided "to educate me in a sexual life". This period (of sexual re-socialisation) is evaluated as a different one. "My upbringing led me to the conclusion that sexual desire is not normal. But then I understood that since sexuality exists I should not struggle against it. And I stopped this struggling. It is great that sexuality exists". The "re-socialised" sexuality was expressed in relationships with steady and casual lovers, in paid sex, in lesbian sex, and in sex as "adventure". The main sense of sex is "to give and to receive pleasure, [which] is given and received on the bodily level and on the level of the unconscious".

Hence the following logic can be reconstructed. Sexuality is a natural drive, which gives pleasure on the level of the body and the unconscious. Culture (the way of upbringing) suppresses sexuality, binding it to marriage. In order to "receive and give pleasure" it is enough to let "the body act". There is no necessity to teach a woman about sex. Nevertheless men and relationships suffer from the lack of experience. The learning process is necessary to free sexuality. As opposed to natural and bodily characteristics of the partner, love is tied to his personal characteristics, and "should not be confused with sex".

The separation of sex from love is described as "decision making": "I decided not to confuse sex and love, that is, not to make the mistake, which women usually make. Men never confuse them". Thus the informant distinguishes herself from *other* "genetic" women. *Otherness* helps her to justify sexual pleasure as an autonomous sphere. She compares herself with *others* – with her youth, her parents, those women "who confuse sex and love", and with those who suppress their sexuality (both women and men). Therefore the main distinction is made between those "who suppress their sexuality" and those "who release it". It was necessary for her to make the decision to "free" her sexuality and to separate sex from love ("as men do"). "The natural expression of sexuality" implicitly becomes a cultural construction. She represents her contemporary sexual behaviour as an active decision and a choice in process. This makes sex into "an art".

There are some conclusions to be made from these two cases. The interpretation of sex as pleasure includes the following opposition: on the one hand, sex is not in accordance with upbringing and education, where it is tied exclusively to marriage. Sex is separated from marriage. On the other hand, sex is separated from love. The feelings which are necessary for having sex, are different from love. Love could emerge from such feelings and from sex, but for sex it is enough to attract and to be attracted. It is important to like one's own and the partner's body, but many more characteristics are required ("common interests", "intimacy", "intelligence", etc.) in order to fall in love.

In both cases the development of sexuality is emphasised. In the first case (M) sexuality is explicitly tied to the learning process, in the second case (S) sexuality is implicitly learned in order to release "suppressed sexuality". Sexual relationships oriented towards autonomous sexual pleasure are connected with knowledge, and experience. In both cases receiving pleasure from sex includes a separation from certain categories of women, that is, a construction of *otherness*. In the first case the construction is based in a turn from a position of pupil to teacher. In the second case male categorisation of sexual relationships (the separation of sex from love) is internalised. The construction of *other* women takes place in both cases. "Other women" have generally no sexual experience and/or are sexually repressed. However, simultaneously the informants ascribe themselves as having "typical female characteristics", as wanting to be liked, to love and to be loved. Thus woman as a category becomes differentiated.

Case 3. "Sexuality as a quest". T, 27 years old

"A young man or woman is looking for their own style, trying to understand what is more suitable."

During her first marriage T was unfaithful and is now married for the second time. Between the marriages she had different steady and casual sexual relations. Her understanding of sexuality can be described as "sex in a happy marriage" or sex as "obedience to sexual hunger". In her descriptions of her sexual relationships the following types of relations can be noticed: love, marriage, passion, and casual sexual contacts. The main frame of reference here is her happy second marriage and the relationship with her second husband (combination of love, marriage and sex as pleasure). All other sexual experiences are compared to the second marriage.

Parental education represents the first frame of reference. Education is characterised in a double sense. "My mother told me about it (sexual experience) in a negative sense... A woman should take care of herself". This meant that she was responsible for her own sexual satisfaction – a man does not care about this. The next frame of reference is the first experience of sexual intercourse. She lost her virginity with her first husband. She had felt no sexual desire and no previous sexual experience. Her husband is also depicted as an inexperienced person, and the sexual contacts within the marriage are described as rare and unsatisfactory. "I don't know what was the reason – either his (quiet) temperament or our inexperience". Her understanding of sexuality includes two dimensions: the "natural" one (passionate temperament is the opposite of the quiet one), and the cultural or "educational" one. She describes the experience of infidelity during the last period of her first marriage and evaluates it as "normal": "I didn't think I did anything bad to anybody". This marriage was generally unsatisfactory. She had had the intention of having only one partner for her whole life, but the choice of partner was wrong and therefore sex was separated from marriage.

The main frame of reference is her second marriage. This is the relationship of love and passion. It is also depicted as belonging and male responsibility: "He gives me a lot, he gives me happiness and the feeling of being loved". The husband is also responsible for her bodily image: "He has changed my attitude to my body, he continuously reminds me that I am a very beautiful woman... He respects and admires me... He always tries to satisfy me". Compared to the first marriage, her current sense of belonging has resulted in negative attitudes toward adultery. She applies the category of sexual experience to describe her present relations. They both have a rich experience, which gives them the opportunity to "be attentive to sexual relations, to discuss them". Thus sexual experience and male responsibility in the relationship serve as the basis for the interpretation of sex as pleasure.

The comparison between the two husbands includes such parameters as attitude to the body, ability to speak about sex, presence of sexual experience and sexual desire, possibility of adultery. Implicitly the qualities of personal relations are compared when the man is responsible for respect and for love. Sexual and personal dimensions are distinguished in the description of sex relationships.

T mentions that she had multiple partners between her marriages. The reason was twofold. First, "I was miserable and missed the attention". Secondly, "I didn't find my identity before my (first) marriage". Thus, having multiple partners where sex is separated from love and marriage is recognised as permissible for the adolescent when experience is searched for. "A young man or woman is looking for their own style, trying to understand what is more suitable." This "search" is the opposite of the informant's previous assumption "to have only one man for life". The separation of sex and love for her has another reason. She also describes sex as the "satisfaction of hunger" and as "sport". Between the marriages she considered sex as "if you are hungry – you can have sex". Now she thinks that the only reason for sex is love. Therefore she re-evaluates her previous opinions. "This was a necessity of love. I was looking for love". Now she, however, gives a negative view of her behaviour between the marriages. "I would refuse all sexual contacts with pleasure in order to belong to only one partner – my husband". "I was crazy at that time". The question occurs – how to obtain experience in a situation where one belongs to only one person? There are two possibilities: either to obtain it before (when multiple partners are permissible) or to make the man responsible for providing experience and teaching his partner.

Thus sex as separate from love and marriage is justifiable under certain conditions. It is permissible at a certain age and status for those who have no experience, and for the satisfaction of sexual appetite. The frame of reference for such a separation is a happy marriage (with love and sexual satisfaction). Sexual experience is necessary, but it should be obtained in youth. At an older age feelings become the basis for sexual relations.

T's case shows that there is no necessity for creating a new gender identity if there are no discrepancies between sex, love and marriage, if autonomous sex is limited to a certain (age) period, if a man is responsible for sexual satisfaction, and if relations with him are described as "belonging". At the same time the quality of sexual relations depends on the experience of both partners, an experience that should be obtained in youth. The main distinction is made between those "who have experience" and those "who have not". It is possible to separate sex from love in order to obtain experience. The cultural construction of sexuality includes skills and abilities for which mainly the man is responsible.

Conclusion

Sexual relationships, oriented towards autonomous sexual pleasure are, according to the three cases (M, S, and T), connected to status, age, knowledge, and experience. At the same time they prefer sex as tied with love and one partner. The most preferable type of sex is a combination of love and pleasure as opposed to marriage (pronatal script), which represents a denial of sex as pleasure.

Sex can be separated from love, but the conditions for this differ. The main condition is experience: all cases represent sexuality as a process which is learned during the course of life through experience. Parental education and relations with husbands and steady partners are the frame of reference for the construction of sexuality. Ideas in youth on sexuality are reproduced according to its contemporary concept. Categorisation of different relationships creates different meanings and binds them together.

There are differences between the cases in the interpretation of sex as pleasure. These are connected to different stages of life. In the first case (M), experience comes with age and makes it possible to realise sexuality autonomously. In the second case (S), experience is necessary to release "natural" sexuality. In the third case (T) experience should be obtained while young.

Those informants who regard sex as an autonomous sphere and take personal responsibility for it, reflect upon the formation of their identity in comparison with *other* women. Those who consider autonomous sex permissible in a certain age, have no need to interpret themselves in comparison with other women. They compare themselves only with their own previous experience.

Finally a remark on the methodology of social constructionism and its limitations in the research of sexuality. In analysing the meanings of sexuality, the dichotomy between "realists" and "constructionist"[10] does not exist. It does not matter, whether the sexual practices are "real" or not, because they are significant for the informants in their construction of certain meanings of sex and in justifying them. Interpretations of sexual behaviour, the analysis of which is my primary task, are cultural constructs. One can find the learning processes in the background even when sexuality is referred to as "natural expression". Besides this the reconstruction of gendered stereotypes demonstrate the construction of sexuality as a cultural process.

Notes:

[1] J.H. Gagnon and W. Simon, Sexual Conduct (Aldine, 1973); J. Weeks, 'Sexual Values Revisited' in L. Segal (ed.) *New Sexual Agendas* (Macmillan Press, 1997); J. Weeks, 'History, Desire and Identities', in R. Parker and J. Gagnon (eds.) *Conceiving Sexuality. Approaches to Sex Research in a Postmodern World* (New York: Routledge, 1995).

[2] J. Gagnon, 'The Explicit and Implicit Use of the Scripting Perspective in Sex Research', In J. Bancroft (ed), *Annual Review of Sex Research.* , vol. 1 (1990).

[3] E. Laumann, J. Gagnon, R. Michael and S. Michael (1994), *The Social Organization of Sexuality. Sexual Practices in the United States.* (Chicago: The University of Chicago Press, 1994), p.4.

[4] For example, M. Hynie, Y. Lydon, S. Cote and S. Wiener, 'Relational Sexual Scripts and Women Condom Use: The Importance of Internalized Norms', *The Journal of Sex Research,* vol.35. no. 4 (1998), pp. 370–380.

[5] For example, L. Carpenter, 'From Girls into Women: Script for Sexuality and Romance in *Seventeen* Magazine', *The Journal of Sex Research,* vol. 35, no. 2 (1998), pp. 158–168.

[6] D. Silverman, *Interpreting Qualitative Data. Methods for Analysing Talk, Test and Interaction* (London: Sage Publications, 1997).

[7] A. Giddens, *The Transformation of Intimacy. Sexuality, Love and Eroticism in Modern Societies* (Stanford: Stanford University Press, 1992).

[8] Certain similarities with intimacy in the terms of Giddens could be found.

[9] A.Temkina, 'Dinamika tsenariev seksual'nosti v avtobigrafiiakh sovremennykh rossiiskikh zhenshchin: opyt konstruktivistskogo issledovania seksual'nogo udovol'stviia', in A. Kletsin (ed). *Gendernye tetradi,* vol. 2 (1999).

[10] See for discussion, for example, D. Bertaux and M. Kohli, 'The Life Story Approach: A Continental View', *Annual Review of Sociology,* vol. 10, pp. 215–237 (1984).

A Cultural Paradigm of Sexual Violence Reconstructed from a Woman's Biographical Interview

Elena Zdravomyslova

Introduction

The research presented here on sexual biographies of Russian women of three generations is based on 25 interviews with middle class women from St. Petersburg during the period of 1997–1998. By middle class I mean people with higher education. These life-stories give a great deal of material for analysis of Russian gender relations, including sexual relations. One of the topics covered in the study is that of sexual violence and abuse experienced by women. The issue of sexual violence is extremely private and sensitive, and women narrate it with certain constraint even when the incidents are quite distant in time. The purpose of this paper is to analyse one frame of sexual violence – the one where a woman is not actually raped but beaten by a man when she refused to have sex with him. The framing of the incident of sexual violence in the interview refers to the cultural paradigm of violence. The cultural paradigm is the pattern embedded in common everyday practices and meanings, and reproduced regularly in social settings. The cultural paradigm is reconstructed from the framing of the incident in the narrative and contains messages on the following issues: the context conducive to a certain sexual violence case; the actors during the incident of sexual violence; the rules of the game reconstructed during the incident of sexual violence; moral statement on the experience.

The text will proceed in the following way. First, I will provide a short discussion of the biographical research in Russia and make certain statements that will help to situate this research on sexuality (and sexual violence) in a general context. Second, I will concentrate on the sociological version of the text analysis that was used in the study. Third, I will turn to the narrative itself and try to show what conclusions were made from the analysis of the narrative. Fourth, I will present the analysis of different sections of the narrative.

Methodological Retreat. The Socio-Biographical discursive situation in contemporary Russia

The Socio-Biographical discursive situation is a term which is used here to describe the discursive practices of life-story telling or reports on individual lives now common in Russian society. It is important to take into account that different periods in history are characterised by different patterns of life stories and thus provide different contexts for the life-story research. There are periods when individual life-stories of ordinary people are kept in private diaries and do not enter public discussion, and periods when they are written and kept in files for future generations. There are other periods when biographies and life-stories attract massive public attention, showing shifts in identity construction. In different periods different topics are tabooed in the life-stories. The reasons for inhibitions on reporting certain events are both individual and cultural-temporal. We do not, for example, expect to find vivid pictures of sexual life, contraception and venereal diseases in 19th century autobiographies, though there can be certain exceptions. However, in contemporary coherent autobiography and life-story the issues of sexuality are seldom abandoned. One possible explanation for this can be the inclusion of sexuality in public discourse (media, culture). I am not going to elaborate on this idea here, but it should be discussed at length elsewhere. However, I consider identification of the biographical discursive context to be an important methodological assumption for the biographical research one carries out.

If we identify a biographical discursive context (or situation) we can expect a certain level of authenticity of the individual life-story, on the one hand, and a certain level of representativeness of the life-story for the culture it comes from, on the other hand. Here authenticity does not mean truth, but rather adequacy of a narrative in reference to the frames and categories used by the informant in his/her identity construction as presented in the life-story. Knowing the features of the biographical discursive context we can also expect both methodological opportunities and barriers for research. Thus, for example, if we know that people consider financial issues to be a confidential topic and these issues are of interest for a researcher, we should develop research techniques that will enable us to enter this secret segment of life. A feminist researcher (as I identify myself) should be sensitive to the discursive context of research.[1] Discursive context should be taken into account as it has at least a three-fold consequence: it influences research design, frames the research situation, and gives a clue to the preferred interpretation of raw data.

The idea of the changing role of biography in the broad social context is developed by Anthony Giddens in his work *Modernity and Identity* (1991). Giddens claims that modernisation is a period of biographisation of society when individuals as agents construct their lives within the frames settled by social structures. This general statement on biographisation of society should be specified for different cultures and societies. Thus the purpose of this methodological introduction is to identify discursive contexts of my research and to understand how they influence my study. I distinguish here three dimensions of discursive context: first, the revival of initiative biographical work in the Russian transition; second, the Soviet biographical legacy; third, the openness of the discourse of sexuality. I will now clarify what I mean by each of these aspects and consider their possible impact on the study.

Context 1. Revival of initiative biographical work in the Russian transition

The breakdown of the Soviet society and the emerging opportunities and barriers caused by the Russian reforms in the last decade brought about the phenomenon which is referred to as identity crisis.[2] Former Soviet identifications often do not work in a current context – the borders of states, the political configuration, the stratification design of society is undergoing change. These changes demand active reflexive work of post-Soviet citizens who are looking for their identities – new and old. The revival of old identifications – class, ethnic, gender, political – and the establishment of new ones are typical features of the transitory intellectual climate in Russia. Using the term of Fischer-Rosenthal,[3] this kind of identity search can be labelled as biographical work. In the course of this intensive biographical work new emerging social agents – individuals and groups – not only invent their own life-stories, but biographical work becomes part of their identity construction and a pivot of their copying strategies through which they clarify their potential assets in structuring their lives (life-worlds).The indicators of such biographical initiative work are numerous. To mention only a few: growth of the publication of life-stories, biographies, memoirs of the leaders of mass opinion and members of elite groups, genealogical search for the families of origin in which thousands of citizens are involved, formations of oral history collections of different milieus, competitions of autobiographies, urban renaming campaigns, etc. Biographical social research with its interest in life-stories is just a small part of this flow.

Mass initiative biographical work gives the biographical research situation a specific blend. It has both positive and negative influence on the study. On the one hand, interest in self-identity construction, which is substituting memory-blocking of Soviet copying strategies, makes people eager to share their self-understandings and self-constructions. The intellectual atmosphere of voicing identities is favourable for a biographical researcher who can expect willingness and openness from informants and their emotional involvement in the study. However, the same context can have a negative effect on the study, or at least make the research situation more difficult. Cathartic involvement in biographical work, being a part and parcel of an individual's copying strategy in the situation of social instability, makes a narrator very sensitive to the professional biographical research. An informant may believe that a sociologist is a political intruder in his/her private life, and could very well misinterpret it. Because of the fact that informants carry out autobiographical research themselves, they are very carefully following professional interpretations that could be damaging for their self-identity construction and that could be a misfit for their self-interpretations. Agent-constructors of their biographies see themselves as biographical experts, they expect respect for their self-reflections and are ready to oppose our judgements. Such research situation claims for specific research design and specific interview techniques. Not only anonymity and confidentiality should be guaranteed (which is normal in most studies), but it is important to share with informants the ideology and the concept of research. It is important to make the study interactive and to convert an interview into a dialogue of two partners. In certain cases it is also necessary to present the research results in the presence of the informants and to consider their agreements/disagreements.

These simple rules of research are necessary to follow, if one does not want to ruin not only his/her research field but also his/her professional reputation. In my case I deliberately tried to take into account this discursive context by addressing in the research of sexual violence only persons whom I knew personally from before (advice of Anna Rotkirch), actually women whose story of sexual violence and harassment I already knew. This choice of informants gave me the opportunity to discuss the topics, which are often taboo in the life-story interview. Another technical device was to initiate the issue of violence in the last part of the interview and to carry out an interview in the interactive fashion that is sharing experiences.

Context 2. Soviet biographical legacy

Soviet rules of the game still influence our everyday lives, our attitudes and communicative expectations. They have an impact on our professional settings. The Soviet legacy in biographical research can be considered two-fold. On the one hand, the Soviet system blocked initiative biographical work. A great number of experiences had to be eliminated from individual and collective memory: these blockages were part of copying strategies adapted by individuals and groups. People preferred to keep silent or just to forget not only certain personal experiences but those of their families as well. Certain memories were not only psychologically harmful – as is always the case with human beings – but they could be dangerous for their life-strategies. In the

Soviet era people were not openly engaged in the search for their roots and certain stories were concealed from younger generations in order to make their life smoother and less traumatic. People changed their family names so as not to be identified as Jews or Germans or Finns, they forgot or did not know if they had kulak, upper class or White Guard ancestors. It was safer to live with an individual biography, to a be a Soviet orphan, a *mankurt* (a person without memory) as the Soviet writer Chingiz Aitmatov put it in his utopia. This is one part of the Soviet legacy.

The other side of the same coin is the official biographical formulas that were designed by the Soviet bureaucracy and filled in by Soviet citizens hundreds of times in their lives. People were obliged to fill in extremely detailed questionnaires, which covered not only multiple aspects of an individual's public and private life, but also those of his/her close relatives, descendants and ancestors. On multiple occasions Soviet citizens provided detailed information on official biographical formulas – in the medical offices, in educational institutions, in the work places, etc. These records, put in archives as personnel files were attainable from the KGB and used in career promotion or prohibition. In the course of this official biographical work, Soviet citizens did their best to construct politically correct biographies that fitted the demands of the party-state ideology.

These official formulas can be understood as imposed life-stories, which the informants used in their public self-presentations. Such self-presentations became part and parcel of the Soviet double self-identity. For the inner circle of friends and family individuals had other, "true" stories, less selective and less politically correct. However, for the purposes of self-preservation people sometimes stayed loyal to their official life-story even in private. Soviet formal biographical work was obviously a part of the social control and self-censorship system.[4]

The influence of such a legacy on the contemporary biographical research situation is severe.[5] The Soviet sociologists, equipped with questionnaires validated by the CPSU departments, were seen as interrogators who implemented official biographical work. People provided them with the imposed life-stories developed for official occasions. Thus a sociologist has still today to invest a lot of energy if s/he wants to get an authentic life-story from an informant. Any narrator has at least two, but in fact multiple stories at his/her disposal – one for official purposes, another for trustworthy people.[6] To take into account such a legacy emphasises the importance to build up a basic trust as the ground for interaction between researcher and informant. This trust will make authenticity of the story more plausible. However, this trust is always an extremely fragile attitude. Let me consider some of the techniques for building trust in a research situation.

I believe that the warming up part of the interview should be expanded compared to established interview practice. A researcher has to share his/her understanding of a research problem with the informant. It is necessary to build bridges between the two agents of interaction, bridges that could challenge the inevitable hierarchy of the interview situation. To discover a variety of common grounds, as for example gender, the same political platform, the same generational experiences and ethnicity, is important. Some sort of commonality is a necessary part of the dialogue in the research situation. I would like to emphasise that the demand to organise interactive interview situations is a methodological consequence of the Soviet legacy in biographical work. In addition it is necessary to combine the biographical interview with participant observation. This can take a long time because a researcher has to surpass boundaries of exclusion. I strove in my research to take this into account and presented myself as a feminist researcher on sexuality. I had mostly been acquainted for a longer time with my informants, and therefore I used feminist research as a framework that enabled me to bring attention to the topics of risks and disadvantages for women in everyday life.

And the last remark: a biographical boom is characteristic for the contemporary Russian discursive situation. This boom takes the form of numerous TV talk shows; wide publication and discussion of biographies, memoirs and personal notes; competition of biographies stimulated by for example social scientists; families engaged in genealogical search etc. The boom is a part of the transformation of identity, which means that the discursive context is favourable for research on biography. On the other hand, the same context creates certain research problems: people being both widely interested in research studies and personally engaged in the construction of biography make them extremely sensitive to interpretations.

Context 3. Discursive context of research on sexuality

Research on sexuality is a specific issue which until recently has been taboo in Russian public discussion. Today it is very topical – a terrain of discovery. Very often people verbalise their sexual experiences openly for the first time, and though this happens only to the interviewer it is nevertheless not easy. Because Russian feminists and media in general have been concerned with issues connected to sexual violence, it has become possible to discuss them more openly. The life-story method appeared to be very suitable for the study of sexuality. When informants narrate their experiences, they select from the memory banks those life events, which they consider relevant for the presentation requested by an interviewer. In the interviews emotional emphases appear in vivid colours and are attached to those pieces of the story which are seen as important for one's identity. However, sexual violence in one's life-story is often a taboo. Usually informants do not tell about violence without being prompted to do so. Every request to tell about sexual violence or abuse resulted, however, in several narratives. The biographical interviews that we collected are filled with different stories of sexual violence and abuse, including domestic violence, street hooliganism, rape, beatings, etc. These stories inform about the normalcy of violent incidents in women's experiences. When these traumatic memories are articulated in the interview they are charged with emotion and thus difficult to narrate.

The Cultural Paradigm of Sexual Violence

I believe that by means of discursive analysis it is possible to identify cultural paradigms of sexual violence in contemporary Russian society. The concept of cultural paradigm is borrowed from Irina Paperno's research on suicide as a cultural institution in 19th century Russian society.[7] She based her work on the ideas of Yuri Lotman. Cultural paradigm is a script that makes the event understandable, an event that is justified and rationalised. Irina Paperno considers stories of famous suicides as units of meaning. Cultural paradigm embraces certain types of circumstances conducive to suicide, certain types of persons or identities that are vulnerable to suicide. She understands cultural paradigm as a more or less stable construction that is reproduced and reformulated in other contexts. She describes, for example, the paradigmatic suicide of Socrates in the following syllogism: Socrates is immortal, Socrates committed suicide, thus suicides are immortal. Deliberate death is seen as the action of an immortal soul.[8] In a similar fashion I am looking for paradigmatic cases of sexual violence against women. My data material differs, however, substantially from the one used by Paperno. I look for paradigmatic cases of sexual violence in life-stories of ordinary people. However, it is precisely the commonality of experiences that makes them paradigmatic.

This article aims at the reconstruction of one paradigmatic script of sexual violence. The story of violence is understood as a meaningful, coherent piece of presentation that has its own narrative logic: a prelude, the story per se and a finale. The following issues give a picture of the logistics of the violence story: the narrator's self-presentation, i.e. a person who became the object of sexual violence; the context of the story; the sequence of events that resulted in the violent incident; presentation of the abuser; the justification where the responsibility for the sexual violence is ascribed; and interpretation of the case.

In reconstructing a cultural paradigm of sexual violence I use a technique of text analysis which is called MCD (Membership Categorisation Device) developed by H. Sacks and A. Schutze.[9] According to this method the text is by different criteria divided into macro-sequences: authentic sequences that are provided by a narrator and/or authorised sequences in accordance with the topics that are of interest to the researcher. Each macro-sequence is analysed as a shorter narrative with a specific topic. The macro-sequence is thereafter divided into meaningful fragments based on a certain category. It is important to identify category-bound activities deriving them either from the text or from supplementary sources. Thus, such behavioural patterns are reconstructed, which are commonly ascribed to identities, actions or rules of the game that the narrator refers to and make the story understandable and interaction accountable. After that it is necessary to identify standardised pairs of related categories.

This method is based on the conviction that each statement or category of the narrative involves certain intentional or unintentional assessment, which refers to value conventions of the narrator, and therefore making the text accountable.These assessments or justifications, if identified, can help to reconstruct potentially shared meanings of the narrator's community. A configuration of such meanings combined with the logic of the incidents are conceived as a cultural pattern or a cultural paradigm. This method shows how a narrative description works as a socially organised activity. The following is the story of sexual abuse and violence from the interview with Olga, born in 1960.

Olga's story

I: Did someone ever try to rape you?

O. Yes, yes. I have one very unpleasant story. There was no sex but the situation was rather strange. I have to start from the beginning when I was in the South at summer camp.

I: Tell me how old you were.

O: 21 years old, probably. I was at this sport camp. The camp was situated in a small village (in the mountains near the sea), so I knew all the village people who often came to the camp. We were always told not to have any relationships with the locals there as there were a lot of stories. I always told the girls not to go anywhere with them even though they seemed to be such nice guys. They'd give you something to eat and to drink, but they would always push for sex. And every time there were situations when the girls got beaten up, or something like that happened periodically, let's say twice per season, it would happen where someone had agreed to go out with them... Of course there were romances with the locals. So there was one guy over there who liked me. Every time we met, he would ask if everything was OK., if any of the locals had bothered me, and if anything happened to tell him, because people were different. He brought me fruit from his garden, just cared about me all the season, and every time we met he asked if something was worrying me, or bothered me. At the end of the training season he came up to me, – I was there with my friend, – and said: you know, tomorrow my friend with whom I was together in the military service comes here in his car, so let's go together with Larisa to some river in the mountains, have a picnic, sit there, talk and then come back. So I was listening to him even nodding my head, and I was thinking at the same time that if it were not him, not Ruslan, whom I knew so well, who has always been so good to me, I wouldn't even talk about it. But because there were so many signs of attention and good feeling I didn't feel that it was right to say "no" straight away. So when we finished talking, he said: so, we are coming tomorrow to pick you up. I came up to Larisa and said: Ruslan offered to go, but let's not go. Tomorrow when they come we'll say that we don't feel well, and won't go. They didn't come next evening. And on our last day there, we had to leave the next morning, and in the afternoon Ruslan, that local guy, came and invited us to come to his place. He said that his friend hadn't come at the agreed time, but now he invited me, my friend, another girl, a few other guys, so all this company was invited to come. We were eating-drinking, had lunch and came back to the camp. In half an hour he came back, saying that his friend had managed to come, maybe we could go now, and there were our friends, the wrestlers, who came up to us and said: Olga, go with them, they are nice guys; go with them to the mountains, there's nothing wrong in it. It was 2 p.m., and the whole situation seemed to be quite safe. So as we were there at that time – Larisa came right from the beach in her swimming suit and robe, and I was in sports wear, we sat in their car and left. He said that there was a mountain river nearby, but first we needed to go to the shop to buy something to eat and drink, then to the market place, to buy some fruit, and then we'd go to the river. First we went to the wine shop. I didn't like it that they were speaking in their mother language between themselves, as we didn't understand a word. And when we got to the wine shop and I saw how much alcohol they bought I understood that we were in trouble - they got a box full of wine. Then we bought fruit and food and came to that river. We were drinking, but I was not getting drunk, and I felt in danger. We had one glass of wine after another, the kind of wine I liked, but I didn't want to drink and I was not getting drunk or relaxed; I only got a headache. And they were pouring wine into big glasses and making toasts, and every time we were supposed to drink it all down.

I: Of course, there is such a drinking tradition for men, but not for women.

O: Yes, you have to. That friend of mine – I felt she understood nothing, she was having fun, and she looked at me asking what was wrong with me. And I was thinking how to get out of this. We couldn't leave without a car. It was hot over there, we had lots of food, and we were tired of those men, so I began to talk about going home. They said - look, so much food and wine left and the sun is still up, let's go swimming, and then we can continue. And then they said, let's go to the bar at the closest small town. We couldn't go there without changing our clothes, so I grabbed a hold of this thought. Let's go, let's go! They had to take us back to the camp where I could ask our guys to tell those men that we weren't going anywhere with them, and tomorrow we had to leave anyway. So I said, yes, yes, let's go to the bar; I even relaxed a bit, and I thought that everything was fine now. We got into the car, we sang songs, I felt that it was passing over, 'cause the main thing was to get home. And suddenly the car made a turn. We were on the road where they had to go straight, but they were turning away; they said that they were going to the beach to spend some more time there. I thought – oh, my God. So we got out of the car, took out the wine and fruit. Larisa went somewhere with Ruslan. First, because she wasn't a very smart girl, and second, she wasn't in touch with the reality. I stayed with Ruslan's Army friend. First, we sat and had a talk. He told me about his wife, that he had studied in Leningrad, where he had liked to go out there, so, it was OK. And then he said to me – let's make love. I tried to joke about it, and said "no". And suddenly he hit me in the face. I was so shocked, I couldn't even understand what's going on. I remember he was saying – something like he wanted me so much, but at the same time he didn't do anything, he didn't try to undress me, nothing, but was beating me. He beat me just to make me say that "yes, I want it, too". He said something like – "let's just do it fast, then we'll forget everything about it, it's nothing for you, why are you torturing me, I want you so much". He began to undress and I saw that he was not aroused and I didn't understand what he wanted from me. Later, when I thought about it, I was amazed at why I didn't resist him, why I only looked at him, saying that I didn't want it and I was not going to, didn't try to hit him or push him back. Because he didn't do anything. He beat me up all through that time. And on the other hand, I had this thought all the time, what if I'd said "yes", what was he going to do with me then, he was not sexually aroused...(Ha-ha-ha!). I didn't understand what he wanted from me. But then I became really scared.

I: But you didn't say "yes".

O: I didn't say "yes", and I continued to say "no". Then, you know, he took the bottle and broke it. And I got so scared but on the other hand, I was thinking that I should've done it from the very beginning, why was I letting him beat me. He kicked me, I was all dirty. My face was all bruised after it. I was so shocked, so passive. When I was a child I was always fighting, and here I did nothing. He wasn't a big man. When he broke that bottle I got so afraid, that I was ready to say "yes". And then Ruslan came with Larisa. He looked on it all with horror. Larisa began to scream – what happened?! And I just began to cry. Wasn't able to say even a word. Ruslan said – get into the car, he sat in the driver's seat, even though it wasn't his car. I said that I didn't want to leave Larisa alone, he said I need not worry. He took me to the camp. On the way back I didn't see that my face was bruised, but I saw that I was all dirty. I got into my room which I was sharing with a girl, didn't talk to anyone, just lay down on my bed. That girl saw me and went out to get the wrestler guys who had told me to go with those men. There were similar cases before, but in those cases it was possible to say that it was the fault of those girls who agreed to go to some restaurant, so they gave those men a reason. In my case they decided to call the militia. It was a very unpleasant story. The militia came and began to ask me why that man hadn't raped me after all. I tried to

> explain. He asked if this guy had tried to undress me. I said, "no, he just beat me up". The militia asked why I thought then that he wanted to rape me, because it looked as if he didn't. There was the camp director who screamed at me that I was a hooker, because I went out with someone I didn't know and after it all even called the militia. But even those locals were mostly on my side, one of the locals came up to me and said that he thought that I had a good reputation with them, and he apologised that it all happened like that. It was our last night in the camp and everyone was concerned for me. I stayed in a separate room and there was one guy – we weren't even friends – who spent all night sitting there next to me. I was so shocked that I wasn't really able to talk about anything else but what had happened. So all the night I was telling him about it. In the morning we left and that was the end of the story.

Macro-sequence I – Prelude

I divide the narrative into several macro-sequences. Each of them describes aspects of a certain cluster of conditions that made the violent story possible.

In this part the context of the story is presented in its specified time, a space dimension. The action takes place in the seasonal sports' training camp in the Southern resort area where a group of young sports people live independent of their families. They had visited the place before. This training season was the third or fourth. The story takes place in the summer of 1980. The narrator, Olga, gives the background to the violent incident. She identifies the context of communication with the local village residents. The local population is presented as a community of young men. Although women obviously lived there, they were not once mentioned in the story.

Olga formulates the security rules for women in this environment. She speaks of herself as an experienced young woman who is knowledgeable of the risks of sexual abuse – she refers to multiple cases of sexual abuse and rape experienced by women who did not follow the security rules. The knowledge of the frequency of sexual violence in this area is structurally important for her story. She refers to it emphatically. She calls the victims of abuse *silly women* whose behaviour was provocative as they did not follow the security rules.

Local men are presented as dangerous strangers, and the camp differs from the local community in that no credit is given to the locals. The security rules are presented in the story as common knowledge, shared by everyone, including the narrator herself. The basic safety rules for women are: *do not trust local men, avoid contact with them.* The category of (mis)trust is central in the description of the communicative patterns between the locals and the sportswomen.

Another category of the Prelude is presentation of the narrator's self. Olga constructs herself as a reasonable young woman. She is a sportswoman, she knows the safety rules and follows them consciously. She places herself in opposition to those foolish women who did not follow the rules, who provoked sexual abuse and thus got into trouble and were raped. Olga is not only "a good girl" but she also represents herself as a *different* woman – a woman capable of developing friendly, non-erotic relationships with men. She describes her status in the company of friends, the wrestlers, as their comrade. Her reputation, she imagines, helps her also to develop specific contacts with certain local men. She presents these contacts as exceptional, based on concern and respect.

Another character presented in the Prelude is the local man, Ruslan (R). This character is functionally very important for the story. He is the one who brings Olga to the scene of violence. I call him a mediator. Olga gives several justifications that aim to convince herself and the interviewer that she had enough reasons to trust R. Let's see how she argues for a trustful relationship with a local man in order to justify her violation of the known safety rules.

Olga presents R as exceptional among local men. He treated Olga in a special way – he was bridging the gap between herself and other local men. Olga names the strategies used by him to create trust: there was a long-term friendly relationship between them, and he brought small presents from his garden (the presumption is that he did not spend money on those presents, which gave them a non-interested character). Another argument that convinced her of R's trustworthiness was his good reputation among Olga's male friends, the wrestlers. They convinced Olga that the man was reliable, that there was no risk to communicate with him and that she could be safe with him. The picnic party with R, planned to take place by the end of the training period, seemed thus quite safe to Olga. The fact that she was invited with her friend Larisa (not alone) and in the daytime (not at night or late evening) convinced her of the secure setting of the forthcoming adventure. Thus Olga's actions can be justified: once the trustful communication was established there were good reasons to break the common cautions and rules for women's safety. Olga established her trust in a basic attitude of communication with R, based on a traditional gender configuration – she saw him as her safeguard and his respectful attitude was a guarantee for her safety. Thus she constructed herself as an object of a man's concern and admiration.

Macro-sequence 2 – the picnic invitation

The core of this sequence is the description of the picnic invitation. R invites Olga and her friend Larisa to a picnic party organised because of the visit of his Army friend. The invitation is an *occasion of choice*: Olga is free to decide whether to accept it or not. In retrospect she realises that it was her own choice that put her in a potential situation of sexual violence. By creating justifications for her actions she reconstructs the arguments that brought her to the decision to participate, and its consequences. In this sequence Olga presents other features of her *self identity*. She describes herself as a *relational woman,* that is a woman who is oriented towards trustful communication and does her best to sustain such communication. She is afraid that her distrust may offend the person who makes the invitation. So, when she gets invited she does not immediately reject it but leaves it for further consideration. Such *relationalism* is the pivot of her self-presentation in the whole life-story. While making the choice, Olga has to choose between two sets of rules that organise her conduct – rules of relation-orientedness and rules of security. Olga gives another supportive argument in acceptance of the invitation: she recollects the *rehearsal,* the sequence where she describes her visit to R's place with her wrestler-friends and the disastrous picnic with the expected friend of R.

The first two macro-sequences form together the exposition of the story of violence. Their main message is that Olga's understanding of proper behaviour under the given circumstances is bifurcated. Olga presents herself as an adherent of two contradicting groups of rules: safety rules for women and rules of trusting relationships. She is a reasonable person that follows the rules of safety for women, and if she makes any exceptions she has sufficient reasons, which are supposed to guarantee her safety. The feeling of trust in communication with R is supported by different arguments that justify Olga's decision to go on a picnic.

Macro-sequence 3 – the picnic: a story of violence

The violence story starts with the introduction of the abuser. He is presented as the *Army Friend (*AF) of R, the mediator, a trusted person. The naming of a person as an AF (Olga never calls him by name) is a category that connotes with certain credentials of trust. In this piece Olga implicitly refers to the mythology of male friendship that was formed during conscription – relations where true masculinity is learned and tested. According to the shared social patterns AF should be considered as positive and trustworthy as R himself. AF is Ruslan's *alter ego*, because the military service is conceived as a crucial institution of masculine socialisation. Friendship between men created as homosocial communication during the conscription period is considered as a sacred value of true masculinity. Respect for the relationship and obligations of men's friendship are shared by both men and women. The category-bound activities implied by the term – the Army friend – made him similar to R with whom he shared difficult and crucial experiences in a formative age. It is assumed that mutual support and help was the basis of their relationship. According to this implied logic the attitude of trust, the feeling of security in the relationship with R could thus be transferred to his AF. It is presumed also that army friendship has its own customs and rituals. The narrative does not give us a description of these rituals but refers to them, and they can be reconstructed from other sources. Army friends can meet more or less regularly, remember the common past and talk of the present. Usually women are excluded as partners in these traditional rituals. They can, however, be included as exchange gifts[10] or decoration. Exclusively male rituals reconstruct the traditional image of women as sexual or at least as objects of entertainment. The presentation of the abuser as R's Army Friend is a sufficient argument for Olga to accept the picnic invitation. Olga motivates her agreement by her unwillingness to break the relationship of trust, which has a fundamental value for her. This motivation is supported by her self-image as a relational woman, abiding by safety rules.

Let's return to the story. AF comes to visit R from some distant place where he permanently lives. For R this is a special occasion to show his hospitality. The main category of reconstruction in this connection is the *picnic as a celebration of men's friendship*. R was responsible for the party. He wanted to make it as splendid as possible, to make it really memorable. To make this happen he chose the "conventional" picnic in the picturesque mountains by the sea decorated by two beautiful and nice women as the party setting. When Olga and her friend Larisa accepted the invitation, they symbolically agreed to follow the rules of the picnic as a celebration of male friendship. The presumed rules of the celebration of this friendship ascribe certain *roles for women at the party*. The rules are traditional: women are expected to play their roles as decorations, muses of amusement and entertainment, to be sexual objects and gifts in the communicative exchange between men. The way Olga presents this situation leaves no doubt about young women's subconscious perception of this role division as normal and acceptance of it. Men have good reasons for interpreting the acceptance of the invitation as a success in their script of seduction. Being precious gifts women are seduced by the car trip, fruits, beautiful mountain landscape and friendly communication with the men. Olga's story shows that she is conscious of being a part of the gift for the friend – an object of admiration and amusement. Perhaps unconsciously, but she shares the same imagery of herself as the men do. At the same time Olga thinks that she can manage the situation and be sexually safe. The situation would have been different and unsafe if she had agreed to the invitation immediately, if the picnic had been planned for a night, if she had not known R., if she had gone alone, if her friends, the wrestlers, had considered it unsafe. She knows that in other circumstances the situation creates insecurity and ends in rape and sexual violence.

The next micro-sequence concerns a *change of the modus of the story from a secure situation to a risky one*, a change from trust to distrust. Olga exposes how she began to recognise the danger and names its indicators. From the narrative we can reconstruct the *semantics of trust, destruction and danger*. In her retrospective reflection it is possible to distinguish several categories of change of meaning. The fragile bridge of trust is broken by at least five incidents of interference: First, on their way to the picnic, the men speak their native language that the women do not understand, and which excluded them from communication. Second, the men buy large quantities of alcohol, which Olga deciphers as a signal that they are not supposed to be sober. Drunkenness is interpreted as a context of abuse and violation of communicative rules. Third, Larisa does not see the situation as dangerous. She is presented as a frivolous person. As a result, Olga feels herself alone in her interpretation of the situation as insecure. Fourth, when the picnic starts, the men insist that the women drink more and more. To convince them to drink they refer to local customs according to which they offend the rules of guest behaviour if they do not drink. Fifth, the final incident, which intensifies Olga's growing feeling of insecurity is the change in the original route. They look for a new setting to continue the picnic. The women are manipulated and taken to another place. In the end of this sequence L and R leave the scene and Olga and the AF are left tête-à-tête. Olga feels alone and in danger, she expects trouble with the AF.

Macro-sequence 4 – culmination

The AF tries to build a communicative bridge between himself and Olga by presenting certain arguments that could enable them to develop mutual sympathy. He positions himself as a person who has certain common ground with Olga. To show that he is trustworthy, he tells her that he is married, and that he knows St. Petersburg where Olga comes from. This "warming up" is followed by the abrupt proposal "to have sex" immediately. Olga does not accept the proposal and tries to make a joke of it. At this point there is a *break in communication*. When rejected the abuser gets aggressive, he beats Olga up in anger. This is his response to her "misconduct". The brutal scene is interrupted by the appearance of the other pair. Olga describes the break in their communicative interaction by using two main categories, *his beating* and *her shock*. The communication is broken by the AF – he is active and Olga is passive. The beating is a violent break in the communication, which was implemented by the AF.

The beating as a break in the communication indicates that Olga and the abuser *ascribe different meanings to the situation.* In the abuser's view the picnic should culminate in sexual intercourse. He expected Olga to follow the implicit rules of his script, the authors of which were himself and R. Women are expected to follow the prescribed roles of gifts. Olga's picnic script was different from the men's, though not as clear and coherent as theirs. On the one hand, she shared the idea of herself as a picnic-gift. On the other, she imagined herself and the script rules as allowing her to develop an alternative script. She obviously underestimated the fact that the script was formulated by the men and mastered by them, though the rules that they followed were tacit.

The beating indicates that *power relations in the picnic situation are relations of male dominance.* The AF is the one who decides whether Olga's conduct is proper or not. He sees her reaction as a violation of picnic rules. He decides how to react to her conduct. Her shock allows him to react in a brutal way. The beating is understood as a brutal but conventional way to implement male dominance and to punish the woman's rejection of the rules of the men's party celebration.

I will now turn to Olga's description of her reaction to the beating as a *shock.* The shock metaphor shows that Olga misinterpreted both the situation and her position in the power relations on the picnic. She tells that the shock blocked her capability to fight back, her resistance or appeal for help. She says that this paralysis was caused by the *unexpectedness of violence* and seeming *irrelevance of the beating* to the sexual intentions of the abuser. She is surprised that he did not try to convince her to have sex, to court or undress her. He showed himself as a non-communicative person. The shock is caused by Olga's failure to implement her own version of the script. Her basic confidence that she could rule out the situation was obviously based on her self-image as a relational and rule-abiding woman, on the one hand, and on her misinterpretation of the picnic situation in which she could trust her rules of safety, on the other. However, she could not rule out the situation because the male dominance dictated what she was supposed to do, and the power to reformulate the rules was not in her hands.

Olga's story is a narrative about the clash of two interpretations of the expected set of rules and a woman's disobedience to follow men's interpretation. The case shows that Olga's exceptionalism and relationalism do not guarantee her safety. Following the standards and axioms of relation-orientedness a woman easily falls into a trap. For Olga, relation-orientedness is more important than safety rules. In the context of male dominance (the picnic) the two sets of rules, rules of relationism and rules of safety, are contradictory. Olga tries in vain to reconcile them. It is her relation-orientedness that makes her at least partially accept the men's rules. The clash of the men's and women's interpretations turns a woman into a victim because the rules are mastered by men. Women have few resources to break the rules, and if they do they are still punished for it. The end of the story shows that the abuser is not punished, while Olga hardly avoids blaming for her misbehaviour her only consolation is apologies from other local men, and some sympathy from her male friends. The AF does not care about the trustful communication, which is so valuable for Olga. Trust is for him just a necessary precondition for sexual intercourse, his final objective. He sees Olga as a desirable sexual object, a possible gift, and he considers the warming-up talk as a prelude for sex, which for him is one of the rules of the game. He thinks that Olga knows the rules of the picnic and that she accepts them. Her rejection to have sex with him (to say No) is looked upon as a violation (a break of the salient contract guaranteed by his friend) and thus her misbehaviour should be punished. In Russian her behaviour is called "to run dynamo". A "Dynamo Woman" is the label for a woman who "uses" her sex appeal in communication with men but then refuses to have sexual intercourse expected by men. The term "dynamo" is used to indicate that such a woman makes the man work on the contact in vain without sexual accomplishment. Olga's logic is different: for her trusting communication is of prior value, and she thinks that it has equal value for men. She believes that the established trustful communication is a guarantee for her safety. She thinks that rules of safety are subordinate to the rules of trustful communication. She believes that her *no* will be respected but she was wrong. Therefore she is shocked by her own misinterpretation of the situation. In the AF's eyes she is *a dynamo woman (dinamistka),* while in her eyes he is a wild beast. As a result of the clash of the two interpretative schemes Olga is physically damaged – beaten.

Macro-sequence 5 – epilogue

Olga does not want to tell about the incident, and she tries to hide, but her female neighbour sees her, informs her friends who come to console her. The militia comes, Olga is interrogated, her evidence is questioned, she is being blamed for provocative behaviour. Her friends understand her and try to comfort her. The next day the camp is broken up. Olga interprets her case as exceptional, as a result of communicative breakdown and of shock.

Conclusion

I perceive this story of violence as culturally paradigmatic. It belongs to those stories of sexual abuse and violence where women know the abusive men. The semantic core of the story is the clash of two versions of women's roles in the picnic script, and the resulting misinterpretation of the situation by the actors in the context of male dominance. Olga orients herself within two basic frames. Each frame is presented in her self-images and activities bound to those images. The frames operate simultaneously and are constructed hierarchically. When she needs to make a choice she prefers one of the frames. The first frame is centred on her self-image as a relation-oriented woman. Relation-orientedness means that trustful communication is her main value. As a relational woman she wants to sustain trustful communication in different situations, even in insecure situations. She looks for arguments that allow her to define the communication as safe. Because she highly values communicative relationships it is not hard for her to find these arguments.

The second frame is focused on the value of security, which Olga considers as a derivative of trustful communication. She decides to violate common security rules, because she appreciates communication as a guarantee for security and subordinates security rules to the rules of women's relation-orientedness. This hierarchisation of rules brings her to the violent scene, which results from men's different interpretation of her relation-orientedness, as her being prepared to accept the picnic rules formulated by them. These rules define a woman as a gift and a sexual object of men celebrating their friendship. The clash in the interpretations between Olga and the abuser results not in a mere communication breakdown, but the picnic is constructed as a setting where men dominate and control women's conduct. The AF beats Olga as a rule violator, and his power takes a brutal form.

Notes

[1] S. Harding, 'Introduction. Is there a Feminist Method?', in: S. Harding (ed.) *Feminism and Methodology* (Open University Press, 1987) pp. 1–14, and D. Smith, 'Sociological Theory: Methods of Writing Patriarchy' in *Feminism and Sociological Theory. Key Issues in Sociological Theory* (Sage 1989) N 4. pp. 34–64.
[2] See L. Ionin, *Sotsiologiia kultury: put v novoe tysyacheletie* (M: Logos 2000).
[3] W. Fischer-Rosenthal, 'The Problems with Identity: Biography as Solution to Some (Post)modernist Dilemmas', *Cornenius*, 3/1995, pp. 250–266.
[4] V. Voronkov and E. Chikadze 'Leningrad Jews: Ethnicity and Context', in *Biographical Perspectives on Post-socialist Societies*. CISR Working Papers 5/1997, St. Petersburg, pp. 187–191.
[5] V. Voronkov and E. Zdravomyslova, 'Emerging Political Sociology in Russia and Russian Transformation', *Current Sociology*, vol. 44, #3, Winter 1996, pp. 41–52, and V. Voronkov and E. Zdravomyslova, E. 'Becoming of Political Sociology in Russia: The First Steps', in P. Sztompka (ed.) *Building Open Society and Perspectives of Sociology in East-Central Europe* (ISA. Alain Mongeu 1998).
[6] Voronkov and Chikadze 1997.
[7] L. Paperno, *Suicide as a Cultural Institution in Dostoevsky's' Russia* (Cornell University Press 1997).
[8] L. Paperno, *Samoubistvo kak kulturnyi institut* (M.: NLO 1999) p. 10.
[9] F. Schutze, 'Biographieforschung und Narrative Interview', *Neue Praxis* (3), 8(1983), pp. 283–294, and H. Sacks, "On Doing Being Ordinary", in: M. Atkinson and J.Heritage (eds.) *Structures of Social Actions* (Cambridge University Press 1989).
[10] G. Rubin, 'The Traffic in Women. Notes on the 'Political Economy' of Sex', in R. Reiter Rapp (ed.) *Toward an Antropology of Women* (Monthly Review Press 1975) pp. 157–210.

Loving With and Without Words

Same-Sex Experiences in Russian Women's Autobiographies during Late Socialism

Anna Rotkirch

To many people in late modern Western societies, sexuality appears as closely connected to, if not the fundament of, personal identity and self-representation. The personal is the private is the sexual, we are used to think, while sexuality is being increasingly verbalised and visualised for political or commercial interests. A look at the representations of sexuality in Soviet Russia reveals a different pattern. From the 1930s to the late 1980s, explicit references to sexuality were practically banned from the Soviet public sphere. In everyday life, sexuality was not perceived and articulated as a distinctly separate sphere of life. Rather, the domains of erotic desire, romantic love and human reproduction were denoted by the vague concept of *intimnaia zhizn'* or intimate life, on the one hand, and the pejorative notion of *poshlost'* which refers to something embarrassingly trivial or dirty, on the other hand.[1]

These different paths of approaching "the sexual" in Eastern and Western Europe evidently have their deep historical roots. Eve Levin has documented how the teachings of the Orthodox Slavs in medieval Russia understood sexual desire as a force external to the human soul:

something which lured from the outside, and from which one could thus also be cleaned. This teaching "denied that love, an emotion of generosity and devotion, could be connected to sexual desire".[2] By contrast, the Catholic and later the Protestant churches emphasised the inborn nature of sexuality: although sexual desire in Western religious ideology was certainly perceived of as problematic, it was earlier intertwined with the concept of love. The division in Russian cultural history between (elevated) love and (banal) sexuality can be seen as yet one example of the famous binary opposition that is said to permeate Russian culture.[3] It seems to continue in the clear lines many Russians still like to make between elevated love and banal sexuality - in the words of the writer and journalist Svetlana Alekseyeva, Russians speak about sexual love either in the language of cruelty or that of romance.[4]

However, the Eastern/Russian experience also shows us an approach to sexuality that does not posit sex as the main defining personal characteristics. Living through the 20th century without being immersed in everyday vulgarised freudianism clearly also has its benefits. For instance, Russians have largely refused to confirm to the type of rigid sexual identity politics that prevailed in the US and many other Western countries in the 1980s and 1990s. In her book about queer sexualities in Russia Laurie Essig quotes her Russian interviewees as repeatedly stating "I don't want to be what I do in bed".[5] Although Essig is careful not to idealise this reluctance to be labelled by one's sexual practices, she does seem to find it – just as I do – an attractive alternative to the more rigid forms of our Western policies of naming.

What, then, does such an alternative look like in the stories of actual lives, and what are its conditions and limits? In this article,[6] I will discuss various perceptions of the role of words and the sexual policy of naming. I will concentrate on two autobiographical accounts about same-sex love, written by women from St Petersburg in 1996 and describing events in Leningrad in the 1970s and 1980s. I will use the term same-sex love as homosexuality is a notion that is often rejected by Russians who love persons of the same sex.[7]

Physical and symbolic threats against same-sex love

During the late 1960s and the 1970s, Soviet sexual behaviour grew increasingly varied in two senses: people's sexual practices became more pluralistic, and distinct sexual subcultures emerged (see also Anna Temkina's article in this book). The period of late socialism can be called the time of behavioural sexual revolution. It took place about twenty years before the revolution of articulation: in the 1970s there was still strictly limited information and public discussion about sexuality and sexual identities, while the post-Soviet 1990s witnessed a sexual revolution in the Russian public sphere.[8] This peculiar, two-phased structure of the Russian sexual revolution had interesting consequences for the role of explicit discourse in the formation of behaviour and sexual identity.

While sexual behaviour grew more liberal during late socialism, the Soviet regime remained extremely negative to both male and female same-sex relations. Male homosexuality was seen as anti-social behaviour, a crime against the interests of the state. Men could be sentenced to as much as five years in prison for same-sex relations (*muzhelovstvo*). Over five hundred such convictions were made in Soviet Russia annually in the 1960s. The men who had been sentenced for homosexuality belonged to the most despised cast in the prison system.[9] Female same-sex relations were, by contrast, seen not as a crime against society, but against Nature – they were a disease. They were also without a proper name: Soviet science labelled them a special – "sluggishly manifesting" (*vyalotekushchaya*) – type of schizophrenia. Women who loved women were thus considered medically ill and could be sent to psychiatric treatment. The treatment they received ranged from psychotherapy to an official change of sex (not necessarily including a sex-change operation).[10]

Laurie Essig underscores the symbolic threat that silenced many women:

> The possibility of being diagnosed as sexually/mentally ill and the resulting forcible internment in a Soviet psychiatric institution worked primarily at a symbolic level. [It] circulated as a threat. (...) Even women who enacted same-sex desire generally also enacted – or at least *play-acted* – heterosexual desire. Many lesboerotic women married men and/or had children, sure signs of health. If a woman stepped too far

> out of line, the threat of the Cure could force her to return to the family of man. Many women told me of threats from the internal security apparatus as well as the KGB: if the women did not 'co-operate' they would be outed to their families, at their place of employment, to their neighbours. Places of employment would fire them, neighbours would blackmail them, families would shun them, or worse, commit them to a psychiatric institution.[11]

The existence of a general, influential "symbolic threat" does not, however, automatically tell us about the severity and scope of symbolic power. Everyday attitudes to homosexuality were in the period of late socialism, the 1960s-1980s, a mixture of crude discrimination, conventional stereotypes and moral permissiveness, depending on place and social milieu. Not all same-sex lovers were in prison or hospitalised; the majority "merely" faced discrimination and lack of support and information. As Essig also notes, Russian queer women's conformity to the heterosexual institutions, e.g. by marriage to a man, was not only due to state repression and the necessity to hide one's sexual life style. Heterosexual marriages could also be entered as a result of wanting to have children, or an apartment.

In my autobiographical material there are examples of blossoming same-sex relations between women that appear to have developed without much of a symbolic threat (nor guidance). Teresa de Lauretis talks about two types of consent for sexual activities, namely *consent in action* and *symbolic consent*: "[T]he consent to homosexual activity and gratification may be provided by a discourse that permits them, as well as by participation in the activity itself".[12] I will use her distinction between action and discourse to compare the autobiographies of the pseudonyms "Tatyana" and "Nadya".

My reading of the autobiographies uses an adaptation of C.S. Pierce's "triad of experience", which aims at grasping the dynamics between bodily feelings and personal emotions; institutional practices; and cultural interpretations.[13] My evidence of emotions, social institutions and interpretations come from the autobiographical texts and can of course not be accessed in a "pure" mode. Nevertheless, I believe that these differences in writing may reflect different ways of experiencing, that there are models of experience where words and naming are centrally involved, and other models were they are less so.

Introducing Tatyana and Nadya

"Tatyana", born in the mid-50s and "Nadya", born in 1960, came from socially and professionally very different milieus, which is reflected in their styles of writing. (In what follows, I will use the present tense in referring to the author of the text and the past tense when referring to the protagonist of the autobiography.)

In the late 1960s, Tatyana moved from a southern Soviet republic to Leningrad to study, probably in a professional institute. She acquired a technical specialisation and, through relations of sexual blat (with the aid of her female lover's male lover, who had a high social position), a decent work place in the city.[14] That job was jeopardised during Tatyana's period of drug usage and petty crime (*fartsovka*) at the end of the 1970s. Her life straightened up after she married, divorced and gave birth to a child. At the moment of writing, in 1996, she was living in a communal apartment with her child, working hard – shifts every fourth night. She seemed generally content with her life, except for her love relations. Tatyana's autobiography begins and ends in acute suffering: "I am in pain right now, and I don't need your prizes, I need to write this." We are told that the immediate reason is that one woman, whom she recently found through a personal advertisement, had ended a beginning relationship. A deeper, enduring pain stemmed from Tatyana's biggest passion, an affair with her class teacher during the first half of the 1970s, when she was in her late teens.

Nadya, by contrast, was raised in an educated Leningrad family and acquired a high and for a Soviet woman rare position in the field of arts. Her autobiography is lighter in tone, depicting an active, curious, spontaneous tomboy. Like Tatyana, Nadya writes very little about her professional life, but concentrates on her successive love affairs. Nadya has had sexual relationships with many women and some men, and was in 1996 involved with a married woman. She stresses that sex had never been a determining ingredient in her life. She was at the moment more interested in philosophy and social and political questions, including feminism, to the point of naming her autobiography "Confessions of a radical feminist".

Turning points

Tatyana writes that she always knew what she wanted in her love life. On the first page, she states that "I have been and still am of the opinion that all love relations are normal", including her own "unordinary" (*neordirnaya*) tastes. When she fell in love with her teacher it was her first important relationship but something already fully "mature" in her inner self, the opening night after the "general repetition":

> My father helped me get settled and returned home after two weeks. No control! Freedom!!! Super!!! It seems to me, that inside my unfinished essence a desire to pay attention to what I paid attention to had matured already long ago. It was as if the general repetition of my brain had transformed into real life. (Tatyana)

By contrast, Nadya's sexual tastes did not develop as immediately. As a young girl, Nadya fell in love with different guys and was infatuated with the famous pop singer Alla Pugacheva. At seventeen, she dated a man described as extremely attractive, somewhat older, and in many ways unique: "He was the incarnation of gallant masculinity, but at the same time he did not have a shadow of sexual harassment (*seksual'noe domogatel'stvo*) in his behaviour with me, it was a purely spiritual friendship, a union of reason and soul". The two of them talked half-jokingly about getting married, which Nadya thinks she actually wanted at the time, in order to "feel myself a woman" – supposedly a feminine and heterosexual woman. But she writes about how, the first time they undressed and he touched her, she – completely unexpectedly for herself – suddenly pushed him away in an intense feeling of disgust and horror.

> It was a purely impulsive, unconscious movement, with my reason I understood the tactlessness and crudity of my attack, but my body protested against his attempt to get close. (Nadya)

This sudden revulsion is something Nadya writes she still cannot understand, and one which was not repeated: "Later on I never had a similar reaction, I found some men agreeable and others disagreeable". She was very confused by her reaction to her boyfriend, guessing with daisies about her own feelings: "I love him, I love him not...". Some years later, when Nadya was in her late twenties, she became close friends with a fellow student and discovered her preference for women. It was not something she was immediately ready to approve of.

> Don't you think that our relation is a little pathological? she suddenly asked me one day. I shrugged my shoulders and answered that I had not noticed any pathology with myself. But the seeds of suspicions were sown. And then one time, when A. once again touched my hand, desire sparked inside me. I was a mature woman and knew the value of all my sensations. There could be no mistake. It was that very same 'pathology'. (Nadya)

What Tatyana knew early in life, Nadya learnt as an adult. In both cases, the autobiographies present bodily desire (and revulsion) as the crucial guiding force. But Nadya speaks of "pathology", echoing the official Soviet view of female homosexuality as a disease, and was at first suspicious and guarded about love between women. In her case, the symbolic threat was clearly present in the form of, at least, a social stigma. On the other hand, once she felt bodily desire, the label of "pathology" did not seem to pose any major obstacle.

In Tatyana's story, there are no similar references to social taboos and threats. As mentioned above, she writes about "unordinary love", a neutral word that she may have picked up during the last years of public writings about sex in Russia. Her autobiography makes only two short references to the social obstacles facing same-sex love, and they have a formal, almost obligatory ring to them: "Love relations with unordinary sexual orientations are obstructed by problems that have to do with society." And a little later Tatyana specifies how, during her long-lasting affair with her teacher, there were "problems having to do with society: the husband [of her lover – AR], my mother, the relatives". But such social problems with spouses and relatives could surely have haunted any Soviet teenager that had fallen madly in love with an older, married teacher.

In the beginning of Tatyana's autobiography it is stated that "you will understand the reason of my enforced marriage", but the reader who thinks Tatyana will present her marriage as an attempt to conform to heterosexual standards is mistaken. According to Tatyana, her husband and she both understood that she married him in order to leave her circle of criminals and drug addicts. And although she now considers her marriage a "necessitated, blatant mistake in my life", she enumerates many of the most usual reasons for divorce – namely, her husband's drinking, jealousy, and insensitivity in bed – without giving her sexual preferences a leading role in the drama.[15]

Consent in action and in discourse

In Tatyana's text, *feelings* and sexual *practices* – how she felt and what she and her partner did in bed – are the most important. Her sexual life course seems to evolve around consent in action, with little reflection about naming. Nadya, by contrast, provides us with a classical example of identity construction and of the role of discursive consent. Before she had had any relations with women she discussed homosexuality with her friends, and was surprised to learn that they approved of it (see below). She then writes extensively about how she renamed and reinterpreted her own self after her deep friendship had evolved into her first sexual relation with a woman.

> The happiness I experienced with her cannot be compared to anything else. Never had sex been so joyful and tender and the affinity of souls so deep. That love made me look anew on my whole previous life, to re-evaluate and understand many things. I remembered that, as it turned out, I had fallen in love with women my whole life, without paying any notice to it – in female teachers and doctors, and in Alla Pugacheva, and those feelings had a clear erotic quality. (Nadya)

The previously inexplicable revulsion towards her ex-boyfriend could also be interpreted from her new perspective: "It was the first male touching of me, and I rejected it with my whole being." Nadya notes how her feminism, after her sexual experience with a woman,

> acquired an impeccable theoretical clarity, the missing link had finally been found. Until then my heterosexual intentions were at dissonance with my convictions and my whole style of living and behaving. In relations with men there is always the duplicity and subservience that belong to the female gender. I do not want to say that those characteristics are immanent for us – no, they have been forced upon us by the men, but we have adopted them! (Nadya).

If women have adopted characteristics given by men, Nadya has, for her part, adopted the view that all real feminists are lesbians, and the other way around.

Tatyana's life story has no similar identity revelation or prescriptions. Instead of Nadya's "impeccable theoretical clarity", Tatyana relates, clearly amused, how surprised one of her lovers was by her rich repertoire of sexual techniques. The lover, in her turn, surprised Tatyana with "having read much Western literature, about what to do and when". Habits Tatyana had developed herself, such as keeping short and tidy nails, turned out to be recommended in Western books. However, there are no signs of the reverse process – that theoretical knowledge would have significantly influenced her behaviour. True, Tatyana describes intercourse in detail and with current popularised sexological terminology (using words such as masturbation, orgasm, heterosexual orientation). Her autobiography is among the most sexually detailed of those written by women in my autobiographical material. But these terms were learnt later in life and do not seem to have altered her profound sense of herself as a woman and sexual being.

I have abstracted these two models of selves into the following triads of experience :

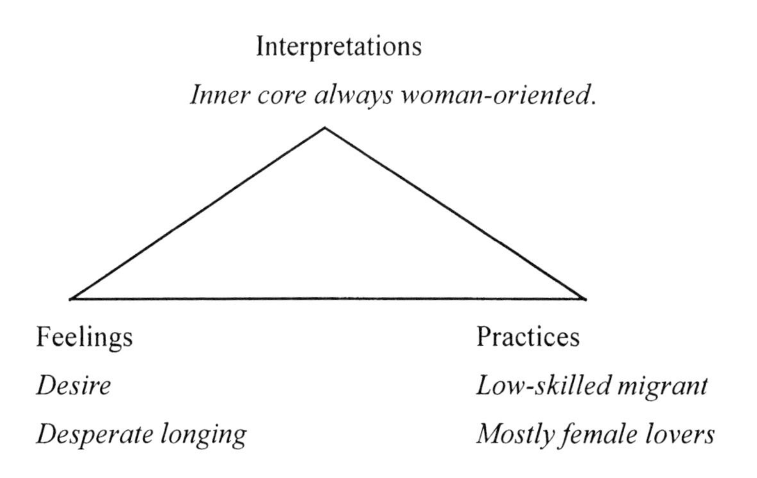

Figure 1. *"Tatyana", born 1955, a model of consent in action*

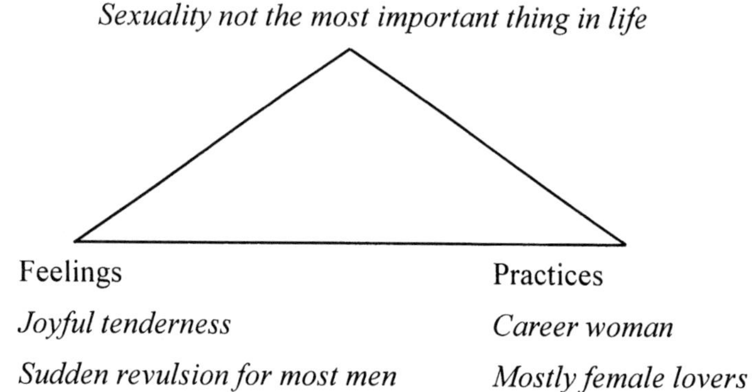

Figure 2. *"Nadya", born 1960, a model of discursive consent*

In the first case, exemplified by Tatyana's autobiography, the emphasis is on feelings and social practices. Her life has had severe social problems, but they are not presented as directly related to her sexuality. Her feelings of loneliness may of course be related to the difficulty of finding suitable female partners, but at least Tatyana perceives of this as a purely personal problem. Her self understanding is not a bit sociological. For instance, she does not write about the availability of newspaper advertisements – a contact forum absent in the Soviet times and thus an important new way for seeking sexual contacts – as a social improvement, she simply makes use of them to find new partners.

In the second case, Nadya's example, the social practices and her personal feelings are both presented as a reason for, and consequence of, her identity construction. From misinformation and a vague disapproval of same-sex love as a "pathology", she evolved into a conscious radical feminist.

Tatyana's experiences are described by evoking bodily sensations of desire and pain, while Nadya consciously adopts and re-interprets her bodily experiences to suit a Western-type feminist discourse about lesbian identity. Although similar in their sexual practices (mostly female, but some male lovers), the two women interpret their habits very differently. Take, for instance, their current relations to men. Nadya had rejected all her heterosexual relations – with the exception of one short and stormy affair: "I cried on his chest... I really loved him at that moment". Male lovers would, she writes, not conform with her political and sexual identity. But Tatyana still occasionally had sex with men, and the pleasure it gives her is enough to justify it to the reader: "I told him that I do not need any bed relations (...) and that I am not interested in men. (...) But this countryside guy, shapely built and enduring in sex, struck me, and was struck by me."

The difference between consent in action and discursive consent is clearest in the summarising self-evaluations towards the end of the two women's autobiographies. In Tatyana's case, there is none – she ends up being lonely and unhappy, but does not wonder any further about why she loves women more. Nadya, on the contrary, wants to stress that lesbianism is "purely social":

> Whatever they write about the hormonal or chromosomal nature of homosexuality, I am firmly convinced that the reasons for this phenomenon are purely social. People with deep and refined sensations (and all homosexuals are like that) cannot accept duplicity and the alienation it creates, which are at the fundament of the relations between men and women. ...women's lesbianism, if it is sufficiently firm, is nothing else but a form of protest against the discrimination of women and the lack of trust and latent animosity between the sexes that it leads to. In my case it is a conscious protest, more often it is unconscious, but in any case it is a natural and logical manifestation of feminism. (Nadya)

In my reading, Nadya's emphasis on the social origins of her homosexuality seems to contradict her own description of the initial, bodily rejection of her boyfriend. In any case, the word "social" in her vocabulary has to be a wide concept, encompassing such things as personal aesthetic and unconscious motives, in order to fit into her logic of reasoning. As already noted, Tatyana instead disregards most social interpretations, centring her self presentation on the personal and interpersonal.

Tolerant young women

As a third example, distinct from the models exemplified by Tatyana and Nadya, we could take the autobiography of Darya, a young woman born in 1972 who was twenty four years old at the moment of writing. Darya was mainly man-oriented, but had a sexual relationship with one of her good female friends. A few times, she had also tried to meet female partners by putting personal advertisements in newspapers. She describes female lovers as an important if secondary part of her love life:

> Women are very often present in my erotic fantasies – in my thoughts I am making love with one, two three and very many women. And I have no doubts that I will sometimes do it in reality. At the same time I do not think of myself as a lesbian – it is just another sexual experience. (Darya, b.1972)

Darya's autobiography is bold and assertive throughout; in her sexual relations she did not seem to have any problems with any kind of consent. Similar self perceptions, were same-sex relations are present but where the woman does not identify as a lesbian, have been found in autobiographies by young Finnish women.[16] According to our survey data, Darya's kind of young St Petersburg women is even quite usual: of women between 18 and 30 years old, more than 15% answered affirmatively to the question: "Have you experienced sexual interest in the same sex?" Of the whole Petersburg population 12% of women reported sexual interest in the same sex, which is much higher than the numbers for St Petersburg men, or for both men and women in Finland and Sweden.[17] This would indicate that the Soviet symbolic threat against female same-sex relations has weakened relatively fast, at least in St Petersburg, a big city well-known for its liberal values. The reported attitudes of today's Russians are already close to the most tolerant Western nations. Thus the percentage of the St Petersburg population that reports it accepts homosexuality was much higher in Petersburg in the 1990s than in Finland in the 1970s. More than two of three young Petersburg people said they accepted homosexuality, which is almost the same amount as among contemporary young Finns.[18]

On the other hand, gay cafés and homosexual organisations or publishers often face prejudices and physical violence in today's Russia:

the overall picture is far from one of rosy and cosy general tolerance. Essig tells how one of her Russian friends in the mid-1990s decided to "come out" to her family. "Her husband raped her and almost killed her. Her mother told her she deserved it, and so did the police."[19] The Russians' personal preferences for fluid, unlabelled and non-public sexual identities have to be partly understood against this kind of threatening social context.

Class and pain

Why do Tatyana's and Nadya's autobiographies differ so much in their models of subjectivity? The main explaining factors appear to be class and generation. Tatyana had a provincial and lower class background, and her formative years were during the prime time of late socialism, in the early 1970s, when public discussions of intimate issues were extremely limited. Nadya belonged to the Leningrad/St Petersburg upper intelligentsia, and her formative years were during the mid-1980s, when sexual issues were being increasingly articulated, and when Western sexual and gender discourses spread in Russia. The influence of generation is fairly obvious – even if Tatyana is only five years older than Nadya, Nadya had access to many more publications, expert advice and newspaper accounts of lesbianism during her formative years.[20] But that access was perhaps even more due to their class and corresponding sexual subcultures.

For instance, Nadya's autobiography relates a discussion at a small party of friends in 1985, at the beginning of the perestroika. The friends played "do-or-tell" and she got the question "How would you react if a homosexual (*gomoseksualist*) or a lesbian (*lesbianka*) would fall in love with you?" At that time, Nadya responded negatively. "I took the question very seriously, thought about it for a long time and finally I answered that if it would be a primitive person, I would simply ask her to beat it (*poshliu podalshe*)". Her friends then asked what she would do if it was not a "primitive person", to which she more hesitantly answered that she would still tell her just the same, to beat it. Evidently, some of those present at the party approved of homosexuality. The whole event is a good illustration of how sexuality, and homosexuality, became an acceptable – fashionably daring – topic during the 1980s and acquired words that had not earlier been in use in Russia, such as lesbianka. Nevertheless, the same kind of discussion was present in more limited spheres also earlier: it could well have taken place in certain middle-class, student milieus already in the 1970s (not to mention the beginning of the 20th century).

Indeed, Nadya's emphasis on self-reflection and naming seems to be typical, if not defining, for the middle class both in Eastern and Western Europe, for men and women who experienced rising social mobility through education and professionalisation. We know that the Western homosexual life style was tied to the development of the middle and upper classes in a capitalist society.[21] In these autobiographies, it is not the question of a distinct way of life, but certainly of a specific model of self. In my material, as in most autobiographical corpuses, the middle-class authors are the ones that spend much time on cognitive reflection and use literary metaphors and scientific terminology. The agrarian and/or working-class women more often refer to bodily sensations, especially physical pain (although in Russia, all members of all classes write poems). The use of pain may seem paradoxical: pain is often understood as something intensely individual, something which overshadows other experiences and is hard to share with other people or convey through writing. This notion sees pain as a separating and individualising experience and belongs to the contemporary Western understanding of emotions.[22] On the other hand, pain can be a transcending experience, and telling about pain can be a very effective way of connecting to other people. For instance, pain appears as a collective and ritualised female experience, as "a transpersonal and allegorical paradigm of pain", in Greek traditions.[23] A similar paradigm of pain is clearly represented especially in poor and working class Russian women's autobiographies. Usually, the pain is not directly sexualised, but connected to reproduction – typically, recovering from a pregnancy or an abortion.[24]

Tatyana's story is partly an example of writing as a way of embodying experiences of pain. Her text begins and ends with her being in tears; the sentences are fragmentary and often end with ellipsis. But she also writes directly about touching, talking, and experiencing sexual pleasure. That is more rarely found in the women's autobiographies of my material, although, among the few exceptions is another poor working woman from the oldest generation. Tatyana's very direct style and abundance of intimate details may also be a trace of the bohemian and semi-criminal subcultures she used to belong to in the 1970s. Her model of self was thus formed both by her provincial (agrarian/working class) background and her participation in a metropolitan subculture.

Nadya again, as most other middle-class women writers in this material, rarely describes sexual pleasure as such. Notwithstanding her radical political views, her descriptions of love and sexuality are typical for her class and in the middle of the Russian mainstream: Sex is better in connection with love, or submerged by love and respect– as Nadya puts it, the ideal relation is “a unit of soul and reason”.

Gender differences

Finally, we may ask what might be specifically female in the different experiential selves outlined above? In my material, two men (born in 1960 and 1968) wrote about mainly same-sex experiences. Without any claim of generalisations, a short comparison of these two stories shows both interesting similarities and differences with the life stories of Tatyana and Nadya.

The slightly older man (born in 1960) describes unproblematic and happy same-sex love during his first student years, when he had a five-year relationship with his roommate:

> I first received a possibility to experience all the sweetness of real love when I was already studying at the institute. That was the only really bright period in my sexual biography. I was studying in another town, due to family reasons. Because there were not enough rooms in the dormitory it so happened that I and another guy from my class had to rent a room. And because of the high prices we had not only to move into the same tiny room, but to make do with only one, shared, bed. (...) And, of course, the situation with 'spatial' proximity in bed with my friend, with whom I already also had quite a strong friendship, facilitated even closer advances. There were caresses (mainly from my side), which my friend did not object to. We ended up living almost five years in total peace, understanding and, probably, happiness, loving each other and spending the nights together. This, by the way, did not hamper my friend from 'chasing women' and he even got married the fourth year. Now he is far from Piter, continuing to be happy in his family life, and has two children. (Man, born in 1960)

This autobiography is divided in two parts. The first is written as an open letter, which the author suggests could be published in a newspaper. The second one is his personal life story, together with speculations about the causes of his homosexuality. The personal life story has a calm tone. By contrast, the public letter is – as the author himself points out – very emotional, desperate in tone, blaming other people (he addresses himself to male, heterosexual readers) for not understanding his conception of love and condemning him to loneliness:

> I will not depict all the denigration I have, without any reason whatsoever, been subjected to by people who were convinced of their absolute righteousness. I am not guilty of anything before them, nor myself, nor God. I am a normal, moral, sensible person. And I do not know, why I am that way. (Man, higher education, b. 1960)

The younger man (born in 1968) had a much longer road towards sexual self-realisation, a road which partly follows a classical coming-out story familiar to Western reader. This man acknowledged his homosexuality when, after several years of dissatisfying relationships with women and depression, he finally, in 1986, dared to buy and read a book by James Baldwin, the openly homosexual American author.

If we compare these two life stories with the female autobiographies analysed above, we find two main things. First, the difference between consent in action and discursive consent is partly mirrored in the male stories. The older man (b. 1960) had his happiest relationship in the student dormitory, while the younger man (b. 1968) figured out what he really longed for only after having read Freud and Baldwin. At the same time, both male autobiographies were full of reflective speculations, justifications and literary quotations of a kind that were absent from Tatyana's autobiography. One simple reason for this is that both male authors came from the Soviet upper middle class.

Second, both male autobiographies discuss, apologise for and justify their sexual preferences. Here lies a crucial difference to the women: neither Tatyana nor Nadya saw their sexual orientation per se as any crucial problem. A similar gender difference has been found on the basis of descriptions of same-sex love in Finnish autobiographies.[25]

Thus my short comparison supports the interpretation that class explains the biggest difference between Tatyana's and Nadya's experiences, with generation as a close second. It also indicates that is was more problematic for men to begin to live with a mainly homosexual identity. The repression of same-sex relations in Soviet society was more extensive and real for men, including the very real threat of imprisonment. Same-sex love between women was less visible. It may also have been less "tainted" by the label of homosexuality – one interpretation to the survey findings reported above, that Russian women more often report sexual interest in the same sex, is that a Western person would read the same survey question as meaning "are you homosexual?" and answer "no", thus deliberately excluding feelings of desire which did not fit the person's sexual identity from the answer.

Concluding remarks: The limits of discourse

This article has analysed the Soviet Russian experiences of same-sex love by using the distinction made by Teresa de Lauretis between consent in action and symbolic or discursive consent. The Soviet Russian historical experience serves to remind us that words are not everything when bodies are involved. In the beginning of this article, I approached the question of less linguistically influenced models of sexual experience from the perspective of Russian cultural history. For many reasons, sexuality has not been as articulated, visible and central in Soviet and Russian conceptions of the human being as in many Western countries.

However, we have seen how this national specificity intertwines with the question of class. I have suggested that the particular weight often given in the West to printed sexual information and to scientific (psychological, psychoanalytical and medical) terminology is partly tied to the middle-class. Life stories from less educated milieus employ another kind of language, where bodily experiences of pain and pleasure have a more central role. Here, the Soviet Russian experience is echoed in recent research on homosexuality in other countries, such as Finland and France.[26]

Notes

[1] Svetlana Boym, *Common Places. Mythologies of Everyday Life in Russia* (Cambridge: Harvard University Press 1994).
[2] Eve Levin, *Sex and Society in the World of the Orthodox Slaves, 900–1700* (Ithaca: Cornell University Press 1989), p. 14.
[3] Cf. Jane T. Costlow, Stephanie Sandler and Judith Vowles, 'Introduction.' In Jane T. Costlow, Stephanie Sandler and Judith Vowles (eds.) *Sexuality and the Body in Russian Culture*, (Stanford University Press 1989), pp. 1–39, and Igor Kon, *The Sexual Revolution in Russia. From the Age of the Czars to Today.* (New York: The Free Press 1995).
[4] Anna Rotkirch, *The Man Question. Loves and Lives in Late 20th Century Russia* (Department of Social Policy, Research reports 1/2000, University of Helsinki).
[5] Laurie Essig, *Queer in Russia. A Story of Sex, Self and the Other (*Durham: Duke University Press 1999) p. 41 and 127.
[6] An earlier version of this article has been printed as part of chapter 9 in Rotkirch 2000.
[7] Essig 1999.
[8] Rotkirch 2000.
[9] Essig 1999, p. 8–14.
[10] Ibid., pp. 28–29.
[11] Ibid., pp. 28–29, original emphasis.
[12] Teresa de Lauretis, *The Practice of Love. Lesbian Sexuality and Perverse Desire* (Bloomington: Indiana University Press 1994), p. 7.
[13] Cf. Rotkirch 2000.
[14] On Soviet blat relations, see Alena V. Ledeneva, *Russia's Economy of Favours. Blat, Networking and Informal Exchange* (Cambridge: Cambridge University Press 1998).
[15] The autobiographies belong to a corpus of 47 materials, collected in an autobiographical competition about love and sexuality organised in St Petersburg in 1996 by the Institute of Sociology in St Petersburg and the University of Helsinki. The autobiographical material has been compared to the results from a representative survey from St Petersburg, conducted in 1996 (N=2081). Similar materials, both autobiographical and statistical, have been collected in Finland, Estonia and Lithuania during the 1990s. Cf. Elina Haavio-Mannila and Anna Rotkirch, 'Generational and Gender Differences in Sexual Life in St.Petersburg and Urban Finland'. *Yearbook of Population Research in Finland* (Helsinki: The Population Research Institute 1998) pp. 133-160.
[16] Marja Kaskisaaari, 'Rakkauden täyttymys. Seksuaaliset erot ja romanttinen rakkaus' (Sexual differences and romantic love), in Matti Hyvärinen, Eeva Peltonen ja Anni Vilkko (eds) *Liikkuvat erot. Sukupuoli elämäkertatutkimuksessa* (Moving differences. Gender in autobiographical studies), (Tampere: Vastapaino 1998) pp. 273–310.

[17] All the latter are around seven per cent, see Haavio-Mannila & Rotkirch 2000.
[18] Ibid.
[19] Essig 1999, p. 126.
[20] Masha Gessen, 'Sex in the Media and the Birth of the Sex Media in Russia', in Ellen Berry (ed.) *Postcommunism and the Body Politic*, GENDER 22 (New York: New York University Press 1995) pp. 197–228.
[21] George Chauncey, *Gay New York: Gender, Urban Culture and the Making of the Gay Male World* (New York: Basic Books 1994).
[22] Similarly, Russian women's late 19th-century literature has been characterized by pain and illnesses occupying a central place (see Arja Rosenholm, *Engendering Awakening*. Helsinki: Kikimora publications 1999). It may well be that feminine suffering is especially present in the Orthodox Christian tradition, or that other social and cultural similarities can explain why pain and suffering play such a central role in both Greek and Russian women's cultural repertoires.
[23] Nadya C. Seremetakis, (1998) 'Durations of pains. A genealogy of pain'. In Jonas Frykman, Nadya Seremetakis & Susanne Evert (eds.) *Identities in Pain* (Lund: Nordic Academic Press 1998) pp. 151–168.
[24] Rotkirch 2000, pp. 98–101.
[25] Kaskisaari 1998.
[26] Ibid., and Pierre-Olivier de Busscher, Romel Mendès-Leite & Bruno Proth, 'Lieux de rencontre et back-rooms'. *Actes de la recherche en sciences sociales* 128, June 1999.

Contributors

Hilde Hoogenboom is Assistant Professor at the Department of Modern Languages, Stetson University in Florida, USA. She is currently co-editing two forthcoming books "Mapping the Feminine: Russian Women and Cultural Difference" and "Nadezhda Khvoshchinskaia", and doing research for a book entitled *Identity and Realism: Russian Women Writers in the Nineteenth Century.*

Catriona Kelly is Reader in Russian at New College, Oxford University, UK. Her latest publications include *Refining Russia: Advice Literature, Polite Culture, and Gender from Catherine to Yeltsin* (Oxford University Press, 2001), *Constructing Russian Culture in the Age of Revolution* (Oxford University Press, 1998), edited with David Shephard, and *Russian Cultural Studies: An Introduction* (Oxford University Press, 1998), edited with David Shephard. Currently she is working on a book entitled *Children's World: Growing Up in Russia, 1891–1991*, a general cultural history of childhood in Russia and the Soviet Union.

Marianne Liljeström is Senior Assistant Professor at the Department of Women's Studies, University of Tampere, Finland, and Docent in Women's History at the Abo Akademi University, Finland. She has published articles on Nordic and Soviet Women's History, and edited textbooks in Finnish on feminist theory. She is the author of *Emancipated to Subordination. The Discursive Reproduction of the Soviet Gender System* (1995, in Swedish), and is currently working on a book about Soviet women's autobiographical texts from the late Soviet period.

Irina Novikova has a Ph.D in American literature and she is Docent at the Department of Literatures and Cultures, University of Latvia. She is Director of the Centre for Gender Studies at the University of Latvia. She has edited the book *Too Early? Too Late? Feminist Theories, Issues, Discussions* (1999) and an anthology of Contemporary Feminist Theories (2000). She is also the editor of the quarterly newsletter "Women of Baltia" in Russian. Her research deals with questions concerning the national and gender order in Latvia (19th–20th centuries); gender and genre – autobiography and Bildungsroman in women's literatures (comparative perspectives); and masculinities in a post-Soviet context.

Arja Rosenholm, Ph.D., is researcher at the Department of Slavonic Languages,University of Tampere, Finland. She is author of the book *Gendering Awakening. Femininity and the Russian Woman Question of the 1860s* (1999). Her current research concerns aesthetic concepts of Russian women writers of the 19th century and gendered meanings of animals in Russian literature and culture.

Anna Rotkirch is Lecturer at the Department of Social Policy, University of Helsinki, Finland. She is the author of the book *The Man Question. Loves and Lives in Late 20th Century Russia* (2000), and has together with Elina Haavio-Mannila edited the anthology *Women's Voices in Russia Today* (Aldershot: Dartmouth publishers, 1996). Her research fields are comparative family research, sexual studies and autobiographical studies. Internet home page: www.valt.helsinki.fi/staff/rotkirch/

Marja Rytkönen is researcher at the Department of Slavonic languages,University of Tampere, Finland. She has published articles on Russian women's autobiographical texts in the (post)perestroika period, which is also the topic of her Ph.D. thesis she is currently working on.

Irina Savkina, Phil. Lic. is Lecturer at the Department of Slavonic Languages, University of Tampere, Finland. Her latest book is *'Provincialki russkoi literatury' (zhenskaja proza 30–40-kh godov XIX veka.* (FrauenLiteraturGeschichte: Texte und Materialien zur russischen Frauenliteratur. Verlag F.K. Göpfert. Wilhelmshorst, 1998). The subject of her current research is autodocumentary texts (memories, diaries, letters) of Russian women in the first half of the 19th century.

Romy Taylor is a graduate student in Slavic Languages and Literatures at the University of Southern California, USA. Her dissertation sketches the history of the friendly epistle genre in Russian poetry, 1750–1860.

Anna Temkina is Associate Professor at the Department of Political Sciences and Sociology, European University, St Petersburg, Russia. She has published articles on the theory and methodology of gender studies, and on the sociology of sexuality.

Elena Zdravomyslova is Associate Professor at European University in St Petersburg, Russia, and Research program co-ordinator at the Centre for Independent Social Research (St Petersburg). Most recently she has co-edited a Reader in feminist theory in Russian, and she is currently doing research on gender relations and social movements in Russia.

KIKIMORA PUBLICATIONS

Series A

Temkina, Anna (1997): Russia in Transition: The Case of New Collective Actors and New Collective Actions. ISBN 951-45-7843-0

Мустонен, Петер (1998): Собственная его императорского величества канцелярия в механизме властвования института самодержца 1812–1858: К типологии основ имперского управления. ISBN 951-45-8074-5

3 Rosenholm, Arja (1999): Gendering Awakening : Femininity and the Russian Woman Question of the 1860s. ISBN 951-45-8892-4

4 Lonkila, Markku (1999): Social Networks in Post-Soviet Russia: Continuity and Change in the Everyday Life of St. Petersburg Teachers. ISBN 951-45-8911-4

Series B

Vihavainen, Timo ja Takala, Irina (red.) (1998): В семье единой: Национальная политика партии большевиков и ее осуществление на Северо-Западе России в 1920–1950-е годы. ISBN 5-230

Granberg, Leo (ed.) (1998): The Snowbelt: Studies on the European North in Transition. ISBN 951-45-8253-5

Sutela, Pekka (1998): The Road to the Russian Market Economy: Selected Essays 1993–1998. ISBN 951-45-8409-0

4 Törnroos, Jan-Åke & Nieminen, Jarmo (eds.) (1999): Business Entry in Eastern Europe: A Network and Learning Approach with Case Studies. ISBN 951-45-8860-6

5 Miklóssy, Katalin (toim.) (1999): Syitä ja seurauksia: Jugoslavian hajoaminen ja seuraajavaltioiden nykytilanne: seminaari 8.4.1999, Helsinki. ISBN 951-45-8861-4

Винников, Александр (1998): Цена свободы. ISBN 5-89739-002-9

Лебина, Н. Б. (1999): Повседневная жизнь советского города : нормы и аномалии : 1920 и 1930 годы. ISBN 5-87516-133-7, 5-87940-004-0

8 Lejins, Atis (ed.) (1999): Baltic Security Prospects at the Turn of the 21st Century. ISBN 951-45-9067-8

9 Komulainen, Tuomas & Korhonen, Iikka (ed.) (2000): Russian Crisis and Its Effects. ISBN 951-45-9100-3

10 Salminen, Ari & Temmes, Markku (2000): Transitioteoriaa etsimässä. ISBN 951-45-9238-7

11 Yanitsky, Oleg (2000): Russian Greens in a Risk Society: A Structural Analysis. ISBN 951-45-9226-3

12 Vihavainen, Timo ja Takala, Irina (toim.) (2000): Yhtä suurta perhettä: Bolševikkien kansallisuuspolitiikka Luoteis-Venäjällä 1920–1950-luvuilla. ISBN 951-45-9275-1

13 Oittinen, Vesa (ed.) (2000): Evald Ilyenkov's Philosophy Revisited. ISBN 951-45-9263-8

14 Tolonen, Juha (ed.) (2000): Legal Foundations of Russian Economy. ISBN 951-45-9276-X

15 Kotiranta, Matti (ed.) (2000): Religious Transition in Russia. ISBN 951-45-9447-9

16 Kangaspuro, Markku (ed.) (2000): Russia: More different than most. ISBN 951-45-9423-1

18 Liljeström, Marianne, Rosenholm, Arja and Savkina, Irina (ed.) (2000): Models of Self. Russian Women's Autobiographical Texts. ISBN 951-45-9575-0

Orders:
Aleksanteri Institute
P.O.Box 4
00014 University of Helsinki
Telephone +358-9-191 24175
Telefax +358-9-191 23822
E-mail: kikimora-publications@helsinki.fi